Praise for

The Great Escape

"Describes the crossroads where art and politics meet, the perils of dictatorship and the horrors of war, all of it punctuated by the frantic struggle to create the atomic bomb. . . . Deserves a special place on bookshelves alongside *Budapest 1900.*"
—ROBERT LEITER, *THE NEW YORK TIMES BOOK REVIEW*

"No exaggeration at all is needed to stress the importance of these individuals, who really did 'change the world,' as the book's subtitle has it. . . . No false melodrama is needed for Marton to make this an intensely gripping story. . . . For a European, this story—with its reminder of horrors still within living memory—is painful and absorbing to read."
—GEOFFREY WHEATCROFT, *THE WASHINGTON POST BOOK WORLD*

"Marton, who fled Hungary as a child in 1957, illuminates Budapest's vertiginous Golden Age and the darkness that followed. . . . By looking at these nine lives—salvaged, and crucial—Marton provides a moving measure of how much was lost."
—*THE NEW YORKER*

"*The Great Escape* is a good fit for Kati Marton's multifarious talents, requiring deep knowledge of the history and culture of Budapest, the analytical abilities of a seasoned reporter and a keen understanding of what it means to leave one's country behind. . . . While the work of uncovering this neglected piece of history required the skills of a worldly journalist, the telling came from the heart. . . . This is a book that should be read with special care."
—KIMBERLY MARLOWE HARTNETT, *THE SEATTLE TIMES*

"Marton writes with passion and the journalist's eye for telling detail as she creates an integrated story of nine who thought and dreamed large."
—SANDEE BRAWARSKY, *JEWISH WEEK*

"Engaging. . . . The book's subtitle 'Nine Jews Who Fled Hitler and Changed the World' could hardly be called an exaggeration."
—EDWARD SEROTTA, *THE FORWARD*

"Marton's compelling narrative zigzags in and out of [her characters'] lives throughout the book, tying the men together and disbanding them eerily, perhaps unconsciously mimicking the fragmented futures they would face as exiles forced to run for their lives."
—ELAINE MARGOLIN, *THE JERUSALEM POST*

"Our Fave. . . . These were individualists who marked indelibly the worlds of physics, cinema, literature, photography and mathematics for all time. As she seamlessly weaves their stories across the years, Marton underscores the particular dreams that took them far from their birthplace, even as it remained part of their souls."
—MICHAEL J. BANDLER, *GO* MAGAZINE

"Noted journalist and bestselling author Marton offers a haunting tale of the wartime Hungarian diaspora. . . . Marton intricately charts each man's career in the context of WWII and Cold War history. . . . Marton captures her fellow Hungarians' nostalgia for prewar Budapest, evoking its flamboyant cafes, its trams, boulevards and cosmopolitan Jewish community. Marton writes beautifully, balancing sharply defined character studies of each man with insights into their shared cultural traits and uprootedness."

— *PUBLISHERS WEEKLY* (STARRED REVIEW)

"An engrossing book. . . . Marton does such a good job of introducing her subjects, showing how they persevered through prejudice and personal problems to shape their times, that she leaves the reader wanting to learn more. Highly recommended."

— *LIBRARY JOURNAL*

"For award-winning journalist Kati Marton, *The Great Escape* is a love letter—not just to the nine amazing men she profiles but to her native Hungary. She writes almost insistently, with historical detail packed into every sentence, passionate that we never forget the Hungarian story. We are swept from Budapest's once-glittering grandeur to the suffocating darkness that followed and into the lives of artists and scientists who fled Hitler and spread their brilliance throughout America and Europe."

— JULIE HEABERLIN, *FORT WORTH STAR-TELEGRAM*

"Thoughtful. . . . Tells the story of nine men who fled anti-Semitism and went on to stunning accomplishments. . . . Their stories are all compelling."

— DENNIS LYTHGOE, *DESERET MORNING NEWS*

"This is the fascinating true story of nine remarkable men who survived the Nazi terror and went on to play vital roles in shaping the twentieth century. The men, all products of Budapest's Golden Age, reinvented themselves and assimilated cultures as they moved westward to Vienna, Berlin, Paris, London, New York, and Hollywood. *The Great Escape* is an inspirational account of human survival and triumph against the greatest odds."

— *TUCSON CITIZEN*

"A wonderfully written and thoroughly readable account. . . . Endlessly enjoyable. . . . A magnificent adventure story."

— DAVID M. KINCHEN, *THE HUNTINGTON NEWS*

"Filled with a number of wonderful anecdotes. . . . Marton's book makes you want to reread *Darkness at Noon* and get to Blockbuster to rent *Casablanca*."

— JENNIFER HUNTER, *CHICAGO SUN-TIMES*

"A prodigious feat of research. . . . Ms. Marton combines the craft of a seasoned journalist with empathy for her subjects. . . . Reading *The Great Escape* is a painless way to absorb history, its vast sweep made comprehensible . . . through individual narratives. . . . Marton has done us the great service of capturing an evanescent era, the last of whose witnesses will soon be gone."

— ALEXANDRA SHELLEY, *THE EAST HAMPTON STAR* (NEW YORK)

"Born in Budapest and a refugee of the abortive Hungarian rebellion of 1956, Marton relates these stories with the passion of a proud daughter of a country that is famous for countrymen that needed to flee to be free.... The pictures are stunning."
— LARRY SHIELD, *THE ROANOKE TIMES* (VIRGINIA)

"Fascinating!... The story of nine men who grew up in Budapest and were driven from Hungary by fascism, just one step ahead of Hitler's era of terror. They came to the West, especially the United States, and their tremendous achievements changed life for us all."
— BETTY E. STEIN, *FORT WAYNE NEWS SENTINEL* (INDIANA)

"Kati Marton's wonderful book celebrates what is glorious and eternal in the human condition."
— ELIE WIESEL, NOBEL LAUREATE AND PROFESSOR OF HUMANITIES, BOSTON UNIVERSITY

"Just when you thought you'd heard all the stories about World War II, along comes *The Great Escape*, a great read and a long overdue account of the remarkable lives of a small band of greatly gifted Hungarians who made profoundly important contributions to the American effort. Kati Marton tells this astonishing story with grace and passion, a sharp eye for the telling detail and the broad sweep of history."
— TOM BROKAW, AUTHOR OF *THE GREATEST GENERATION*

"Kati Marton captures beautifully the genius and flair, as well as the insecurity and essential loneliness, of nine brilliant Jewish refugees from Hungary. Not only is this great biography, it gives a touching insight into human nature and the wellsprings of creative ambition."
— WALTER ISAACSON, AUTHOR OF *BENJAMIN FRANKLIN*

"*The Great Escape* is a tangy history of key moments in twentieth-century history as well as a glittering gallery of the boulevardiers, bon vivants, and dandies who were the makers of history. Who else but a gifted ex-Hungarian writing about the epochal gifts of other ex-Hungarians could have produced this paprika-and-champagne book? Bravissima, Kati Marton!"
— FREDERIC MORTON, AUTHOR OF *A NERVOUS SPLENDOR* AND *RUNAWAY WALTZ*

"Hungarians, those men from Mars, escaped west in the years before World War II and gave us great scientists, filmmakers, photographers, and engineers. Kati Marton's lively, engaging group portrait recovers for us the lives and work of the extraordinary men who invented Hollywood and the atomic bomb."
— RICHARD RHODES, AUTHOR OF *THE MAKING OF THE ATOMIC BOMB*

"*The Great Escape* is an evocation of genius in exile, a panoramic view of nine twentieth-century giants from Hungary who in Nazi times had to flee their country and often against great odds realized their genius in the West. Kati Marton, a seasoned American writer whose native language was the Magyar that is so unmanageable for the rest of us, has set her imaginatively researched, finely drawn individual biographies in the context of the Euro-American world of the last century and has given them a spice of Budapest nostalgia. Her book is an instructive, moving delight."
— FRITZ STERN, AUTHOR OF *FIVE GERMANYS I HAVE KNOWN*

"A remarkable woman writes about nine remarkable men who fled from Hitler and from fascism. These men, scientists and artists, were united by a shared search for freedom. They made their way to America and to England and made their impact on the free world. Kati Marton, who took this trip herself, relates their journey and the choices in their lives. She writes with passion and commitment about a world which too many could not escape, but some were fortunate enough to do so. It is a story that is gripping and a book that should be read."

— FELIX G. ROHATYN

"One of the great advantages of America as an open society is that it has welcomed people of different continents, faiths, ideologies, and ethnic and racial backgrounds who in turn have helped to ensure both the progress of our society and enriched its culture, as well. Those who have been cast off by or fled from totalitarian regimes such as Nazi Germany, Fascist Italy, and the Soviet Union personify the wealth of knowledge and talent that might have been lost to the world had the U.S. not provided them with more than a sanctuary but also a new country, a new home, and citizenship. In this insightful, moving, and deftly researched book, Kati Marton writes about nine Hungarians whose experiences are a prism through which we can see the quest and ultimate triumph of humanity seeking the right to dream and the freedom to create."

— VARTAN GREGORIAN, PRESIDENT, CARNEGIE CORPORATION OF NEW YORK

"A moving account of nine emigrants from Hungary who changed our world and their professions—a remarkable testament to the intrepid human spirit."

— HENRY KISSINGER

"Kati Marton has not written a book about Hungarians. The tale she tells, grippingly and poignantly, is a universal one—about a group of scientists, artists, and thinkers driven from their homes and forced to confront strange new lands and people. As these restive exiles ran from their memories of a lost world, Marton shows, they managed to harness their pain, tap their latent genius, and forever alter history. At a time when anti-Americanism mounts and foreigners are increasingly turned away from America's shores, Marton's story is also a timely one—there has hardly been a more urgent time to reflect on the immigrant roots and principled foundation of American greatness."

— SAMANTHA POWER, AUTHOR OF *A PROBLEM FROM HELL: AMERICA AND THE AGE OF GENOCIDE*

KATI MARTON

THE GREAT

SIMON & SCHUSTER PAPERBACKS
NEW YORK   LONDON   TORONTO   SYDNEY

To Barry

Best wishes

ESCAPE

NINE JEWS WHO FLED HITLER
AND CHANGED THE WORLD

Kati Marton

SIMON & SCHUSTER PAPERBACKS

A Division of Simon & Schuster, Inc.

1230 Avenue of the Americas

New York, NY 10020

First Simon & Schuster trade paperback edition November 2007

SIMON & SCHUSTER PAPERBACKS and colophon are registered trademarks of Simon & Schuster, Inc.

For information about special discounts for bulk purchases,
please contact Simon & Schuster Special Sales at
1-800-456-6798 or business@simonandschuster.com

Designed by Karolina Harris

Map by Paul Pugliese

Manufactured in the United States of America

7   9   10   8   6

The Library of Congress has cataloged the hardcover edition as follows:

Marton, Kati.

The great escape : nine Jews who fled Hitler and changed the world / Kati Marton.

p.   cm.

Includes bibliographical references (p.   ) and index.

1. Jews—Hungary—Budapest—Biography.   2. Jews, Hungarian—United States—Biography.
3. Exiles—Hungary—Budapest—Biography.   4. Exiles—Hungary—Budapest—History—
20th century.   I. Title.

DS135.H93A153 2006

940.53'180922—dc22   [B]   2006049162

ISBN-13: 978-0-7432-6115-9

ISBN-10: 0-7432-6115-1

ISBN-13: 978-0-7432-6116-6 (pbk)

ISBN-10: 0-7432-6116-X (pbk)

Photo credits will be found on page 272.

To my parents, Ilona Marton (1912–2004)

and Endre Marton (1910–2005)

CONTENTS

Hungarians are the only people in Europe without racial or linguistic relatives in Europe, therefore they are the loneliest on this continent. This . . . perhaps explains the peculiar intensity of their existence. . . . Hopeless solitude feeds their creativity, their desire for achieving. . . . To be Hungarian is a collective neurosis.

—ARTHUR KOESTLER

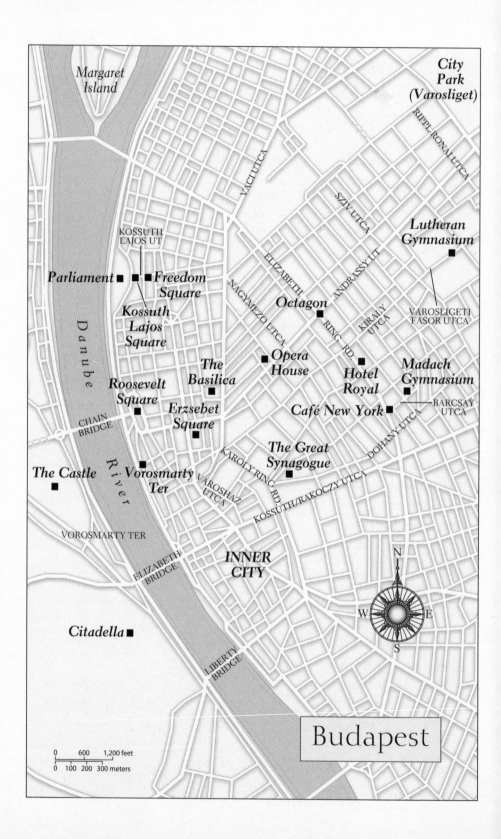

Margaret Island

City Park (Varosliget)

RIPPL-RONAI UTCA

VACI UTCA

KOSSUTH LAJOS UT

SZIV UTCA

ELIZABETH

ANDRASSY UT

Lutheran Gymnasium

Parliament ■ ■ Freedom Square

Kossuth Lajos Square

NAGYMEZO UTCA

RING RD

Octagon ■

KIRALY UTCA

VAROSLIGETI FASOR UTCA

Danube

The Basilica ■

Opera House ■

Hotel Royal ■

Madach Gymnasium ■

Roosevelt Square ■

CHAIN BRIDGE

Erzsebet Square ■

Café New York ■

BARCSAY UTCA

River

Vorosmarty Ter ■

KAROLY RING RD

The Great Synagogue ■

DOHANY UTCA

The Castle ■

VAROSHAZ UTCA

KOSSUTH/RAKOCZY UTCA

VOROSMARTY TER

INNER CITY

ELIZABETH BRIDGE

N

W   E

S

Citadella ■

LIBERTY BRIDGE

Budapest

0   600   1,200 feet
0 100 200 300 meters

INTRODUCTION

MAGIC IN THEIR POCKETS

O n a muggy day in July of 1939, two young physicists got into a blue Dodge coupé, crossed the Triborough Bridge, and drove past the futuristic World's Fair pavilion, passing fruit stands, vineyards, and modest farmhouses along Route 25, much of which was still unpaved, looking for the world's most famous scientist, Albert Einstein, who was spending the summer on Long Island. Their trip, and a second shortly thereafter, would have historic consequences.

Inside the car, which was his, Eugene Wigner, wispy-voiced and as un-prepossessing as a small-town pharmacist, listened patiently to the intense, curly-haired Leo Szilard. Wigner always let his friend, whom he called "The General," think he was in charge, but Wigner's piercing eyes, hidden behind steel-rimmed glasses, missed nothing. As they drove, they argued in their native tongue, Hungarian, about what they would say to the great man.

Deep in a typically heated conversation, the two Hungarians got lost. For two hours they drove around the South Shore; Einstein's retreat, however, was in Peconic, on the North. Finally, they found Peconic, but the roads and gray shingle houses all looked identical to the pudgy Szilard, sweaty in his gray wool suit. Agitated, he began to think that fate might be against their bold step. The cooler Wigner calmed him down. "Let's just ask somebody where Einstein lives," he suggested. "Everybody knows who Einstein is." Finally, a boy of about seven pointed his fishing rod toward a one-story house with a screened front porch.

The sixty-year-old Einstein welcomed his visitors, old friends from

Berlin days, wearing a white undershirt and rolled-up trousers. He had spent the morning sailing. Szilard and Wigner now switched to German and went straight to the point; they were in no mood for small talk. Einstein was aware of recent experiments in Germany suggesting that if neutrons bombarded uranium a nuclear chain reaction could be created. But the second part of the Hungarians' message was news to Einstein: that a nuclear chain reaction could lead to incredibly powerful bombs — atomic bombs! Shaking his famous white mane, Einstein said, "Daran habe ich gar nicht gedacht" — I had not thought of that at all. But Einstein's former colleagues at the Kaiser Wilhelm Institute for Physics in Berlin, Szilard warned, appeared to be closing in on the discovery. Until that moment, Einstein, the man whose theories had launched the revolution in physics, had not believed that atomic energy would be liberated "in my lifetime." Now he saw how his famous equation of 1905, $E=mc^2$, might apply to the explosive release of energy from mass, using uranium bombs.

Though a pacifist, Einstein well understood the Nazi threat; like Szilard and Wigner, he had left Germany because of Adolf Hitler. So the father of relativity signed a letter, prepared primarily by Szilard, to the Belgian ambassador in Washington, warning the Belgian government that bombs of unimaginable power could be made out of uranium, whose primary source was the Belgian Congo. Then Einstein returned to his dinghy, and the two Hungarians drove back to the city.

Szilard worried that this would not be enough: should they not also alert President Franklin Delano Roosevelt? "We did not know our way around in America," Szilard later recalled. But he knew an investment banker named Alexander Sachs, a friend of the president who did know Washington. After Szilard talked to Sachs, the banker concurred: the president must be told.

So two weeks later, on Sunday, July 30, Szilard returned to Einstein's cottage. Wigner was in California, so Szilard — who did not know how to drive — turned to another Hungarian, who owned a 1935 Plymouth: a young physics professor at Columbia University named Edward Teller. (Teller would later joke that he entered history as Leo Szilard's chauffeur.) Together Szilard and his bushy-browed driver extracted a second letter from Einstein. It was probably the most important letter of the twentieth century.

"I believe," the greatest scientist of the century wrote to the most important political leader of the age, "it is my duty to bring to your attention . . . that it may become possible to set up a nuclear chain reaction in a large mass of uranium, by which vast amounts of power and large quantities of new radium-like elements would be generated. Now it appears almost certain that this could be achieved in the immediate future. This new phenomenon would also lead to the construction of bombs, and it is conceivable—though much less certain—that extremely powerful bombs of a new type may thus be constructed. A single bomb of this type, carried by boat and exploded in a port, might very well destroy the whole port together with some of the surrounding territory.

"The United States has only very poor ores of uranium in moderate quantities. There is some good ore in Canada and the former Czechoslovakia, while the most important source of uranium is Belgian Congo.

"In view of this situation you may think it desirable *to have some permanent contact maintained between the Administration and the group of physicists working on chain reactions in America.*" (Emphasis added.)

Szilard believed that such a letter, signed by none other than Albert Einstein, would get immediate attention. But it did not. On September 1, 1939, when Hitler attacked Poland, Einstein's letter lay unread somewhere in FDR's in-box.

Einstein's letter was finally brought directly to FDR's attention by Sachs on October 11, and began the process that would lead to the creation of the Manhattan Project—the top secret government effort to build the atom bomb. But Roosevelt had no idea that the letter was the work of three Hungarian refugees who were not yet American citizens.

It was altogether fitting that these products of Budapest's Golden Age would stimulate the most momentous scientific-military enterprise of the twentieth century, leading to the Manhattan Project, and, after that, Hiroshima. Szilard, Wigner, and Teller—these men were just part of a group of Hungarians who, after fleeing fascist Budapest in the 1920s and 1930s, brought their distinctive outlook on life, science, and culture to the United States and Western Europe—and played immensely important roles in shaping the mid-twentieth-century world. Forced into exile by the rising tide of fascism, they would alter the way we fight and prevent wars, help shape those most modern art forms, photography and the movies, and transform the music we listen to.

This is the tale of some of them—specifically, four scientists, two photographers, two film directors, and a writer—who, collectively, helped usher in the nuclear age and the age of the computer, who left us some of our most beloved movies and many of the most enduring images of the violent century they navigated. The currents of twentieth-century history, science, culture, and politics entered them as young men in Budapest, and as they crossed borders and oceans in search of safety, they carried with them only their genius and ideas—truly they had magic in their pockets.

WHO WERE these men, and where did they come from? Was it simply a coincidence that they were from such a strange little country, with a language incomprehensible to the rest of the world? Or was there something peculiar about that country and that city at that time that created, in so many different fields, so many unusual people?

LEO SZILARD, Edward Teller, and Eugene Wigner—along with another genius from Budapest, John von Neumann—brought to America more than the physics revolution. Having saved themselves from Hitler, they were determined to alert their new nation to the mounting danger. Buffeted by every political upheaval of the century, the four scientists, and the others in this narrative, were in the vanguard of an early warning system. Working in vastly different fields, they tried to rouse a world still averting its gaze from the gathering storm. As the scientists pushed for the atom bomb, Arthur Koestler was writing *Darkness at Noon*, the first real exposé of Stalinist brutality to achieve worldwide fame. Michael Curtiz was making *Casablanca*, as much a call to anti-fascist arms as it is a romance. Robert Capa was making an immortal photographic record of the helpless victims of Generalissimo Francisco Franco's indiscriminate aerial bombs, photographs to stand alongside Pablo Picasso's *Guernica* in the field of art as political statement.

This is the chronicle of the remarkable journey of nine men from Budapest to the New World, how they strove and what they learned along the way, and the imprint they made on America and the world.

Some of the nine—Robert Capa and Edward Teller—are famous, others less so, but of equal consequence. John von Neumann, widely believed by his contemporaries to be the smartest of them all, pioneered the electronic computer and invented Game Theory. Andre Kertesz, along with Capa and Henri Cartier-Bresson, virtually invented modern photo-journalism. The names of Michael Curtiz and Alexander Korda may be less well known today, but their work is immortal. Curtiz's *Casablanca* is the most popular romantic film of all time. Korda, whose life story is more fanciful than any Hollywood fabrication, also left enduring movies; in 1994 the *New York Times* called Korda's *The Third Man* "one of the finest films ever made," a widely held judgment. Arthur Koestler is on every list of the twentieth century's greatest political writers.

They had in common, first of all, a time and a place. They were members of the same generation, roughly spanning the last decade of the nineteenth century until the outbreak of World War I. All they would become started in the city of their birth, Budapest. They were by no means unique in Budapest in its brief Golden Age; gifted men, and transforming figures, but these nine were but the tip of an iceberg of talent that came out of Budapest. Over a dozen Nobel Prize winners emerged from roughly the same generation of Hungarians. (There is some dispute as to their numbers, twelve to eighteen, depending on whether one counts areas of the country the Treaty of Trianon stripped away in 1920.) Among them were George de Hevesy, John Polanyi, and George Olah, awarded Nobel Prizes in chemistry; Albert Szent-Gyorgyi and Georg von Bekesy, awarded Nobel Prizes in medicine; Dennis Gabor and Philipp Lenard, who joined Eugene Wigner in winning the physics Nobel; and in economics, John Harsanyi, who won a Nobel for his work in Game Theory, the field pioneered by von Neumann, whose early death probably denied him his own Nobel. There were others—not all of them Nobel laureates. Marcel Breuer designed his famous chair and other Bauhaus masterpieces, as well as the Whitney Museum in New York. Bela Bartok's disturbing harmonies started in Budapest and reached the world. For decades, Bartok's students, as well as other products of Budapest's Franz Liszt Academy, among them Fritz Reiner, George Szell, Eugene Ormandy, Georg Solti, and Antal Dorati, created the sound of the world's great orchestras.

Of course, many other places have spurred such creative energy: Athens, Rome, Florence, Amsterdam, Paris, London, Edinburgh, New York have all had their day—some more than once. In each case a certain set of unique circumstances combined to create a moment of special creativity. But what makes this moment dramatically different is that the geniuses of Budapest had to leave their homeland to achieve greatness. One can only wonder how much more potential was trapped inside the city as its brief moment of magic and opportunity turned into a fascist hell in 1944. But before all that—before Admiral Nicholas Horthy, Europe's first proto-fascist, before Adolf Hitler and Adolf Eichmann, before the communist leader Bela Kun—Budapest between 1890 and 1918 was relatively secure, tolerant of new people and ideas and bursting with civic pride. It was also a secular city.

It is important to note that the men who make up this narrative were all double outsiders once they left their native land. They were not only from a small, linguistically impenetrable, landlocked country, they were also Jews. (One could argue that, in fact, they were even triple outsiders, since they were all nonobservant Jews whose families had consciously rejected the *shtetl* for the modern, secular, cosmopolitan world that, briefly, lay glistening in front of them.)

The nine men who are the subject of *The Great Escape* were Jews in a city that briefly welcomed and encouraged their ambition. Unlike the Jews of Russia and Romania, Budapest Jews were integrated into the city's great academic and cultural—though not its political—institutions. Budapest, like New York, Paris, and Berlin, became a magnet for the brightest from all over the region. The multiethnic cauldron of the Austro-Hungarian Empire in its closing years helped to ignite creative explosions in both Budapest and Vienna. It is no accident that another secular Jew, Theodor Herzl, born in Budapest in similar circumstances only a few years earlier, created modern Zionism out of the ferment of the Austro-Hungarian Empire.

All nine were big thinkers, with big dreams. The small, the political, or the bureaucratic were neither open nor appealing to them. It was no accident that they excelled in new fields where they could break new ground, and where official or institutional support was less important than talent: mathematics, physics, literature, photography, and film. Their forefathers had lived on the margins, but this generation believed they could change the world, just as their world had itself changed.

Then, just as most of them were reaching manhood—though the youngest, Robert Capa, was still a boy—in the wake of the catastrophic

First World War, these daring young men collided with the realities of hate and violence. Creative life could not flourish in a climate of fear. First wearing the guise of nationalism and then murderous racism, fear marched into Budapest in the 1920s and 1930s. Jolted out of the comfort of their lives, they would never again feel entirely secure; fame and fortune would not alter that condition. Their westward journey took them to Vienna, Berlin, Paris, New York, and, for some, Hollywood—through a boiling continent and beyond. They reinvented themselves and assimilated cultures as they moved west. But the city of their youth, pulsing with energy and in love with the new, and, however briefly, secure but not smug, marked them for life.

When it came to politics, they were as sensitive as burn victims. All nine had experienced how quickly things can change. Some, particularly Korda, Capa, and von Neumann, masked their insecurity better than the others. But as Sir Georg Solti, one of the most celebrated conductors of our time, wrote of his childhood in post–World War I Budapest: "Since that time, I have never been able to rid myself of the fear of anyone wearing a military or police uniform, or even a customs office uniform, because in Hungary uniforms always meant persecution in one form or another." Such feelings were buried deep within all the men in this narrative.

WHY HAS the tale of this remarkable Hungarian diaspora not been told in this manner before? The answer is twofold: language and history. The Hungarian language, my mother tongue, is virtually impenetrable—a member of the Finno-Ugric family, but not really similar to other European languages—and limits outside research into the culture and the people. And history—the Cold War and the Soviet occupation, which shut Hungary and her neighbors off from the West—turned Mitteleuropa into a frozen, uniformly gray mass. By 1989, when the Iron Curtain crumbled, this generation had dispersed. Budapest, emerging from almost half a century of Soviet rule, its World War II scars still painfully apparent, was barely recognizable. The world had moved on—and so had they.

The nine men who form this narrative also played a part by obscuring their own history. While the United States had welcomed them, their own country had shunned them—or tried to exterminate them. In exile they restyled themselves into urbane Europeans and turned their back on a homeland tearing itself apart. Why look back? The past was a minefield. Their blazing triumph enabled them to obscure their Budapest origins: von Neumann transformed into the genius of German physics; Kertesz became Andre of Paris; Capa "The World's Greatest War Photographer"; Korda, Sir Alexander, friend to Sir Winston Churchill; Koestler, the continent's mournful prophet of totalitarianism; and so on. But, as we shall see, there was an emotional cost to their skillful reinvention.

A PERSONAL WORD is necessary: this tale is in my bloodstream. Like the cast of *The Great Escape*, my family, too, rode the great crest of Budapest's golden years. My great-grandfather, Maurice Mandl, born in 1848, the year revolution swept Europe, was the son of the chief rabbi of Dobris, Bohemia. German was his mother tongue, Franz Joseph his emperor. In his early twenties he jumped onto a rickety train to Budapest. Maurice soon learned Hungarian and prospered as an accountant in the boomtown of Budapest. His rabbi father traveled from Bohemia to Budapest only once, in 1876, to officiate at Maurice's wedding in the great synagogue that still sits—recently restored—on Dohany Street. Maurice and his wife, Tekla, had six children, among them, in the fashion of the newly emerging, emancipated, and primarily secular Hungarian Jews, a lawyer, an engineer, a teacher, and a grain merchant (my grandfather).

In 1900, like many other aspiring Jews in Hungary, the family Magyarized its name to Marton, and entered the city's prosperous middle class. Great-grandfather Maurice's apartment was in the fashionable Leopoldtown area, near the Parliament, overlooking the Danube. Maurice's sons were decorated in the First World War, which Europeans call, without irony, the Great War. Less than thirty years later, his grandsons would not be allowed to wear their country's uniform nor bear arms, but were instead sent off to forced labor on the Russian Front. Unlike the central figures in this book, the Martons stayed through the Nazi terror— which they miraculously survived. Though my father, Endre, was called up by the Nazis for forced labor on the Eastern Front, he managed to escape and from then on he and my mother, Ilona, were hidden by Christian friends. My maternal grandparents were not so lucky. Living in a northeastern city called Miskolc, they were among the first Jews rounded up by Adolf Eichmann and his Hungarian allies and forced on an

Auschwitz-bound transport. The last word my mother ever had from them was a postcard slipped through the crack of a cattle car headed for Auschwitz. My mother, a historian, and my father, an economist, became journalists for the two American wire services, United Press and Associated Press, after the war, as the communists seized Hungary. Early in 1955, they were arrested by the communists and convicted of being spies for a country neither of them had set foot in, the United States of America. Their story attracted international attention and made the front page of the *New York Times*. For nearly two years, while my parents were incarcerated in Budapest's maximum-security Fo Street prison, my sister and I were placed in the care of strangers.

My parents were released from prison in the brief thaw just prior to the outbreak of the Hungarian Revolution in October 1956, and resumed their reporting for the Associated Press and the United Press. When the Soviet forces, which had briefly withdrawn from Budapest in the face of a national uprising, returned to crush the revolt, my father sent the last cable from Budapest, alerting the world that Soviet tanks and troops were rolling toward the capital. Then all communications with the outside world were cut. (These are among my most enduring childhood memories.) Again in danger of arrest for their coverage of the revolt, my parents and my sister and I were granted asylum in the American embassy in Budapest, along with the world-famous cardinal, Josef Mindszenty, who, I remember clearly, blessed us each night. (Not only did the cardinal think we were good little Catholic girls, so did we; our parents had raised us as Catholics, and never told us our true family history.) In early 1957, a brave American diplomat named Tom Rogers drove us across the Austria-Hungary frontier to freedom—and exile. Today, only one of Maurice Mandl's offspring remains in Budapest, my father's first cousin, my aunt Tekla, now in her eighties, who, along with my mother's younger sister, Magda, are my only surviving relatives left in Budapest.

This family saga partly accounts for this book, which fills in a missing chapter in the history of the tumultuous twentieth century. These nine people seemed very familiar to me; I felt I almost knew them personally. Their anxiety—born of their own history and their fear that peace cannot last—resonated inside me. As I did research about Leo Szilard, who always kept two packed bags with him in case he had to flee again, I thought of my mother; forty years after she fled Hungary for the security of the United States, she still answered the telephone with a somewhat tremulous "Hello?" as if braced for bad news.

IN ADDITION to being insecure, driven, and *lonely* once they fled Budapest, most of the nine characters in *The Great Escape* were hedonists with a love of the good things in life, for whom appearances were all-important. (Leo Szilard, in his rumpled raincoat, is the sole exception.) My father once told me if he ever wrote a novel, it would be about Andre Kertesz's older brother, Imre. Why? I asked, when Andre is the one who achieved so much. "Imre," my father said, "interested me more. In the 1930s, I used to see him at my parents' open house on Sundays. The anti-Semitic laws were already in effect and Kertesz had lost his job. But he always looked like a million dollars." That, to me, summed up the Hungarian credo, by which my parents lived: whatever hand life deals you, put a good face on it and the rest will follow. This credo was the impulse behind Alexander Korda, who lived in the grandest hotels when he could least afford them, Robert Capa, who bought an elegant Burberry raincoat for the Normandy invasion, and John von Neumann, who wore a three-piece suit and tie for a mule ride down the Grand Canyon. Young Arthur Koestler was the only student at his German boarding school to wear an elegant Eton suit. Later, with his precisely parted hair and his soft Harris tweeds, Koestler was among Europe's most dapper intellectuals. In a similar vein, I recall my mother, while awaiting her arrest by the Hungarian secret police (she had been warned), carefully choosing what she would wear to prison. Comfort was important, but style, partly as a manifestation of defiance, played an equal part in her choice of a Scottish tartan skirt for her year in a communist cell.

Like the nine men profiled here, my parents (and I, to a lesser extent) were touched by a sense of perpetual exile, of never quite belonging, of having been reinvented in the New World, without escaping the burdens of the Old. Something sad and distant hung over them, the legacy perhaps of having once been marked for death by their own people. That, too, was part of their inheritance.

Millions of other people were displaced by the wars of the last century. But for Hungarians, exile was magnified by linguistic and cultural isolation. "Hungarians," Arthur Koestler wrote, "are the only people in Europe without racial and linguistic relatives in Europe, therefore they are the loneliest on this continent. This . . . perhaps explains the peculiar intensity of their existence. . . . Hopeless solitude feeds their creativity, their desire for achieving. . . . To be Hungarian is a collective neurosis."

For Hungarian Jews the loss of *their* Budapest ran even deeper. The pain was sharpened by the speed with which they had gained—and lost— their Zion on the Danube. It happened, after all, in less than forty years. Describing the mood in Budapest at the time of her wedding day on April 25, 1897, Leo Szilard's mother, Tekla, reflected the boundless optimism of the age and the opportunity it was suddenly providing Jews. "The city was growing by leaps and bounds. I felt as if this were all my progress, my development."

Yet by 1945, Budapest, which the (non-Jewish) Hungarian poet Endre Ady described as "built by the Jews for the rest of us," was no more— smashed by World War II, its spirit snuffed out earlier by the fascists—and about to disappear inside the Soviet empire for another forty years.

I had a sense of this longing for what was irretrievably lost during an interview with a great chronicler of the Hungarian Holocaust, Randolph Braham. As we began, sitting in my New York apartment as the sun set, Professor Braham, eighty years old, whose own family had been destroyed by Hungarian fascists, closed his eyes. He had retreated to a faraway place. After some moments of silence, he switched to our mother tongue, "Meg nyilnak a kertben a nyari viragok . . ." recalling a well-loved poem by Sandor Petofi, a favorite revolutionary-romantic bard. "The summer flowers are still in bloom in the garden . . ."

I LOVED my hometown as a child, but it was not *their* Budapest, that glittering, elegant metropolis on a hill, which was as remote from the Stalinist gray city of my mid-1950s childhood as the Emerald City of Oz. But it came alive to me through the eyes, the letters, the faded old photographs of that era, and I could imagine—and share—the excitement of those faraway days. It is in that showy place, over a century ago, that this chronicle begins.

PART ONE

PLENTY

Y ou must remember this . . ." Rick's Café in Casablanca—or to be precise, in *Casablanca*—is a refuge from the outside world, a smoky microcosm of the early war years. A woman trades her diamonds for quick cash, an elderly refugee couple practice fractured English ("Vitch Vatch? Such Much!"), a beautiful woman offers to sell herself to the corrupt Vichy police chief, while another gets drunk at the bar.

It was in a place like Rick's that Mihaly Kaminer first dreamed of escape. His café was the New York and it towered like a cathedral over the young man's universe. The New York was (and in its newly restored state, is once again) Budapest's most flamboyant café, a gold and marble temple that welcomed the city's leading writers and journalists into its smoky, vaulted chambers. When a playwright was temporarily down on his luck and could not pay for a meal or even an espresso, the café's owner, Willy Tarjan, shrugged it off. The café featured a special low-cost platter of cold cuts for hungry artists. The headwaiter was also known to advance small loans to his struggling but promising customers. Writers and poets worked at their tables from morning until late at night. Their editors sat at separate tables. In the New York, originality and wit determined your fate. Colorful characters were good for business.

More than half a century after he first set foot in the New York, Kaminer, now Michael Curtiz, would bring elements of his beloved Budapest café to a Hollywood back lot and win the Best Director Oscar for *Casablanca*, the most popular romantic film of all time. And the film would have an unbelievable staying power, remaining at or near the top of every poll of all-time favorite films. It was set in Casablanca, but Rick's Café, right down to the actors playing the waiters, was straight out of Budapest. "I am sometimes overcome by a feeling," Curtiz wrote from Los Angeles in 1960 to a friend in Budapest, "that I am living—not surrounded by American mansions—but gazing at the hour hand of the clock at the New York Café, through the mist, at dawn."

It is not surprising that Curtiz's memory of the city of his birth had a Camelot-like quality. Like King Arthur's mythical citadel, Budapest, too, had its season, as shining and as brief as Camelot's. It began in 1867, when Vienna, the capital of the still mighty Austrian Empire, granted it equal status as co-capital of the newly formed Austro-Hungarian Empire. The thousand-year-old Magyar nation had struggled for centuries for acknowledgment of its special place on the continent. The fiercely proud Magyars had submitted to various armies of occupation, including the Ottomans from 1526 until 1699. When Austrians rolled back the Turks in 1699, they imposed their own rule over Hungary. In 1848 the Austrian Habsburgs brutally extinguished a Hungarian war for independence, scorching Magyar earth and pride. In 1867, as co-capital of the Austro-Hungarian Empire, recognition seemed to have finally arrived. Budapest, formerly a provincial outpost (made up of three small towns, Buda, Pest, and Obuda), would embody the nation's long pent up aspirations for grandeur.

Between 1870 and 1910 the city, pulsing with energy and ambition, became a magnet for the region's brightest and best, ballooning from 300,000 residents to over one million. Budapest had become Europe's fastest growing metropolis. The grandest Parliament and the largest Stock Exchange in Europe, the continent's first underground train, a boulevard to rival the Champs-Elysées, and an extravagant jumble of architectural fantasies soon altered the once provincial cityscape.

THIS THEN was the stage that welcomed the future Michael Curtiz in 1888. Curtiz, who would later blur details of his modest beginnings, neither wrote his memoirs nor wanted them written. (Even his birth date, variously given as 1886 or 1888, is subject to debate.) Nor is it clear when he changed his name from the distinctly Jewish Kaminer to the Magyarized Kertesz, before finally becoming Curtiz. He could not quite erase the circumstances of his Budapest youth. The child of Orthodox Jews (alone among the group covered in this book), he lived in a crowded Jewish neighborhood, the Joseph district. A world away from the grand boulevards, it was a small town of dusty courtyards, dark taverns, shabby tailor shops, and dark smithies, tucked inside the city. It was neither his parents nor his schools that shaped Curtiz. It was Budapest.

Perhaps no one benefited more from Hungary's new status and Budapest's explosive growth than the empire's Jewish population. For the first time, Jews could aim almost as high as Christians, at least in certain fields. Budapest welcomed their contribution. Hungarian Jews and other enlightened Hungarians had similar ambitions and values. Each valued learning, education, and culture. Each had recently won long-dreamed-of rights from the Habsburgs. Hungarians—Jewish and non-Jewish—had much to prove and were eager to do so. "In the hierarchy of social prestige," Franz Alexander, one of the founders of psychoanalysis and a Budapest Jew who came of age during this period, wrote, "creative artists and scientists ranked first." What mattered were brains, drive, and talent.

Starting in 1867, when a law emancipating Hungary's Jews was enacted, Jews (including my great-grandfather) streamed into Budapest from Moravia and Bohemia. Though only 5 percent of the country's overall population, by 1900, Jews were one-fifth of Budapest's residents. For a generation, Hungarians regarded Judaism as a faith, not an ethnicity. In 1912, a Jew, Ferenc Heltai, was elected mayor of the city. Ironically, Heltai's uncle was Theodor Herzl, the founder of Zionism, who moved to Vienna as a youth. Although both his parents were Hungarian, Herzl would have been hard-pressed to find people in Budapest sympathetic to his dream of a Jewish state; Hungarian Jews thought they had already found their Promised Land on the banks of the Danube, and had no interest in going to Palestine or anywhere else.

Nineteen hundred, around the time Curtiz—though that was not yet his name—prepared his bar mitzvah, was high noon for a city reinventing itself. Those arriving for the first time were surprised to find a modern city, the largest between Vienna and St. Petersburg. Budapest's dream of world stature, of catching up and even passing Vienna, was now within reach.

The country, however, was still composed of land-rich aristocrats and semiliterate peasants. Magyar aristocrats and lesser gentry were not interested in swapping their tradition-bound lives for urban bustle. They enjoyed the new luxury hotels that soon lined the Pest side of the Danube and, a block or so away, savored their cigars in the paneled elegance of the National Casino, a perfect replica of an English gentlemen's club. But building things, or running, selling, creating, or editing—that was work unsuitable for a hereditary landowner. A well-known anecdote from the period summed it up. In 1900, Count Karolyi invited the German consul-general in Budapest to dine at his palace. At the end of an evening of lavish entertainment, the diplomat asked the count how it was that no one in the Karolyi household played music. "Why should we?" asked the count. "We keep the Gypsies to play music for us, since we are too lazy to do it for ourselves, and the Jews to do the work for us." All parties seemed satisfied with this arrangement.

With only a few occupations formally closed to them, Jews eagerly provided the brainpower for the emerging capitalist economy. Jewish assimilation happened faster here than anywhere else in Europe. There was no ghetto in Budapest, though certain densely packed parts of Pest—such as the young Curtiz's neighborhood—were up to 70 percent Jewish. But even there, Jews spoke Hungarian, not Yiddish. Both the Magyar language and the culture were orphans in Europe. The Magyars welcomed the Jews' loyalty, for without them Hungarians would have remained a minority within the multinational empire. By 1910, Jews made up half the lawyers and doctors, one-third of the engineers, and one-quarter of artists and writers in Budapest. Jews were largely responsible for Budapest's transformation into a bustling financial and cultural hub. Over 40 percent of the journalists working at the city's thirty-nine daily newspapers were Jews.

A popular joke of Curtiz's childhood is revealing. A local is showing an Englishman around the city: "Here, on Calvin Square, is the Calvinists' Church, and," pointing to the river, "on the Danube, the Greek Orthodox Church. The crumbling one over there belongs to the Lutherans, and the one with the big dome, that's the Basilica of the Catholics." "And the big one with the twin towers?" the visitor inquired. "That, Your Lordship, is the synagogue of the people of Budapest."

The offspring of the new arrivals filled the newly reformed schools, built new monuments, and invented new art forms. Tellingly, the city did not have an artistic or literary quarter, no Greenwich Village, Bloomsbury, or Montparnasse. The whole city was open and hungry for the new. Everyone read the same newspapers, and, even if they could not afford tickets, knew the current offering at the National Theater or the Opera. "It was an era," Franz Alexander recalled, "in which literary and theatrical events absorbed our interest as much as today's youth is fascinated by a

baseball game or a prizefight. . . . All this went with an unshakable optimism about human progress." Six hundred cafés, and among the continent's highest concentration of theaters and cabarets, changed the
rhythms of the city. There were streets as crowded at midnight as at nine in
the morning. The moment was ripe to show the world that free at last of
Ottoman and Habsburg occupation, this was *someplace*. Jews—whose
goal was to be Hungarian citizens of the Jewish faith—and Hungarians
seemed equally invested in the dream.

There was reason for urgency. Budapest Jews were born into families
with memories of other places, other lives. One or two generations before
the young men and women who packed the cafés, the publishing houses,
and editorial offices, Jews were locked into small trades in muddy villages
scattered across the Austro-Hungarian Empire. Village rabbi or Talmudic
scholar was the highest intellectual aspiration of their grandparents. Em-
bedded in the newly cosmopolitan Jews' DNA were stories of the narrow
and often perilous provincial life. In Hungary, as elsewhere in Europe,
anti-Semitism had deep roots. The first popular outburst against the Jews
took place during the revolution of 1848, the second during the so-called
"liberal age" in 1882–83. A sense of how quickly events could take an unexpected turn was part of Budapest Jews' genetic inheritance. So was
seamlessly adapting new roles, new identities, as circumstance required it.

E V E R Y few minutes, the bright yellow tram, the city's new symbol, clattered down the cobblestone Ring Road, steps from young Curtiz's house.
For a few pennies a ride, the tram bound the city together. Curtiz's universe was the Inner City, a semicircle bordered by the Danube. Everything seemed to happen inside the Ring Road. The tram rolled by the
National Theater as well as the Comic Opera, where a steady stream of
plays by Ferenc Molnar—the city's most famous playwright, a secular Jew
(best known for *Liliom*, transformed later into the Rodgers and Hammer-
stein musical *Carousel*), mocked the newly rich. Waiting for the tram on
the Ring Road you could catch the strains of musicians rehearsing in the
Franz Liszt Academy, where Bela Bartok taught and composed. The Ring
intersected the new Andrassy Boulevard, a leafy homage to the Champs-
Elysées that boasted a jewel-like Opera House, recently under the baton
of Gustav Mahler himself.

One block away was Budapest's Broadway, Nagymezo Utca, with its string of cabarets, music halls, and the Orpheum, featuring the city's most popular entertainment, the operetta. A hybrid of grand spectacle, lavish costumes, catchy tunes, thumping choreography, sentimental plot, and dry, urbane wit, the operetta distilled mass culture. The Orpheum's proprietor, Desider Balint, combining sharp business sense with an artistic sensibility, embodied the razzle-dazzle of the city at the turn of the century. A few years after arriving from the provinces with nothing but big ideas, Balint became one of the city's most prominent nouveaux riches. Mass entertainment was big business.

Much of the city's creative business was transacted on the terraces and inside the chandeliered chambers of the cafés. Like the Athenian agora or the Roman forum, Budapest's cafés played a civilizing role. A bright idea, a joke, or a whispered tune heard at the Café Japan on Andrassy Boulevard at noon, reached the New York down the Ring Road, by dusk. A respite after a hard day, a safe haven from a bad marriage or a cramped apartment, cafés fulfilled many roles. "They spoiled you there," Hollywood director Andre de Toth remembered, "with the morning papers on their cane frames with handles so the newsprint never smudged your fingers, the always fresh hot coffee, white linen napkins the waiters draped on your knees. They sent you off to face the day not *thinking* but knowing you are the king." Observing the intensity of the interaction on these terraces, a visitor could easily assume that everybody in Budapest was selling something: a surefire stock, a novel way to tan leather, or simply a novel. As the famed French film director Jean Renoir has noted, "The foundation of all great civilization is loitering." No city in Europe took loitering more seriously than Budapest.

WHILE CURTIZ—largely unsupervised—prowled the city's streets, his Orthodox Jewish father, Ignatz, was laying bricks at the Basilica. There was little to keep the youth at home in the family's cramped apartment, much less in the tiny room he shared with his two younger brothers and a sister. "Many times we are hungry," Curtiz recalled half a century later, in his still fractured English. "I tell my brothers then, all my life I will work to keep from being that way. Sleeping with four kids in one room." His mother, once a singer, brought show business into the home. Like the city, young Mihaly was a natural show-off. Show business, one of the city's growth industries, was a perfect outlet for him.

For five years after Curtiz graduated from Budapest's Royal Academy of Theater and Art, he paid his dues on provincial stages. By 1911, he was tapped for a role in Budapest's National Theater. Six feet tall, with even features and steely blue eyes, he was launched on a stage career. But the young man had no illusions about his moderate acting ability, and moderate success was not what he had in mind.

But there was a new art form on the Ring Road and it was the talk of the cafés. The café of the flashy Hotel Royal was projecting the films of the pioneering French Lumière brothers. Other cafés quickly felt compelled to dim their lights and crank grainy bits of film showing such scenes as the arrival of the king of Bulgaria in Budapest, British royalty hare-hunting, the life of vagrant Gypsies, or a drunken cyclist race. The subject did not much matter; it was the medium that mesmerized the city. Sometimes, the same man who ground the coffee would crank the projector; well-developed biceps were useful for both. Literary journals, such as the one edited by another ambitious newcomer named Korda, analyzed the prospects of the movies, *mozi* in Hungarian. The word itself was coined on the Ring Road.

Observing the rapt customers at the normally noisy Café Velence, Curtiz saw his future. Films seemed to appeal to all classes, but especially to the new urban class of workers and professionals looking to be entertained after a long day. The movies were cheaper and more accessible than concerts or the opera. The light and the sound transported the bricklayer and the baron into other worlds. Figures of literature and history jumped to life. By 1914, 108 of Budapest's cafés, cabarets, and theaters doubled as movie houses. Mixing the high and the low, this was the birth of mass entertainment.

Curtiz had a vision for the embryonic art form. "I can see amazing things," he wrote in 1910, "possibilities in film which the narrow confines of the stage can never encompass." The film director should control the plot, he insisted, as well as the action, the sets, and the actors. He made and starred in Hungary's first feature film, *Today and Tomorrow*, of which unfortunately no trace remains. Within the next year, he directed several more silent films, quickly acquiring a reputation as Budapest's premier director.

But Curtiz was restless. He knew that better films and more advanced technology were sprouting beyond Hungary's borders—in Germany, France, and in Denmark. Impatient to learn, in 1913 he took the train to Copenhagen, then a mecca for films. Movie lore has it that he passed himself off as a deaf-mute and was hired by Nordisk, the continent's film industry leader. For six months he absorbed the latest editing and direct-ing techniques, lived in a world of acetone fumes, film draped around his neck, razor blade in hand, literally mastering cutting-edge technology. Returning to Budapest later that year with the sheen of foreign certifica-tion, he cut an even bigger figure in the capital's cultural scene.

Curtiz was not much of a letter writer and did not keep a journal. There is but a single reference among Curtiz's papers to the war that embroiled all of Europe and America, and that was to cost Hungary its new identity, and Budapest its brief tenure as a world capital. "The intoxicating joy of life was interrupted, the world had gone mad," he wrote of World War I in 1960. "We were taught to kill. I was drafted into the Emperor's Army. We were geared up for the terrors of glorious wartime. . . . When we marched out in the mornings and passed by the cemetery, I thought, we are going to the barracks to prepare the raw material for the cemetery. One morning we were ordered into the battlefield. After that, many things happened: destruction, thousands forever silenced, crippled or sent to anonymous graves. Then came the collapse [of Austria-Hungary]. Fate had spared me."

FATE HAD not spared Hungary, however. As the junior partner of the empire, Hungary entered a war that used the excuse of avenging the Sarajevo murder of an Austrian archduke famous for his hostility to all things Hungarian. The assassination of Franz Ferdinand by Serbian na-tionalists on June 28, 1914, gave the empire the chance to absorb Serbia, as Austria-Hungary had absorbed Bosnia and Herzegovina five years ear-lier. Germany assured Austria she would back whatever action she took against Serbia, allied with Russia on the European chessboard. So, as the German chancellor Otto von Bismarck had predicted, "Some damned foolish thing in the Balkans" ignited a world war that ended the Old Order in Europe forever. Caught on the losing side, Hungary began her seventy-five-year slide into the abyss. And among the war's first victims were the Jews.

But the front had been far from Budapest and, for a while, on the surface, the city seemed unchanged. The fine new buildings still stood, the cafés were full, the theaters packed. But, in fact, World War I changed everything for Hungary. The collapse of the empire first led to a peaceful socialist revolution under the liberal Count Michael Karolyi, in late 1918. But this well-meaning but incompetent aristocrat could neither stem the postwar, post-empire chaos, nor the mass starvation of an unraveling society.

THE TWENTY-FIVE-YEAR-OLD Curtiz was not about to allow political turmoil to slow him down. Along with directing, he was writing serious film criticisms, elaborating his vision for the new medium. Each scene must lead to the next, nothing should be extraneous, editing must be tight, while acting should be natural, free of theatrics. Films should reflect real life, real emotions.

"It is sufficient for us to say that this film was directed by [Michael Curtiz]," began a 1917 review in *Mozgofenykep*—"Film News"—of his *Nobody's Son*. By 1918, he was making lavish costume dramas and historical epics as well as mining modern Hungarian literature, the works of Ferenc Molnar and Janos Arany, to packed houses. But packing houses in Budapest was never going to be enough. "Sadly," he wrote, "we cannot even think about [films with international appeal]," he wrote in *Movie Week* in 1918. "The world has no appreciation for Hungarian history or culture. The great thing about films is that they have the potential to appeal to a wide, international audience."

SOON BUDAPEST could claim another first: the capital of Europe's first Soviet republic, after the Soviet Union itself. Freshly demobilized soldiers and refugees from Transylvania and other parts of Hungary awarded to its neighbors by the Versailles powers swarmed into the capital, looking for food and work. A Soviet-trained demagogue named Bela Kun and about five thousand communist activists, with support from the hordes of jobless, forced Count Karolyi to yield power. And one of the most significant facts about Hungary's ill-starred 133-day Soviet republic would be that its reckless leader, Bela Kun, was a Jew.

Curtiz was too prominent not to attract Kun's attention. Soon he was recruited to make communist propaganda films as a member of the Arts

Council of the newly nationalized film industry. Though he had little interest in politics, he was good at this, too. *My Brother Is Coming*, Curtiz's earliest film to have survived, is a rousing, if heavy-handed, tale of a returned POW who becomes a communist.

On November 16, 1919, Admiral Nicholas Horthy, the last commander of the Austro-Hungarian navy, chest ablaze with decorations for service to the fallen empire, rode into Budapest at the head of an armed right-wing militia, and declared himself Regent. Horthy called Budapest the "guilty city," which had "denied its 1,000 year history . . . flung its crown, its national colors into the mud and wrapped itself in red rags." Budapest, now synonymous with anti-Magyar and *Jewish*, would pay for the excesses of a few thousand Communists, among whose top leaders were Jews. In 1919, having seen communism fail, Hungary pioneered another form of twentieth-century rule. Horthy established Europe's first proto-fascist state. In the words of historian Istvan Deak, Horthy was "neither very cultivated nor very bright, [he] was a Hungarian patriot who changed his views and methods often." Variously described as an archreactionary, a dictator, or simply a fascist, what is certain is that with the arrival of this regent without a king, this admiral without a fleet, Budapest's bold experiment with an open, tolerant, urban culture was over, and democracy would not arrive until 1989.

The thirty-one-year-old filmmaker understood that his hometown had become a dangerous place. From the great glass and steel Eastern Rail Road Station—one of the city's proud monuments—Curtiz cast a final backward glance, and boarded the train for Vienna.

B UDAPEST," sixteen-year-old Sandor Kellner—whom the world would later know as Alexander Korda—wrote of his first glimpse of the city at the height of its glory in 1908, "behind this strange word lay new and miraculous mysteries. . . . [I] had known from books that . . . there existed things other than what [I] had experienced and seen in a small town, that there were secrets as strange as an Eastern tale." Korda approached, he wrote later, Budapest, "like a bride waiting for the moment of revelation." It was the beginning of his liberation from "a half-peasant family in a small town [where] there were no mysteries to unlock, no beauty to be born, only tranquility. And tranquility was boredom." Kellner craned his neck out the train window. The city appeared like a stage set: the river banked on one side by sheer cliffs, and on the other by gleaming luxury hotels. Joining the tumult outside the station, he let himself be carried along by the crowd to the boulevard beyond. He would not be bored in Budapest.

In the village he had left only hours before, no building was more than one story, and geese picked their way along the muddy road that led from the Kellners' whitewashed house to the town of Turkeve. But the boy had not wasted his childhood. During the black country nights in the Great Plain, he had devoured the great adventure tales of Verne, Wells, Kipling, and Dickens. His knowledge of the world came from their stories, and like them, he wanted to be a storyteller. He would never look back to the village where he had first dreamed of "new and miraculous mysteries."

Tall and gawky, Sandor Kellner was in a hurry when he reached the city. He was poor, he had already outgrown his clothes, and he was burning with a sense of his own untapped gifts. He had the preternaturally serious air of a youth who, at sixteen, had become the family's chief provider. His mother, Ernesztina, who soon followed her son to the capital, saw her own intelligence mirrored in the eldest of her three sons; she would be the first co-conspirator of his dreams. His gymnasium was on Barcsay Utca just off the Ring Road, in the boisterous heart of the city. When he stepped off the yellow streetcar each morning he could see the gold letters, "New York," carved into the highest tower of the multi-turreted stone pile; for him, like Curtiz, it was the most magical of the city's six hundred cafés. But the country boy was not yet ready to venture through its massive revolving doors.

From the start, Kellner/Korda lived several lives simultaneously—and never played by the rules. With his hungry mind and boundless self-confidence, he and the city were made for each other. Budapest's blend of the sophisticated and the showy appealed to him. He could not afford education above the gymnasium level, but the city's cafés, cabarets, opera, and the National Theater were his advanced education. Like Curtiz, he had a natural gift for showmanship. Actual, stomach-churning hunger fueled his energy and his boldness. Submitting articles and short stories to a liberal newspaper that had no idea the author was still an adolescent, he changed his name to "Korda," which was both easy to remember and vaguely—but not too—Hungarian-sounding. He borrowed the name from *Sursum Corda*—"lift up your hearts"—in the Latin mass. In a city so open to ambition and drive, it did not even seem presumptuous.

Until 1910 Korda's energy lacked focus. Then, one day the lights dimmed in the Café Velence while he was there, and a silent film was projected on a whitewashed wall. Overwhelmed, Korda turned to a friend, Simon Darvas, and whispered, "That's what I want to do." The medium was rough, silent and new, but Korda immediately saw its impact reflected in the faces around him. Unlike the theater, movies did not need an educated audience; they could be shown anywhere, anytime. Who wasn't looking for escape? The movies were about reinvention; the impossible made possible; small, ordinary people suddenly large and radiant on the screen. Who better than Sandor Kellner, reinvented as Alexander Korda, to master this new medium?

Like Curtiz, Korda understood he could not learn the craft in Budapest. He chose Paris, where the Pathé Studio was regarded as the world's most advanced film production company. But Korda was barely earning enough to feed himself and his family, much less pay for a trip to Paris. Lack of funds, however, would never deter Korda. "I would like to go to Paris," he wrote one of his more prosperous relatives, "but, as you know, I am poor. Would you lend me two hundred crowns?" In exchange, Korda promised, "I will become a great man." His relative was unmoved, but his mother scraped together the train fare.

If Budapest made an electrifying impact on the country boy, Paris, the epicenter of civilization in 1911, stunned him. Desperately poor, he was always hungry. All his life he remembered tearing up at the sight of roast beef and *frites* through a Paris restaurant window. Lurking on the fringes of the Pathé Studio, he watched the filming of silent costume epics, learning—and yearning.

In the Louvre, Alex found not only great pictures but a place to keep warm. Within a year, he had picked up a rough French and the right to claim France as one of his spiritual homes. Pale and scrawny, the eighteen-year-old returned to Budapest, his ticket paid for by the Hungarian consul in Paris. He now knew something of the world and the movies it was making and watching. With his new Parisian credentials, Korda pitched himself headlong into the vibrant world of the Ring Road.

Soon Korda was writing movie reviews and working for Projectograph, the first Hungarian film company, owned by Mor Ungerleider. Korda was also developing his own ideas about the infant medium's possibilities. He even created an original and innovative platform for his ideas, a film journal called *Budapest Cinema*. In its pages Korda elaborated the revolutionary notion that a film director was a creative artist, and that movies themselves were more than entertainment, they were a new art form— ideas decades ahead of their time. His editorial office was the Café New York that he had once not dared to enter; now he was a recognized figure there. His publication was sold in the city's movie houses. Together, Korda and his rival Curtiz were helping turn Budapest from a café town into a cinema town.

Budapest was suddenly wide open to the handsome twenty-one-year-old. Headwaiters and fellow *personnages* in the capital's literary café world acknowledged his entrance. Years later, he claimed the most important lesson he learned in Budapest in his youth was to listen. But he also learned how to spellbind and to charm. A naturally gifted actor, Korda assimilated the styles, gestures, and intonations of Budapest's most flamboyantly successful personalities. That gift proved to be more important to his career than a university education. With a country boy's shrewd eye for sizing up character, motives, and vulnerabilities, Korda decided he would be more than a skilled filmmaker. His crowning achievement would be his own carefully crafted persona. If he played the role of a man of consequence convincingly enough, he would soon become one. Korda was only twenty when he added a prop that would become his trademark: the big cigar. "Films were considered something rather lowly," he later explained. "More lowly than newspapers. Cigars were large and cheap at the time. We smoked cigars to show we were important, and to make up for our lack of position." Josef Somlo, a Hungarian producer, recalled Korda during this period as "Always penniless, but always smoking a big cigar. His pockets were bulging with three or four books he had just bought or borrowed. His eyes were red-rimmed from endless reading."

Other props followed: the hat (always a homburg) and, when he could afford it, impeccably tailored suits. Meanwhile, Korda thrived in the cauldron of Budapest café life and befriended people who would help him in his quest to become "a great man."

Korda wanted power and wealth, not for their own sake, but for the lifestyle they made possible. In Budapest, he learned an invaluable lesson: when making a deal do not appear to be doing so. Even while hungry and penniless, he mastered the art of seeming to be nonchalant about money.

By 1914, Korda had served as "apprentice" at Pathé, had become Hungary's first film critic, edited several film and literary journals, and was a bona fide member of the city's literati. But none of this was enough. He had not yet directed a film.

It happened—or, more accurately, Korda made it happen—at the New York. Nursing his espresso at a corner table, Korda waited for Gabor Rajnay, the National Theater's leading man, to make his ritual morning appearance. "My name is Korda," said the lanky youth, gripping the big cigar as he intercepted Gabor Rajnay. "I'd like you to star in my war picture. . . . You'd play the hero, the Captain of the Hussars. . . . We have money, we have cameras, we have everything." Actually, he had nothing. But his pitch was lightning-fast and irresistible and the actor found himself agreeing. The next day, when Rajnay arrived at the railway station where Korda said the shooting would begin, a company of real Hussars marched past. Korda signaled the camera to start rolling and quickly directed his new star to join their ranks. Alexander Korda's first production, *The Officer's Swordknot*, starring Gabor Rajnay and hundreds of unpaid extras, was launched.

Now, with a film credit to his name, things began to break for Korda. In 1916, when Michael Curtiz—several steps ahead of Korda—left his job as Projectograph director, Korda succeeded him. (There is no record of interaction between these two men in Budapest. But the world of Hungarian movies was too small and their ambition too large, for them not to have known each other.) In another deal he hatched at the New York, studio head Jeno Janovics put Korda in charge of Corvin Studio, in Kolozsvar, Transylvania (now Cluj, in Romania). The twenty-three-year-old learned an important lesson during the year he spent working for Janovics. Unlike Curtiz, Korda had low tolerance for authority—of any sort. Even in his twenties he had to run his own shop. Korda's unique gift was persuading others to put their money behind his vision, while he maintained power and control.

His father had served in the Hussars. His brothers fought for the empire in the world war. But Korda himself was exempted because of poor eyesight, and it gave him an advantage in Budapest's cultural life.

And so, between 1916 and 1919, Alexander Korda, future international producer and personality, emerged nearly fully formed, a creation of his own imagination. Though Budapest was too small to contain him, the Korda style was set during those years. As soon as he could afford to, he moved out of the family apartment into the Hotel Royal on the Ring Road. It was the first of the many first-class hotels he would call home, but in some ways it was the grandest, at least to him. Just steps from the New York and the National Theater, the Royal was the city's showplace. Inside its gleaming white marble halls, beneath its crystal chandeliers, Alexander Korda was already living beyond his means. Korda sensed that to attract the powerful you needed not only great intelligence and charm, but an opulent setting. The rich had to feel they were dealing with one of their own.

From Korda's five years as Budapest's leading film producer, only one film remains. Today deemed a national treasure, Korda's 1918 production of the *Man of Gold*, a three-hour epic, is based on a nineteenth-century classic by Hungary's beloved romanticist, Mor Jokai. Korda filmed it on location along the Danube. Viewed today, the acting has the stilted quality of most silent films, but the sets are lavish and Korda's directing had dash.

For a decade, Budapest nourished and shaped Alexander Korda's dreams. He and his brothers, Vincent and Zoltan, were so driven and gifted that eventually they would have sought international careers. But Hungary was home, and they loved it, at least until the fateful year of 1919 and the anti-Semitic backlash to the Red Revolution of Bela Kun. After 1919, more importance was attached to three small letters, "Izr," inscribed on their birth certificates. Except as material for the city's comedians, the subject of being Jewish had not been a big topic in Budapest. Everybody, it was assumed, was Jewish! "The Kordas' Jewishness," Vincent Korda's son, author and editor Michael Korda, noted, "did not have a religious component. It related to their relationships with mostly other Hungarian Jews." In addition to Hungarian, Alex spoke German, and Latin was his favorite language for poetry. Yiddish was alien to him, as it was to most of Budapest's assimilated, middle-class Jews. He was Hungarian, and proudly so.

It was not that the Kordas denied their Jewish roots. But, as Michael Korda noted, "being Hungarian was challenge enough, you did not need to add Jewish on top of that. . . . Alex's way of dealing with anti-Semitism was to pretend he hadn't noticed." Years later, the English writer Evelyn Waugh, seated between Alex and his fiancée (and soon to be third wife) Alexa Boycun, grumbled, "I do not wish to sit between a Jew and his mistress." Alex shrugged it off as boorish manners.

"FILM PEOPLE," Alexander Korda often said, "must make films if they're going to earn their bread, whatever the government." So Korda accommodated himself to each of the short-lived regimes that succeeded the Austro-Hungarian Empire. From his patriotic Habsburg propaganda film *The Officer's Swordknot*, to a pro-republican film for Count Michael Karolyi, under the Hungarian Republic, to supporting Bela Kun as a member of the State Directory for the Film Arts, Korda went with the flow.

With the arrival in power of the openly anti-Semitic Regent Horthy, however, Korda had reason for concern. Korda was everything Horthy despised: Jewish, intellectual, and cosmopolitan. Korda was a member of the Budapest café society Horthy blamed for the communist experiment and the country's moral decline, and which he soon began to purge. Alexander Korda's carefully cultivated high profile now worked against him. The sergeant Horthy dispatched to the Hotel Royal to arrest Korda in the fall of 1919 doubtless relished handcuffing a man who lived so well. Korda was led away to another of the city's legendary hotels, the Gellert, on the opposite bank, but this time he was locked in a room used as an interrogation cell.

Korda's new bride, Maria, rushed to the Gellert, accompanied by his brother Zoltan. In the hotel elevator, the Kordas overheard one of Horthy's men boast, "Tonight, I'm going to beat the shit out of that Communist kike Korda." Maria and Zoltan called Jeno Heltai, an influential politician and writer (and first cousin of Theodor Herzl) and arranged a hearing with the regent's chief of staff. Maria's dramatic threat to turn Korda's arrest into an international incident succeeded in freeing her husband.

THE CAMERA would transform—and be transformed by—another Budapest youth coming of age at the same time as Alexander Korda. But

Andre Kertesz preferred to disappear behind the lens, and let his pictures speak for him. In 1912, only eighteen years old, the first year he picked up a camera, he captured an image that would still be held in awe almost a century later by historians and experts in photography.

Using a cumbersome wood-framed camera and glass plates, Andre Kertesz froze a moment of startling intimacy. Known as *Sleeping Boy*, it revealed his sense of composition: the diagonals and the balance of forms, which later became his signature, are already there. The subject is autobiographical: an aimless youth asleep in a café. This, too, foreshadowed much of Kertesz's work. *Sleeping Boy* was not photography straining to imitate painting. In this early image, fusing form and feeling, the young Kertesz revealed a modernist, independent vision.

Until the day he first peered through the lens of the primitive ICA camera his mother had given him, nothing inspired him. Unfocused and dreamy, Andor Kertesz, a boy with no prospects, had found his joy and his calling. He discovered that the camera was a perfect instrument for self-exploration. "I look for the poetic in everything," he wrote in his diary in January 1912. A few weeks later, on a trip to a small town in northern Hungary, he wrote, "Everything is so enchantingly ancient. I would like to go back there during the summer, but with a camera. What great pictures I could take. All filled with poetry."

In a tumultuous age, Kertesz's camera mirrored his inner world. As with the cinema, the field was wide open. Money and institutional support were unimportant for photography. Nor did language matter. All this made the new field an inviting prospect for a Hungarian Jew, doubly isolated: by ethnicity, as his own country veered right, and by the Magyar tongue—the only one Kertesz ever fully mastered.

Posed studio portraits of people in their Sunday best, with a classical or other heroic backdrop, defined the photography of Kertesz's youth. French photographer Eugene Atget's groundbreaking late-nineteenth and early-twentieth-century experiments, with Paris as his favorite subject, were unknown to the young man. Kertesz only dimly realized that he was pioneering a new mode of expression. A remarkable series of circumstances matched Andre Kertesz and the medium then in its infancy.

As a youth, his family's apartment on the humble side of the Ring Road was mostly a place to escape *from*. His father was an itinerant bookseller and sometimes grain merchant, his mother ran a small café. Their means may have been modest, but their city was not. The Kertesz family was immensely proud of the bustling metropolis they had called home since the middle of the last century. It was partly pride and a sense of finally belonging that had prompted them to change their name from Kohn to the Magyar Kertesz. Like most Budapest Jews, the Kertesz family was largely secular, celebrating Christmas and Easter, the Jewish High Holy Days with equal lack of fervor. For two generations they had been loyal subjects of the Austro-Hungarian Empire, conscripts in its army.

Style was Budapest's substance, and the Kertesz sons, Andor (not yet Andre) and his brothers, Imre and Jeno, had style. In their well-tailored suits, bowler hats, and kid gloves, they strolled proudly up Andrassy Avenue toward the City Park, or, in the summer, raced each other in the Palatinusz swimming pool on Margit Island—debonair participants in the pageant of the city.

Through the camera's lens, Kertesz saw a different Budapest. He saw lights and shadows, ancient streets, and, beyond the city limits, a countryside of meandering rivers, and he saw them not as others saw them. Every detail of Magyar life resonated with the observant young man. Peasant girls in snowy, starched Sunday skirts, a shepherd in massive cloak, the village elders in bowler hats, smoking curved pipes—these were his subjects. From the beginning, he showed a natural sense of composition. In Kertesz's landscapes, the human imprint, a bench or a horse-drawn cart, is always visible. Serene and intimate, these are the work of a photographer who *belongs* in the setting.

Kertesz later said the seeds for all he became were sown at that time, in that place, in Budapest. His craft would improve, but he would never again feel so powerful a connection to a place or a people.

BUT HE was poor and his family saw no future for a fellow without, in his own words, "a drop of ambition," a young man who was interested in the world only as seen through the eye of his camera. From beekeeper to clerk in the Stock Exchange, Kertesz soon exhausted a string of jobs. But he never stopped taking pictures.

It was not the intellectual stimulation of Budapest's schools nor the cafés that nourished the shy, inarticulate young man. Kertesz soon joined a circle of artists exploring unconventional ways of looking at the world. The century was younger even than they were, and the conventions of the Old Empire seemed as musty as a Viennese operetta. Kertesz and his friends—artists, sculptors, and poets—assumed that the future was theirs to shape.

In art, prose, and photography, Kertesz's circle blended the modern, urban culture and the simplicity of Magyar folk art to create something new. Bela Bartok, composing music in the same period, shared their spirit. They sought simplicity and authenticity, the very qualities to which Kertesz instinctively responded. His 1915 photograph *The Lovers* captures this. "The couple," he later recalled, "were friends of mine. They were not yet married and one Sunday we three went out to the City Park. They sat down and kissed. It looked very warm—very sincere and honest. They liked each other. I was present with a camera. They had forgotten me."

Erdekes Ujsag, or "Interesting Newspaper," a new, illustrated journal, was looking for unconventional, intimate glimpses from life. It was "the first modern pictorial magazine," according to Stefan Lorant, a famed pioneer of the illustrated newsmagazine. The kiosks of Budapest soon featured several imitations of the new genre. Kertesz had an outlet for his work now, but still not enough income to quit his day job at the Stock Exchange. Photography was still his guilty pleasure, something he could indulge only when he could steal time.

In 1915, the twenty-year-old Kertesz was drafted into the Austro-Hungarian army. He packed his camera in his kit. At first the war promised adventure. But his excitement did not survive the trip to the front. "The train left at 2:15," Kertesz wrote in his diary, "the crying, the last words of farewell almost drowned out the band that was supposed to fire us with enthusiasm. . . . I saw a desperate, shrieking mother who could hardly be stopped from running after the train. One of the sergeants jumped off the already moving train to go to his wife . . . and gave one last goodbye kiss to this unhappy woman who did not want to let him go." Kertesz's camera recorded such moments.

After a two-day journey, Kertesz's train reached the eastern front. The young man who responded to the harmony of the countryside was stunned by the vista of scorched villages, freshly dug graves, and trains rushing wounded and dead soldiers in the opposite direction. "In the morning," he wrote in his diary, "as I stood in the dugout . . . a bullet flew directly past me. It was the first bullet intended for me."

His camera became his shield against the madness. In the midst of the slaughter, through his lens, Kertesz could isolate a moment of beauty. "We had begun to march at dawn," he wrote in his journal. "All of a sudden I saw a splendid image: a quartered battalion at daybreak. In a foggy landscape, with sleeping soldiers—dreaming peaceful dreams."

Kertesz's diary has little to say about his bloodiest days; about the bullet that pierced his chest and arm, severing a nerve and partially paralyzing his left arm in September 1915. Kertesz chose to avoid scenes of violence—the horror of war would not be his subject.

THE WAR DID, however, open a new field for his explorations. Using a crude self-timer and a tripod he carried on his backpack, his self-portraits are a visual diary of his war years. He was there to fight, not take pictures. So Kertesz learned stealth. Closing in on an intimate scene undetected became his trademark. Like all of his work, his war photographs reveal as much about Kertesz as about the subject: soldiers sitting idly on a row of latrines, another playing a cello. His picture of a soldier taking leave of his family, understated and poignant, perfectly framed, is heartbreaking because the emotions are so contained.

Kertesz's eye was gradually sharpened by the danger and discipline of war. Speed and precision were paramount. Given the technology, expense, and danger, there was no possibility for retakes. His *Long March* captured a column of soldiers snaking beyond the horizon, a geometrically perfect composition, with a lone soldier casting a melancholy backward glance.

Erdekes Ujsag liked his work and asked for more. Kertesz was making a name for himself. His self-confidence as a photographer with a singular vision was growing. Unselfconsciously, he was pioneering a new field: candid war photography.

Kertesz even turned his war injury into a chance to expand his art. In 1917 while in physical therapy in Esztergom, he produced one of his most memorable photographs, a male swimmer underwater, seen from above. "The water of the pool," he later recalled, "shone with a magnificent blue.

We were sitting around it with the others, when suddenly I saw the reflections and the little movements on the surface." The swimmer's head is invisible; his body is like a spectral streak and the water a surreal reflection of light. This was the beginning of Kertesz's fascination with distortions, his search for an artistic breakthrough. A decade later, the Bauhaus and the Surrealists would popularize reflections and distortions. Nearly a century later, *Underwater Swimmer* feels modern.

The war transformed Kertesz. For the rest of his life, he went to great lengths to avoid the violent, the harsh, and the confrontational. In an age of fanaticism, he would cling to the lyrical and the personal, observing and recording the world through his lens, something he alone controlled.

N O ONE was to profit more from the new freedoms of pre–World War I Budapest than an extraordinary group of young men, all Jews, who became mathematicians and physicists just as those sciences entered their own Golden Age. Their names would be engraved in the history of the century: Leo Szilard, John von Neumann, Eugene Wigner, Edward Teller, and many others.

In the span of just one generation, from humble beginnings as Moravian and Bohemian tradesmen, the Szilards, von Neumanns, Wigners, and Tellers joined the ranks of Budapest's upper bourgeoisie, setting the stage for the achievement of their prodigious sons.

The Szilard family's climb was speeded by a name change—from Spitz to the Hungarian-sounding Szilard—in 1900. While conversion from Judaism to Christianity was not required, the Szilards, like most of the capital's middle-class Jews, wore their religion very lightly—and only occasionally. Hungary, and the fabulous city on the Danube, was their new faith, its strange language their own. "We called ourselves 'Magyars,'" the future Nobel Prize–winning physicist Eugene Wigner remembered, "and this word had magical properties."

The man charged by Emperor Franz Joseph (whom Hungarians referred to as King) to reform Hungary's backward education system, a Budapest Jew named Maurice Karman, removed education from church control. Combining the best of the French lycée system with the German gymnasium, Karman imposed a standard curriculum for all high schools. The classics, mathematics, science, and humanities formed the core curriculum, which soon rivaled any in Europe. For his efforts, the emperor ennobled Karman.*

"At school," Tekla Szilard recalled, "the treatment I received was, if anything, preferential. In grade school I had been a favorite pupil of the lady teachers, as later in the middle school I was that of the professors. . . . I saw an advantage in being Jewish, as this preserved me from harboring a prejudice, that of anti-Semitism. But even as a child, I was sensitive to injustice," noted the woman who would have the deepest influence on Leo Szilard.

When Tekla's first child, Leo, was born, "the whole family came to welcome the heir apparent," Mrs. Szilard recalled, "as it was then customary to call the firstborn of bourgeois families . . . though the offspring was not to inherit a throne, his prospective inheritance was nothing to sneeze at."

In 1901, the family moved into a grand villa that embodied their aspirations and optimism. A short walk from the Ring Road in Pest's leafy Garden District, it was just off Andrassy Boulevard. The Szilards' neighbors were old nobility, as well as the new aristocrats of banking and business. "Other members of the [Szilard] family were building even more luxurious homes for themselves," Mrs. Szilard noted. "It was a veritable craze. Everybody was on the move."

The times were good and there was no reason to fear the future. Evenings at the Opera or the National Theater, minutes from their home, often ended at Gundel's open-air restaurant in the City Park. "I was conscious of living in the Golden Age of our middle class," Mrs. Szilard wrote in her diary, "and I told my children so. I would not have changed places with any ruler great or small."

This, then, was the environment, based on faith in science, technology, and Rational Man, which welcomed Leo Szilard and his friends Eugene Wigner, John von Neumann, and Edward Teller into the world.

* Maurice von Karman's son, Theodore, a product of his father's reformed education system, went on to pioneer America's aviation and space programs, for which President John F. Kennedy awarded him the Medal of Freedom in 1963.

"My childhood world," Wigner remembered, "was devoted to reason. . . . Our schools taught us what was reasonable; our friends and neighbors acted reasonably toward us and expected the same in return; the great majority of people I knew were friendly and intelligent, without hatred or power lust."

The parents of this new generation failed to take into account a critical fact: social and intellectual progress was not matched by political reforms, and there were vast areas still closed to Jews. "My parents did not discuss the absence of Jews in national politics," Wigner recalled, "just as they did not discuss whether sexual interaction is needed to produce children. Such topics need not be expressly forbidden; they simply do not arise. Children sense quickly what is taboo. . . . Politics was not a Jewish business."

Leo Szilard's elders created a perfect environment for raising exceptional children. The parents of Wigner, von Neumann, and Teller were similarly obsessed with the development of their offspring. "Once he got home," Leo's mother wrote of her civil engineer husband, "he was totally absorbed in the worship of his children. He was anxious to give them all the comforts and advantages gained by his hard work, and that was his delight." Leo, who, like most Hungarians, cherished his mother tongue, was also fluent in French and German before he even started school. Leatherbound copies of Goethe, Schiller, and Heine filled his parents' library. In common with Budapest's Jewish middle class, Leo never learned Hebrew, and considered organized religion irrelevant.

At age ten, Szilard picked up a book that would shape his life's work—and the course of history. *The Tragedy of Man* by Imre Madach is a long dramatic poem, often compared to Goethe's *Faust*. A theological spectacle in fifteen scenes, its subject is the Devil's temptation of Man. In later life, Szilard considered it, "apart from my mother's tales, the most serious influence," on his life. Szilard was particularly transfixed by the scene in which the Devil shows Adam the future of Man. With the sun slowly losing its strength, and the earth cooling, only Eskimos survive, and they have too few seals to feed themselves. There is a narrow margin for hope, however, if the survivors behave rationally. For the rest of his life, Leo was able to quote this passage verbatim.

His father wanted Leo to follow him into civil engineering, so he was enrolled in the more technical *Realschule,* rather than the humanistic gymnasium. Raised in comfort with the notion that he was smarter than almost anybody else, Leo's social skills lagged behind his intellectual development. As he crossed the busy intersection of the Andrassy and Rippl-Ronai and Szondi Streets each morning, he was dangerously distracted, his mind focused on problems, rarely on people—a trait that would lead him, decades later, to one of the most important conceptual breakthroughs in the history of science. But he loved the spectacle of the city. The New York Café was his favorite haunt; someone was always ready to engage the young man discovering the world of ideas. "In such places," his friend Wigner remembered, "you were not only allowed to linger over coffee, you were *supposed* to linger, making intelligent conversation about science, art, and literature." In a city that published dozens of daily newspapers, Leo became a news addict, racing to grab the latest edition.

Very early, he developed his habit of truth-telling—no matter what the consequences. When war broke out in 1914, the Szilards were on a train from Vienna to Budapest. "More and more troop trains pulled alongside [ours] or passed us," Leo wrote in his memoirs. "Some of [our] fellow passengers . . . remarked to my parents that it was heartening to see all this enthusiasm; and I remember my comment was that I could not see as much enthusiasm as drunkenness."

Drafted into the Austro-Hungarian army as an artillery officer candidate in 1917, Leo was spared from combat when he caught influenza and returned to Budapest in 1918. The end of the war, however, brought political and economic disaster for Hungary—and for families like the Szilards. "The guns were silent," his mother recalled, "but that world of peace we had known did not return." Nor did Budapest's Golden Age. "The greater part of our considerable fortune was lost," Tekla Szilard wrote, "what was left was mostly the elegant villa, and not the proper background for the mean existence we were reduced to. There was no coal for the central heating. Our teeth chattered in the oversized rooms. . . . What good is it to painfully keep up old customs, when the happy old life was missing from it?"

ROVING BANDS of communists scuffled with right-wing nationalists, while Budapest's middle-class residents bolted their doors. On June 4,

1920, black flags flew over Budapest and Hungary. In a palace called Trianon, in the gardens of Versailles, the victorious Allies dismantled the Austro-Hungarian Empire. As punishment for being part of the losing side, Hungary was reduced to one-third its former size, a land-locked* country of seven and a half million people. Historic Hungarian cities, Pozsony, Temesvar, and Kassa, were renamed Bratislava, Timisoara, and Kosice and turned over to Czechoslovakia, Romania, and Yugoslavia. Three million three hundred thousand Hungarians were consigned to foreign rule. Ethnic Hungarians fleeing territory lost to the "successor states" soon flooded Budapest. Hungarian schoolchildren would start each day pledging "Nem, Nem, Soha!"—"No, No Never!"—shall we accept Trianon's diktat. The delicate balance lately achieved between the aspiring largely Jewish, urban middle class and their allies, the Magyar gentry, was swamped by this influx of hungry, provincial job-seekers.

Statues of four grieving women were erected behind Parliament Square to symbolize the lands awarded to Romania, Yugoslavia, Austria, and Czechoslovakia by the victorious Allies at Trianon.

LEO SZILARD feared fascist Hungary, and, breaking with family tradition, he converted to Protestantism. "The thought that I might convert to Christianity," his mother wrote later, "had never occurred to me. It wouldn't be right to deny my origins. There was nothing to hide or be ashamed of."

Conversion did not fool Regent Horthy's vigilantes. That fall, they barred Szilard and his brother Bela from classes at the university. Szilard's document attesting to his new religion only enraged the thugs, who pushed him down the university's marble stairs. For the rest of his life, Leo Szilard avoided the topic of what it had meant to be a Jew in racist Budapest.

At age twenty-one, Szilard packed his bags. He was armed not only with a superb education, but, from his mother, a strong sense of ethics. He had also experienced the lightning speed with which hate and extremism can poison a nation's bloodstream. Along with a love of science and mathematics, Szilard had learned to react fast to shifting political currents. The

---

* It had previously claimed Fiume as its port on the Adriatic.

villa in Budapest's Garden District—and the world it represented—had been perfection. But, like the mist that hangs over the Danube each morning and burns off by noon, that world had vanished. He had no interest in trying to re-create it elsewhere. Hotels would do. Szilard would not really unpack his bags again for almost half a century.

IN THE YEARS before the Allies dashed the city's hopes, between 1913 and 1921, Eugene Wigner and John von Neumann also thrived as students at one of Budapest's fabled gymnasia: the Lutheran. (Unlike Szilard, they were too young to have been drafted.) Minutes away from the Ring Road and Andrassy Boulevard, the Lutheran was a place of exceptional physical grandeur for a secondary school.* Surrounded by grand villas, the school's vaulted ceilings, marble foyer, and murals of Euripides, Homer, and Socrates emanated great expectations. Along with Latin conjugation, intellectual elitism and competitiveness were drilled into its students. Though a cross hung above every blackboard, the Lutheran was humanistic and tolerant. Today, its facade is marked by a black marble tablet honoring three of the school's distinguished graduates—ironically all Jews: John von Neumann, Jeno (Eugene) Wigner, Nobel laureate in Physics, and John C. Harsanyi, Nobel laureate in Economics.

A 1908 photograph of the Lutheran Gymnasium faculty looks more like a gathering of the French Academy than a group of high school teachers. Dignified, formally dressed men in bowler hats, "They had a presence," Wigner recalled, "[and] watched their best students closely . . . To kindle interest and spread knowledge among the young—this was what they truly loved." Half a century later Wigner would still reminisce about two of them: Sandor Mikola, his physics teacher, "a gruff, distant man . . . who told us about Sir Isaac Newton and his equation for the motion of the stars and planets." And for the rest of his nomadic life, he kept a photograph of Laszlo Ratz, his mathematics teacher, on his wall, "because," Wigner recalled, "he had every quality of a miraculous teacher: He loved teaching, he knew his subject and how to kindle interest in it. . . . No one could evoke the beauty of a subject like Ratz . . . [who] took special care to find his better students and to inspire them."

---

* Theodor Herzl had graduated from the Lutheran Gymnasium one generation earlier.

Ratz inspired another student at the Lutheran: John von Neumann. Jancsi, as he was then called, was the son of a wealthy banker who had been ennobled by the Emperor Franz Joseph. "When Ratz saw how intelligent Jancsi was," Wigner said, "he began giving him private lessons. . . . [Ratz] felt so privileged to tutor a phenomenon like Jancsi that he refused any money for it. His compensation was more subtle: the brush with a special kind of mind; the privilege of training that mind in a discipline that both of them loved." Ratz called on von Neumann's parents "to ensure [they] understood the nature and implications of their son's gift . . . [and] put von Neumann in some classes at the University of Budapest," his friend recalled.

Although the two youths, Jancsi and Jeno, would meet after school under the mural *The Age of Pericles* and walk home together, Wigner later said, "I never felt I knew [von Neumann] well at gymnasium. Perhaps no one did; he always kept a bit apart. He loved his mother; and confided in her, but hardly in others . . . He joined in class pranks just enough to avoid unpopularity."

Once, on the way home, the youths wandered into a café where billiards were being played. Fascinated, they asked a waiter who seemed to know the game if he would teach them. "Are you interested in your studies?" the waiter asked. "Are you interested in girls? Because if you really want to learn billiards, you will have to give up both." After some consultation, Jancsi and Jeno decided they could give up one but not both, and never learned to play billiards.

Wigner was amazed by his younger friend's "depth of mathematical knowledge. . . . He was one grade below me, but in mathematics, two classes ahead. He already had an astonishing grasp of advanced mathematics. Budapest had a strong mathematics community, and Jancsi made himself well known in that circle before he even left gymnasium. . . . The way he described set theory and number theory was enchanting. The beauty of the subject, his intensity and facility of description made me feel we were close friends. Jancsi went on and on and I drank it in, hardly speaking myself. Both his knowledge and his desire to relate it seemed inexhaustible. Most people [at the gymnasium] went straight home, already thinking of what they would do when they arrive. Not Jancsi. You got home late after a walk with him."

In 1963, when he received the Nobel Prize for physics, Wigner acknowledged the role of those childhood walks, as well as the teacher who taught them both. "My own history," Wigner related during the Nobel ceremony, "begins in the high school in Hungary where my mathematics teacher, Ratz, gave me books to read and evoked in me a sense for the beauty of the subject. . . . The contemporary from whom I learned most . . . was von Neumann."

Like Szilard's and Wigner's, von Neumann's education was astonishingly well rounded. He learned French, German, and English, as well as the classics and humanities. For the rest of his life, von Neumann could quote Thucydides in Greek, and Voltaire in French. Decades later, when Herman Goldstine was working with von Neumann on the digital computer, he decided to test von Neumann's recall. "Tell me how *A Tale of Two Cities* started," Goldstine challenged his friend, whereupon, without pause, von Neumann "immediately began to recite the first chapter and continued until asked to stop after about ten or fifteen minutes."

Often present at the von Neumanns' elegant dinner table were playwrights and musicians, as well as titans of Budapest's business community. Even as a child, Jancsi loved the city's parade; he never missed the opening of a new play by Ferenc Molnar or a new opera by Bartok. But his greatest joy came from exercising his brain. Once, catching his mother staring off into the distance, he asked, "Mother, what are you calculating?"

For all of them, science was their faith. "I felt," Wigner remembered, "that this great movement of science and technology had . . . raised the moral standards of humanity. . . . In Europe, whole peoples had been slaughtered [during World War I] with little outside protest. This acquiescence to wholesale murder seemed to be ending—chiefly, I felt, due to the advance of the scientific movement. I felt that physics might soon begin to solve important human problems of a social and emotional nature."

No one had to remind these youths that their grandparents could not even dream of such opportunities. They were also aware that the future was unpredictable. "Innovate or die," is how another of their Budapest generation, Nobel laureate in physics Dennis Gabor, summed up this feeling. Only to his most trusted friend did von Neumann confide his own feelings that he had to "produce the unusual, or face extinction."

"Why call ourselves Jews," von Neumann's younger brother Michael once asked their father, "since we don't observe religion?" Max von Neumann replied with a single word: "Tradition." Following his death in 1929, however, the family, still in Budapest, converted to Catholicism. "For the sake of convenience," his brother Nicholas noted, "not conviction."

🕱

O N JULY 28, 1914, a headstrong nine-year-old tore from his governess's grip and joined a mass demonstration surging through his neighborhood. "Death to the Serbian dogs!" the crowd roared, and the boy shouted with them. It was thrilling, being part of something so much bigger than himself, melting into a giant crowd. It gave him the unaccustomed feeling of being part of a family. Marching on, he, too, sang the melancholy "God Bless the Magyar." The Austro-Hungarian Empire had just declared war against the Allied Powers and their Serbian "dogs."

This was Arthur Koestler's first political act—and he felt transported. Koestler's next demonstration was in November 1918, when he was thirteen. This time Budapest marchers celebrated the demise of the same empire. Hungary would soon be punished for joining the German coalition, but the demonstrators and the boy could not have imagined that the treaties of Versailles and Trianon would permanently reduce the size of Hungary and leave millions of Hungarians outside its new borders. The boy was swept up in the frenzy of the day. Cheering mobs blocked Kossuth Lajos Street, where his father, Henrik's, office was located. No longer in the hands of a governess, Arthur now marched with his father. Together they shouted their approval of the lanky aristocrat who appeared on the balcony overhead, Count Michael Karolyi, who proclaimed Hungary's secession from the Austro-Hungarian Empire. "Henceforth," the count exhorted the jubilant crowd, "Hungary will be a free, democratic republic!" Arthur and his father joined in a spontaneous chorus of "God Bless the Magyar."

Four months later, Karolyi resigned and handed power over to Bela Kun's communist dictatorship. Again, Arthur Koestler joined the excited crowds pouring into the streets of Budapest, but this time the celebration turned to bloodshed. A right-wing mob attacked a group of communists and killed several of them. A few days later, Koestler joined the communist funeral march as it wound its way through his neighborhood. "They marched slowly," he later wrote, "with discipline and dignity. Never before had the citizens of Budapest seen a crowd of sturdy proletarians parading through their elegant shopping streets; many of them had probably never seen a factory worker before." For the rest of his tumultuous life, Koestler would associate Chopin's *Funeral March* with communism.

In the coming months the Commune replaced Chopin with the "Internationale" as Budapest's musical theme. Arthur memorized the words:

> To wipe out the past forever, O army of slaves, follow us. We shall lift the globe from its axis, we are nothing, we shall be all.

"During those hundred days of spring," Koestler wrote, "it looked indeed as if the globe was to be lifted from its axis." Everything about the revolution dazzled the boy. The gigantic propaganda posters plastered on every wall were the highest art to his eyes. "They had been designed by the elite of modern Hungarian painters who later on swarmed out over Europe and America. Some of the posters were cubist, some futuristic, all celebrated anonymous workers, peasants and soldiers, not a single one was a portrait of a leader."

Koestler, awkward, an only child, admired the grimy, hulking soldiers who came to requisition his room. Not even the famine provoked by Kun's bungled revolution bothered Arthur — who lived mainly on ice cream. "I suppose," Koestler later speculated, "an imaginative food commissar must have stumbled upon a consignment of vanilla in a government storehouse and decided to turn it into ice cream in some requisitioned refrigerator plant." When his cousin Margit took him to a suburban factory where she lectured the workers on political economy, Arthur's sympathy was ignited. "The pathetic thirst for knowledge written on [the workers'] faces," he wrote later, "made me suddenly feel close to them. I had already taken a liking to these members of a strange race who invaded our streets. . . . Now seeing them transformed into wide-eyed school boys, I understood that they had the same feelings and frustrations and aspirations as I. Then the thought struck me that I was undeservedly lucky to go to school and have books to read while these . . . sweaty characters obviously regarded my cousin's lecture as a rare and special treat."

Thus began the political education of Arthur Koestler, who, two decades later, would rouse millions to the danger of the communist police state with one of the greatest political novels in history.

ARTHUR's lifelong friend Eva Striker (who would later be a famous ceramicist, Eva Zeisel) remembered a kindergarten class with six-year-old Koestler. "We were instructed," she recalled almost ninety years later, but with stunning vividness, "that early man lived in his cave, surrounded by dangers, until he found a stone which he sharpened and eventually used as a weapon to defend himself." The precocious Arthur interrupted the teacher. "But the lion does not wait for the savage to invent his weapon!"

Arthur's insecurity was heightened by his family's precarious social and economic position. His father's business career had fluctuated wildly between prosperity and poverty. Their apartment was on the "right" side of Andrassy Boulevard, but it was small. When the elder Koestler's textile business thrived, the family drove a flashy car and summered on the Dalmatian coast, in the company of well-heeled Austro-Hungarians. But when one of his father's schemes misfired, they moved to a boarding house. His snobbish, Viennese-born mother insisted on the trappings of prosperity—even when they could scarcely afford them. Arthur attended the "right" schools (Szilard had earlier attended the same Realschule on Rippl-Ronai Street) and dancing classes, but he was aware that their gentility was of the shabby variety. Even in his hometown, he observed life as an outsider, looking in. He dreamed of escape.

Koestler's first flight was a journey inside his over-active brain. "One day during the summer holidays in 1919," he wrote, "I was lying on my back under a blue sky on a hill slope in Buda . . . the paradox of infinity suddenly pierced my brain as if it had been stung by a wasp. . . . The idea that infinity would remain an unsolved riddle was unbearable." All his life, Koestler held up a mirror to his every move, and left behind a remarkable set of memoirs. So it was with this first epiphany on a Budapest hillside. "The thirst for the absolute is a stigma which marks those unable to find satisfaction in the relative world of the here and now. . . . The Infinite as a target was replaced by Utopias of one kind or another."

One hundred days after Arthur Koestler joined the communist march, Horthy's militia scraped the colorful posters from Budapest's walls and began to round up those "wide-eyed school boys" and the Jews who had turned them into revolutionaries.*

Koestler's family joined the Vienna-bound exodus of potential enemies of fascist Hungary. Arthur, age fourteen, began his first exile. From now on, the Koestler family had no fixed home and would float between Vienna and Budapest, wherever his father found work.

---

* Arthur's first cousin Margit escaped Horthy's roundup but would not survive its more murderous successor, the gas chambers of Auschwitz.

PART TWO

HARVEST AT
TWILIGHT

R eturned to Budapest from the front in 1919, Andre Kertesz transformed the convulsions of the defeated capital into small, closely observed images. In his photographs of a communist demonstration, the angry mob seems like Sunday strollers. His photograph of refugees converging on one of the city's grand boulevards is unsettling. Where are all these people going? In the same shot, Kertesz's eye catches the joy of two men who suddenly recognize each other in the crowd. His photograph of a mass demonstration in front of the Parliament shows two men perched on a lamppost, straining to view the action. The agitated mob, whose rage Kertesz had seen and felt, is not so much seen as felt. Only later would the psychic cost of all he had witnessed, and sublimated, surface.

Increasingly, it was the countryside that attracted Kertesz and his camera. In 1919, Andor met Elizabeth Salomon at the bank where they both worked. She was ten years his junior, as unsuited to banking as he was, dark-eyed, artistic, and strong-willed; she became the love of his life. Together they explored the countryside, she with her paints and easel, he with his camera.

Just outside the city, Kertesz photographed a scene: the resulting *Budafok* is bathed in an almost magical light. Kertesz catches several events simultaneously, conveying the feeling that something is about to happen. The matriarchal figure in the foreground observes a couple on the grass, while a man in a hat and suit is walking out of the frame. He makes it seem like a chance encounter. But Kertesz had developed the patience of a hunter methodically stalking and waiting for a moment infused with form and personal meaning.

In 1921, he made a photograph called *The Blind Musician*, which blends rigorous composition and emotional power. Again, the moment seems spontaneous, as if the photographer just happened to be strolling by the blind violinist and a little boy guiding him at the very moment two other children arranged themselves in a perfect composition, all under the observant eyes of a peasant girl. Kertesz recalled the precise moment more than half a century later. "I took this picture on a Sunday. The music had woken me up. He was playing so beautifully, this blind musician, that I can still hear it today. Maybe he would have become a great musician, had he been born in Budapest or Vienna, and to a different family."

Though he was happiest behind his lens or in his darkroom working with his younger brother, Jeno ("my most perfect collaborator"), he was still not making a living as a photographer. Postwar Budapest was no longer a place ripe with opportunity. His family was worried. However apolitical Kertesz might be, there was no room in Horthy's Hungary for the magazines that had celebrated Budapest's free spirit and nurtured Kertesz's work. Art and photography were now meant to stimulate Magyar nationalism, not challenge it. *Erdekes Ujsag* and other avant-garde publications like *Ma* and *Nyugat*, outlets for prewar liberalism, were either closing or accommodating to the new nationalism. Many of Kertesz's former editors were packing their bags for Vienna, Berlin, or Paris.

Kertesz continued to search for ways to earn a living in Budapest— and still keep taking photographs. On March 10, 1921, armed with a strong letter of recommendation, he interviewed for a job with the director of Hungarian Steel Products. Kertesz was turned down for a low-level administrative job. "My being Jewish was the problem," he wrote in his diary on April 17, 1921. With no interest in any formal religion, Kertesz regarded himself simply as Hungarian. But in Horthy's Hungary, he was a Jew. Being Jewish now reverted to what it had been for much of history: a sect, an ethnicity, and a tribe, not merely a religion like any other. (Though, oddly, the proportion of Jews in the best-paid professions and in business as well as industry did not dramatically decline until 1938.)

For the rest of Kertesz's life, the "Jewish question" remained the single most sensitive, least-discussed topic. As a Hungarian with poor skills in other languages, he was already isolated. Now, he was isolated even in his own country. But even as his future in his homeland looked uncertain, Kertesz continued to refine his art. He experimented more boldly with night photography. His younger brother, Jeno, was his patient model in such night scenes as *Taban at Night*, with its dark street, full of mystery, which *Erdekes Ujsag* put on its cover in June 1925.

Kertesz was still not making a living. "I am 30 years old," he wrote in his diary, "and I am a nobody!" Elizabeth also had bigger dreams and gave him an ultimatum. If you want to marry me, she told him, "Go away and establish yourself and then come for me."

"All that is treasured in my life," Kertesz declared in 1986, "had its source in Hungary." Yet, in 1925, Hungary, the only place where he really felt at home, was no longer the place where Kertesz could fulfill either Elizabeth's challenge or his own destiny.

E DWARD TELLER was rocked by the turmoil of 1919. Five years von Neumann's junior, Teller was a first-year student at the Minta, another of the city's great secondary schools. The communist marches, their gigantic, unfurled red flags, and their enormous posters frightened the eleven-year-old Teller. "On one of them," Teller remembered half a century later, "a stern man with his arm extended and his fingertips as large as if it were an inch from my nose said, 'You, hiding in the shadows, spreading horror stories, you, counterrevolutionaries, TREMBLE.' The finger seemed to follow me wherever I went." Although Bela Kun's communist regime lasted only four months and ten days, that was long enough to mark Teller for life.

"My father could no longer practice law," Teller recalled. "In fact, we became social outcasts. A lawyer was clearly a capitalist; and unlike a doctor, who provided a service, a lawyer was a thoroughly worthless person in a 'good' society." Not even Teller's home was safe from the regime. Part of the Teller family's apartment was requisitioned by the communists. While Koestler would later associate those four months with vanilla ice cream, one of the few available foods, Teller's memory was of hunger—and a new concern. "My father told me that the communists would soon fall," he recalled, "and that anti-Semitism would follow. 'Too many of the communist leaders are Jews,' he explained, 'and all Jews will be blamed for their excesses.'" Events would confirm the elder Teller's premonition. "Within the first few years after the demise of the Hungarian Soviet," Teller wrote decades later, "5,000 people, most of them Jews, were executed, and many tens of thousands more fled to other lands." By age eleven, Edward had experienced war, communism, revolution, counterrevolution, anti-Semitism, and fascism. "Having seen the end of Hungary as I had known it, I could imagine the end of Western civilization."

But the anxious boy found a way to calm his fears. "Finding the consistency of numbers is the first memory I have of feeling secure." Calculating the number of seconds in an hour or a day, he would drift off to sleep. Edward's father noticed the ease with which the boy tackled his sister's algebra problems. He turned to a friend, a mathematics professor at the University of Budapest, for advice. Give him a copy of Euler's geometry, Professor Leopold Klug advised. "He read Euler," Teller's sister Emmi recalled, "the way I read love stories."

The great moment in which four young men forged friendships that would change the world was about to come. "During my last two years in gymnasium," Teller wrote later, "I became acquainted with three young men from the Jewish community in Budapest who were studying and working in Germany as scientists. . . . Probably my father mentioned to their fathers, whom he knew, that I was also interested in science and would benefit from meeting them. . . . I looked forward to spending a few hours with them when they were home during academic breaks. The only topic we discussed in those days was physics. . . . Most of the time I simply listened to them, but they were willing to explain if I asked, a privilege I used sparingly." They were, of course, Leo Szilard, Eugene Wigner, and John von Neumann. This astonishing trio would have an immense influence on Edward Teller.

Teller was younger than his new friends when he felt the sting of anti-Semitism. When he questioned his mathematics teacher's answer to a problem, the teacher sneered, "So you are a genius, Teller? Well, I don't like geniuses." So openly was Jew-baiting practiced in his elite gymnasium, that Teller wondered whether "being a Jew really was synonymous with being an undesirably different kind of person."

Great scientific discoveries were taking place in Germany and his friends were there. It was the obvious place for Teller after graduation. But even with rising anti-Semitism, it was painful to leave Budapest. "I walked along the Danube. The weather was beautiful. I loved the sunshine. I looked at the bridges, the trees, the flowing river. . . . I knew that I was fortunate . . . but the price of my good fortune felt high. I knew in my heart that my new life away from Budapest would be not only a beginning, but an ending."

⬧

ENDRE FRIEDMANN was one year old when Gavrilo Princip fired the shots in Sarajevo in 1914 that would shatter Budapest's Golden Age. Thus did the twentieth century embark on a course that Friedmann—as Robert Capa—would chronicle with some of the most memorable photographs in history. The city was beautiful and the gymnasia still among Europe's best. The eighteen years Friedmann/Capa lived there—nearly one-half of his short life—shaped the man. Capa remained a city boy, "a street-smart ruffian," in the words of Henri Cartier-Bresson, his friend, partner, and another of the twentieth century's greatest photojournalists. The clamor and rush of central Pest, those were his first experiences of life. It was the soil where he would always thrive. But young Friedmann had missed the exciting possibilities of the decade before, and had to learn to live by his wits.

He was intimate with every scrap of green space, every alley, every stop on the subway and the tram. The young Endre Friedmann had neither money nor social position nor much supervision. He learned to leap on the back of the moving streetcar and jump off before the ticket collector noticed. He learned to calculate risk: to stay indoors when the odds were against him, even at the age of seven, in 1920, when Horthy's thugs prowled the streets looking for troublemakers and Jews. And finally, with his pure animal magnetism, he also learned how to win girls, something at which later, as Robert Capa, he would famously excel.

His home—a good middle-class apartment—was in the heart of Pest, as cosmopolitan a neighborhood as any in Europe. The Friedmanns, like almost everybody in the neighborhood, were secular Jews. His mother, Julia, a sturdy, determined fireplug of a woman, ran a fashion salon while her husband, Dezso, mostly enjoyed the city's café life. From his father Capa inherited a lifelong taste for gambling. Julia absolutely adored her son. In her eyes he was meant for great things. Capa would owe something to each. He was determined to make something of himself—though he had no idea what.

Each morning the youth sprinted through elegant streets of luxury shops and cafés to the Madach Gymnasium on Barcsay Street. He was no scholar, but he was quick enough; despite little effort he graduated in 1931. His poorest grades were in comportment.

Higher education had become increasingly unlikely. In 1920, when Capa was seven, Hungary became the first nation to pass anti-Semitic legislation, the so-called Numerus Clausus law, which limited Jewish admission to Hungary's universities to 5 percent (which was roughly equivalent to Hungary's Jewish population, but dramatically lower than their presence in the country's higher education had been). But his real school was the city. Friedmann and his friends were excited by the avant-garde spirit of poet-painter Lajos Kassak, whose generous view of humanity contrasted with Horthy's nationalism. Kassak was a legendary figure to many young Hungarians looking for the avant-garde; he was supposed to have walked all the way to Paris, and then returned to spread a new spirit to replace the decadent remnants of the empire. Kassak and his friend Laszlo Moholy-Nagy published an activist magazine called *Ma* ("Today"), outlining the Bauhaus and Constructivism. Kassak and Moholy-Nagy introduced a new style of photography to Central Europe: a bold, documentary style that was unsentimental in depicting the hardships of the underclass. Here, in the last years before fascism destroyed Europe as he first knew it, the future Robert Capa developed a passionate engagement in the world's affairs.

At the dawn of the age of militant anti-Semitic nationalism, the young man with glossy black hair, a cocky swagger, and a sly smile looked like trouble. He was only seventeen when Horthy's police hauled him away from a political rally, shoved him in a van, and roughed him up for political agitation. Like some other ambitious young men in Budapest, he understood that he, too, would have to look elsewhere for his future.

<hr />

THE CAFÉS along Vienna's Kartnerstrasse swarmed with exiled intellectuals from the defunct Austro-Hungarian Empire. Almost as many Budapest figures loitered at Vienna's Café Filmhof as at the New York. They were hungry and, during the winter of 1920, cold.

Vienna had been reduced from the capital of an empire of sixty million people to the capital of a small country of six and a half million. Without its grain-producing partner, Hungary, Vienna was starving. But Michael Curtiz, fluent in the only language that mattered to him, the language of film, never stopped working. "On the way to Vienna," Walter Reisch, who was among the first of his screenwriters, recounted, "Curtiz had with him a little German-Hungarian dictionary which had a page on which all the verbs that express motion were enumerated: walk, leap, climb, jump. . . . He learned them by heart and whenever he later had to tell an actor what to do, he would use all the verbs. Not just the verb that was appropriate, but all of them! If he wanted to tell an actor 'You go to this door,' he would say, 'You go, jump, leap, walk, crawl to this door!' . . . He was a sensational director, although he never spoke any languages properly. There was no need to speak his language because he demonstrated everything with his hands."

Determined, relentless, and adaptable, Curtiz was soon directing again. A fellow Hungarian exile in Vienna, S. Z. Sakall, whom Curtiz would later cast in a small but memorable role as Rick's rotund head-waiter in *Casablanca*, stumbled on Curtiz filming in Vienna's Prater amusement park. "The sight before us was impressive," Sakall recalled in his memoirs. "My childhood friend, Mike Curtiz, stood on top of a two story high director's rostrum and gave his orders through a megaphone. A crowd of many hundreds hung on his every word. And he was talking—German!" The film was *Sodom and Gomorrah* and it launched Curtiz on the world stage.

If the postwar movie audience was in the mood to escape into the fantasy world of the Bible, Michael Curtiz would oblige. As he had once turned Hungarian literature into the stuff of screen dreams, he now mined the Old and New Testaments, turning out extravagant, cast-of-thousands spectacles. One of those extras, a fellow refugee from fascist Hungary, Richard Berczeller, auditioned for Curtiz. "The director," Berczeller recalled, "sat chain-smoking. With a quick wave of his hand he indicated that we were to walk past him. He rejected one after another. Finally, I arrived at the desk and stood facing him. His squinting eyes rested on me. Five seconds passed, and five more—I was still not rejected . . . 'Any training in acting?' [Curtiz] asked me. 'Yes,' I said. . . . 'In gymna-

sium.' A roar of laughter greeted this. The man smiled, 'How exciting!'
Then turned to two men standing with him. 'Too bad,' he said, amused.
'The fellow has a biblical face.' Again there was a salvo of mocking laughter, and I felt myself grow hot with rage. 'Someday I hope to meet you
when we are alone!' I shouted at [Curtiz] in Hungarian," Berczeller recalled. "He got up and walked around the desk toward me. He raised
his right hand, and I was preparing for a fistfight, but he placed his hand
gently on my shoulder. 'We Hungarians have a terrible temper, haven't
we?' he said and laughed. . . . [Curtiz] had a terrible temper, shouted,
screamed on all occasions. But I was [hired] as one of the extras."

Berczeller recalled his first day on the set of *Sodom and Gomorrah*.
"Curtiz, from his ladder shouted, 'Let's begin!' " and the cameras rolled.
But not for long. "Fools," the director shouted from high above his extras.
"You stroll as if you were on the Kartnerstrasse. Attack, you sons of bitches!
Again, Again, you . . ."

What the beleaguered extras did not realize—nor much care about—
was the pressure the director was under. "Somber-looking strangers—the
men who financed the venture—watched the shooting," Berczeller recalled, "while [Curtiz] smoked more than usual."

IN 1923, Ufa—Universum Film AG—the great German film studio—
invited Curtiz to Berlin. Founded by the German high command during
World War I as a propaganda medium, by the 1920s Ufa sprawled over the
Berlin suburbs of Babelsberg and Woltersdorf, cranking out six hundred
films a year. Legendary directors like Ernst Lubitsch, Fritz Lang, Leni
Riefenstahl, and Billy Wilder learned their craft on Ufa's stages, as did
Josef von Sternberg, Peter Lorre, and Marlene Dietrich. Ufa made Curtiz
no promises, no guarantees, just a chance to prove himself. It was an op-
portunity every film director in Europe would have killed for.

Curtiz asked Berczeller to accompany him. Arriving at Berlin's Pots-
damer Bahnhof following a fourteen-hour train ride "[Curtiz] was to start
immediately; in a neighboring room, half a dozen cameramen and tech-
nicians were waiting for him. . . . At first, he was jittery, but within a day or
two, he found himself—authoritative, abusive, and ingenious. Only at
night," Berczeller noted, "when we had a nightcap together, did he have
doubts. . . . One night three weeks after our arrival in Berlin, [Curtiz]

stumbled into my room. His face was deadly pale and he was perspiring profusely. With trembling fingers, he took a sheet of paper from his pocket—his contract."

A photograph of the Hungarian director taken at the Ufa around this time shows a man radiating an alarming intensity, surrounded by his production team, ready to pounce.

In 1925 Hollywood producer Harry Warner screened Curtiz's *Moon of Israel* and immediately rang his brother Jack with an urgent message: "Get this man to Hollywood." Jack Warner remembered: "We were laid in the aisles by the impact of Curtiz' camera work. We saw shots and angles that were pure genius." After pursuing Curtiz to Berlin and secretly observing him in action, Jack Warner drew up a contract, which Curtiz signed immediately. Warner Brothers planned to develop Curtiz as their answer to Cecil B. DeMille, the master of the epic, who was under contract to their rival, Paramount Pictures.

✴

KORDA arrived by first-class wagon-lit in Vienna in November 1919. Curtiz was already there, as were Budapest expatriates Peter Lorre, Bela Lugosi, the writer Lajos Biro (Korda's future collaborator), and the film theorist Bela Balazs. All of them were hungry, but none of them had Korda's flair for turning desperation into opportunity.

He checked into the largest suite of the Grand Hotel, where, for the first time, he registered as Alexander Korda. Instructing the chauffeur to wait outside the Grand—as ostentatiously as possible—the twenty-six-year-old waited for his international career to begin.

For two weeks he acted as if he had not a care in the world. Finally, Count Alexander Kolowrat Krakowsky, an Austrian aristocrat with a passion for movies, called with an offer to make a film.

Samson and Delilah was one of the four forgettable films he directed during his Vienna exile. It was a prototype for his future work. Korda was not a bold artist. He mined history and literature for entertainment value, boldly improving on the original with the erotic and the human. He had the same casual attitude toward history's plain facts as he did for his backers' money. He was a showman: equal parts entertainer and businessman.

By 1922, Korda's string had run out in Vienna. The city was dull compared to Budapest. He chafed under his new patron, Count Kolowrat—as he did under any close supervision. And Curtiz's big-budget epic *Sodom and Gomorrah* had bled the count.

In the 1920s, the lights were dimming in Vienna. Alexander Korda wanted to be where the bright lights and action were. And in 1922 that was Berlin.

✦

V IENNA was more important for Arthur Koestler than it was for Curtiz or Korda. Adapting to a cramped Viennese boarding house was not the most challenging part of Koestler's new life. The adolescent had to learn to navigate a new culture.

Koestler later claimed that he came to his first utopia—Zionism—not as a victim, but as a "volunteer." But an early work of fiction, a short story he wrote in Hungarian when he was twenty-two, contradicts that assertion. Entitled "Ball Game," it is the story of a schoolboy who tells his parents that he is emigrating to Jerusalem. His stated reason is that having picked "Jew" as his chosen nationality in a "ball game" that required each player to choose one, he is pummeled by his playmates, while his teacher "stood there with his back to us in another corner of the yard, feeding crumbs to the birds." When he fights back, the boy tells his parents, his teacher has "a fit, and gave me a lecture and entered my name in the form book . . . but I don't mind as I'm emigrating to Palestine anyway." The autobiographical implication of the short story is underlined by the father's use of Hungarian and the mother's use of German, Koestler's parents' habit.

FOR KOESTLER, politics was always a search to fill an interior void, and so with Zionism. "The idea of a 'National Home,' " he wrote, "had this strong attraction for me because I lived in hotels and boarding houses. . . . A 'rootless cosmopolitan' from the days of my youth with a polyglot culture and physically always on the move, there was perhaps an un-conscious craving in me to grow roots, and an urge to create and construct, to build cities in the desert. . . . Zion was a new version of the ["Internationale"] which promised that we would 'lift the globe from its axis.' "

Vienna in the 1920s—twenty years after Theodor Herzl's death—was electric with Zionism. This was uncharted territory for Koestler. "Fed on Hungarian, Russian, French and English literature," he wrote, "the only Jewish literature as far as I knew was the Old Testament." He felt no connection to the religion itself (though his family occasionally attended seder at his cousins' home in Budapest) or even to a centuries old way of life. "I read . . . the tales of ghetto life translated from the Yiddish and felt even more estranged," he wrote. "They exhaled a stale air, saturated with the smell of narrow streets. . . . Every single so-called Jewish trait can be found in varying combinations in these closed communities."

In the hothouse of the Viennese student cafés, teeming with displaced young intellectuals from across the smashed Austro-Hungarian Empire, Koestler found the antidote against this "deformation": a Jewish National Home, and a flag the Jews could finally call their own. "In the absence of these," Koestler asserted, "[Jews] were the paying guests in the houses of strangers, and, whether tolerated or beaten up, were always regarded as different."

In Vienna, Koestler met the first "shaman" to turn his head: Vladimir Jabotinsky, an early Zionist zealot—an important figure in the history of Zionism, and an enduring inspiration to right-wing Israelis like Menachem Begin and Yitzhak Shamir. (Israel's foreign minister, Tzipi Livni, appointed in 2006, is another important follower of Jabotinsky.) Like Koestler, the Odessa-born Jabotinsky had been "brought up in [an] enlightened atmosphere . . . a stranger to Jewish tradition."

Jabotinsky's Zionist Revisionism—whose terrorist offshoots, the Irgun and the Stern Gang, would play a major role in Israel's birth—was the sort of muscular movement to appeal to the young Koestler. "In violent opposition to the Zionist leadership [and its] traditional backdoor approach—Jabotinsky's was the bang at the front door." The Revisionists' aim was "to establish a Jewish state on both sides of the Jordan."

For his part, Jabotinsky "seemed to take an immediate, amused liking to me," Koestler wrote, "and before the end of his short stay in Vienna took me as secretary and co-speaker on . . . his lecture tour." Koestler was mesmerized by Jabotinsky, who "carried himself like a soldier, and talked like a man of letters."

. . .

ON APRIL 1, 1926, just weeks before graduating from Vienna's Technical University, the twenty-year-old Koestler jumped off the career track anticipated by his background and education. "I explained to [my parents] that I was going to Palestine for a year as an assistant engineer in a factory, and that by acquiring . . . practical experience, it would afterwards be much easier for me to find a job in Austria and to make a quick career." In fact, Koestler had no intention of returning to Austria, nor of resuming a bourgeois life. A self-described "romantic fool, in love with unreason," Koestler boarded a train on the start of his journey to Haifa to "the loveliest music . . . the whistle, puff and jolt of the train pulling out of the station." His destination was a kibbutz in the desert of the Valley of Yesreel, one of the least-hospitable landscapes in British-ruled Palestine. The aimless, rootless youth "was launched on the warpath for Zion."

Koestler stayed only three weeks in the kibbutz. He was not much good at agricultural work, and his individualism was out of place in communal life. The next year and a half he spent in a state of semi-destitution, often sleeping on the floor of offices belonging to friends. Koestler did not find the warm fellowship and the sense of *belonging* for which he hungered. A bred-in-the-bone European, he felt alienated in Palestine. "The Palestinian Jews," he wrote, "have a mental attitude and culture patterns completely different from Jews anywhere else. Jewishness is essentially a minority status. What in Europe and America is known as Jewish humor is the salty product of a victimized minority. In Palestine it is drying up."

From his earliest childhood, Koestler had crackled with ideas. "It was as though if you touched him," one girlfriend later said, "you would get an electric shock." He was cocky and intellectually arrogant, and language and words were his coins. He found Hebrew "a petrified language which had ceased to develop . . . unfit to serve as a vehicle for modern thought, to render shades of feeling and meaning of twentieth century man." Nor were Palestine's dusty roads a suitable setting for the fastidious Koestler, who, since adolescence, when he spent his allowance on white kid gloves, had been something of a dandy.

Even while selling lemonade in Tel Aviv, he kept writing—in German. He submitted—then forgot—an article about his impressions of Haifa to the *Neue Freie Presse*, one of Europe's most prestigious dailies. The paper published Koestler's bylined story on its front page. He was a journalist!

Hired by the Ullstein newspaper chain as Middle East correspondent, he suddenly had access to the powerful. (Once, while he was waiting to interview King Abdullah of Transjordan, an aide asked the baby-faced Koestler when his father was arriving. "Mon père," Arthur shot back, "c'est moi.") He was thrilled to be summoned back to Europe by Ullstein, "the embodiment of everything progressive and cosmopolitan in the Weimar Republic," Germany's doomed post–World War I attempt to forge a constitutional democracy.

"I was twenty-three," he wrote, "and had had my fill of the East—both of Arab romantics and Jewish *mystique*. My mind and spirit were longing for Europe, thirsting for Europe, pining for Europe."

COME ON, switch on the lights, give us a chance to see what it's all about: Berlin in lights." Kurt Weill's 1928 song, "Berlin in Lights," summed up the city's allure in the 1920s. Like Budapest and Vienna, Berlin in the 1920s was the capital of a lost empire—but with a difference. "To go to Berlin," wrote the historian Peter Gay, who grew up there, "was the aspiration of the composer, the journalist, the actor . . . with its superb orchestras, its . . . newspapers, its forty theaters. . . . Wherever they started, it was in Berlin that they became, and Berlin that made them famous."

In Berlin, Korda found neither Budapest's beauty nor Paris's refinement. An architectural jumble, Berlin looked more Prussian than continental. The intellectual excitement of the city in the 1920s, however, was equal to that of any other city in the world, even Paris. As in Budapest, people stayed up all night, anxious not to miss anything. Like Budapest, Berlin was a new post-imperial capital, without a fixed establishment or the frozen social rites of older European cities. Artists like Max Beckmann and George Grosz brought their subversive vision to the art world, while Bertolt Brecht, Kurt Weill, and Max Reinhardt were shaking up the rigid rules of drama. Walter Gropius, Mies van der Rohe, and Korda's fellow Hungarian, Laszlo Moholy-Nagy, founded the breakthrough architectural movement known as Bauhaus in the nearby city of Weimar.

In 1923, Alex Korda joined the most gifted and adventuresome filmmakers in the world already gathered in Ufa's sprawling studios. All over Berlin, cinema palaces had sprung up to showcase Ufa's talent. Porters in gold-braided livery patrolled the long lines of the hungry and the jobless, queuing up for an hour's escape at the movies. Cheaper than the theater or cabaret, movies, unlike books, were accessible to all, and in the silent era films from all countries were equal. Which is how Charlie Chaplin became the most recognized face in the world. Until Adolf Hitler.

Outside Ufa's dream palaces, things were not so bright in Berlin. Nineteen twenty-three was a sour year for the Weimar Republic. Hitler failed to ignite a mass movement with his abortive Beer Hall Putsch in Munich. Arrested by Weimar authorities, he spent about a year in jail, working on his memoirs, *Mein Kampf*, which outlined his solution to Europe's "Jewish Problem." The victorious Allies seemed determined to play into Hitler's hands by undermining Weimar Germany. In January 1923, French and Belgian troops occupied the Ruhr to squeeze war reparations from an economy already on life support. Inflation was so high it was said that a diner's bill doubled while he ate his lunch. A suitcase full of nearly worthless marks was required to buy shoes. And worse was coming.

"Only on Sundays," Joseph Roth, one of Berlin's sharpest observers, wrote one year after the Kordas' arrival, "do you come across political scout troops with sandals, walking sticks and knives. In the woods they do round dances, they rave about nature, and have big brawls with each other. It's a strange, baffling generation. . . . You see them at railway stations, the blooming, wheat-blond girls, born to be mothers, but turning into political furies. . . . They have unnaturally long strides and absurdly mannish gestures, but nature takes its revenge on them, because as soon as they shout out their 'Heil!' or their 'Yech!' their voices take on the repellent shrieking edge of hysteria."

True to his dictum that to attract money you must first spend it, Korda moved to the opulent Eden Hotel, and dined conspicuously at Berlin's most expensive restaurants in the company of his actress wife, the radiant Maria. Like bees to honey, backers soon gravitated to the debonair Hungarian and his glamorous wife. "What I remember about him were his exquisite manners," the English director Michael Powell recalled. "He was always in control of himself and always the most important person in the room."

For three years, Korda, with a mostly Hungarian production team, directed commercial costume dramas starring Maria. As usual, his lifestyle was unrelated to his income. Extravagance had become a fixed part of Alex's personality, part of the Korda magic. Alex and Maria soon moved to a vast apartment on the Kurfürstendamm. Though they could afford to furnish only three of the thirteen rooms, their home became a refuge for the Budapest diaspora. One backer recalled Alex's telegrams asking for money to be cabled, while he and Maria toured Italy in grand style in 1924.

Though Alex and Maria tried to float above politics, Korda was an acute observer of political currents. Four years earlier, he had experienced the multiple convulsions of his own country.

Only among themselves, and only in Hungarian, did the three Korda brothers discuss what Europe's descent into madness meant for them. "Alex was always deeply pessimistic," his nephew Michael Korda noted, years later, "despite every evidence of success. But the subject of what happened between 1918 and 1933 was never talked about at home. That was not for the wives or the children." However much Korda enjoyed Berlin's sybaritic pleasures, there was only one place for a filmmaker who had a sharp sense for the demands of the box office, who aspired to international success—and who was Jewish.

Korda's close friend and favorite collaborator, Lajos Biro, was already in Hollywood, preparing the ground for Alex's 1926 arrival. Lifestyle was as ever Alexander Korda's obsession, and America worried him. Could he maintain his present lifestyle on the agreed-upon $350 a week that the First National Company offered him? "In Vienna," he explained to the lawyers, "I lived in the Imperial, ate at Sacher's, and had my suits made at Knize. Here, I live in the Eden, eat in the Bristol, and go to Stavropoulos. Can I do that in Hollywood—with this contract?" No, First National admitted, he could not live like that in Hollywood. But there would be other compensations. Korda shrugged. He could always go back.

FOR THE four scientists, Berlin in the 1920s had the intellectual excitement of Pericles' Athens. Szilard, Wigner, von Neumann, and Teller all spoke fluent German and had cosmopolitan backgrounds. Their education had prepared them to compete with the best of

their European peers. Still, they could hardly have anticipated the intellectual explosion they now plunged into. From 1925 until 1929, they participated in the construction of a cohesive theory of quantum mechanics,
the study of the laws that apply to the behavior of molecules and atoms.

From all over the globe, theoretical physicists gathered in Berlin and in
the medieval university town of Göttingen, three hours away. In those last
years before darkness fell on Germany, a revolution was taking place that
transformed the way we understand space and time. Starting in 1900 with
Max Planck's discoveries about radiation and energy, a remarkable frater-
nity cracked the mystery of the behavior of molecules and atoms. Albert
Einstein's special theory of relativity of 1905 was, of course, the crowning
achievement of the age, but there was much more. A Dane, Niels Bohr,
commuting between Copenhagen and Germany, penetrated the hydrogen atom. Werner Heisenberg—the formulator of the Uncertainty Princi-
ple—formulated matrix mechanics. Erwin Schrödinger developed wave
mechanics. Einstein's close friend Max Born published his paper on prob-
ability and causality. Together, these scientists—including the young
Hungarians—prepared the stage for the nuclear era and the age of the
computer and the Internet.

Life in and around the Greek Revival buildings of Friedrich Wilhelm
University (now renamed Humboldt University), on the Unter den Linden, or at the Kaiser Wilhelm Institute for Physics in the suburb of
Dahlem, crackled with the excitement of cocky young men, competing
with one another to break down old assumptions concerning space and
time. There was unusual academic freedom at the university, with students encouraged to take any courses that inspired them. In a very short
period a generation of physicists revised the fundamental laws of nature,
as Copernicus and Newton had in their day.

Much as the Renaissance attracted the greatest painters in Europe, and
the age of the Baroque drew the best musicians, physics was the magnet
for the brightest minds of the 1920s. Though Leo Szilard had come to
Berlin to study engineering, he was inevitably pulled into their magic circle. "Engineering," Szilard wrote, "attracted me less and less, and physics
attracted me more and more, and finally the attraction became so big that
I was physically unable to listen to any of the lectures through which I sat,
more or less impatiently, at the Institute of Technology."

Szilard had known about these great scientists and their innovations, but now he was in daily contact with them, jostling them in the corridors of the university, and in the cafés that lined the Unter den Linden. He wanted to be on the front lines of the revolution in science.

Another Hungarian physicist in Berlin, Nicholas Kurti, recalled, "Szilard was a regular attendee at the famous, almost fabulous Wednesday [Max] von Laue colloquia, when people, from professors down to doctoral students, gave . . . reports on recently published physics papers. They addressed an audience . . . which usually included seven Nobel laureates, some already honored: Einstein, Max Planck, von Laue, Gustav Hertz—some yet to be: Schrödinger and Wigner."

It was inevitable that Leo Szilard would meet Eugene Wigner at the physics colloquium. Their initial bond was language. "Speaking Hungarian freely," Wigner remembered, "evoked the sweeter days of my childhood." The two Budapest expatriates formed an odd couple in Berlin. Wigner was small, courtly and quiet, carefully dressed and excessively polite. His voice and manner were so wispy that people mistook him for a modest man. "I think so," he would reply when asked on the telephone if it was Wigner on the line. In fact, he was as competitive as his fellow Budapest expatriates. "Johnny von Neumann was a better mathematician," Wigner acknowledged, "and a better scientist. But I knew more physics." A steely ego was tucked inside the modest exterior. He was once asked why he chose chemistry. "Being Jewish," he answered, "I knew I couldn't be prime minister of Hungary. I thought I should do something practical."

Szilard, in a rumpled raincoat, electric with energy and ideas, oblivious to others, brash and impatient, struck strangers as rude. But it was only because his mind respected no boundaries. His mission since reading *The Tragedy of Man* was to save humanity from self-destruction. There was no time to waste. Szilard and Wigner could be seen walking from the Brandenburg Gate through the lush green paths of the Tiergarten, animatedly talking in their incomprehensible language. Their chosen terrain reminded them of the Varosliget—the Budapest City Park.

SZILARD DISCUSSED Albert Einstein's theory of relativity with Max von Laue, who had received the Nobel Prize in physics in 1914. "I went to von Laue," Szilard recalled, "and asked him whether he would give me a problem on which I could work to get my doctor's degree." Surprised by the brash newcomer, von Laue was even more so when Szilard presented his finished work. Szilard had found von Laue's topic (on relativity) insufficiently challenging. The Hungarian always did his best thinking while walking, and in the winter of 1921 he spent a great deal of time trudging through the gray, rain-slicked streets of Berlin. "Within three weeks I had produced a manuscript of something which was really quite original," he modestly admitted, "but I didn't dare take it to von Laue, because it was not what he asked me to do.

"I caught [von Laue] as he was about to leave for class," Szilard recalled, "and I told him that while I had not written the paper which he wanted me to write, I had written something else. . . . He looked somewhat quizzically at me, but he took the manuscript." Early the next morning, the telephone rang at Else Dresel's boarding house, two blocks from the university. "It was von Laue," Szilard recalled. "Your manuscript has been accepted as your thesis for the Ph.D. degree." Szilard had broken through a complex notion of thermodynamics that had baffled scientists for half a century. The twenty-three-year-old Hungarian was awarded a Ph.D. by one of the world's most prestigious academies. Moreover, he had done it by working on his own, outside established channels. It would become his preferred method.

AROUND THE University of Berlin, Albert Einstein's prematurely avuncular features, his distracted air—and his fame—made him instantly recognizable. A permanent member of the Prussian Academy of Sciences and director of the Kaiser Wilhelm Institute for Physics (a position established for him) since 1914, he was as monumental a figure at the university as the great statue of university founder Wilhelm Humboldt. As the most famous scientist in the world, he was already an iconic figure. It was well known that Einstein liked to work alone. Students tended to clear out of his way, but not Leo Szilard.

Szilard and Wigner both attended Einstein's seminar on statistical mechanics. "Einstein's thoughts alone did not content Szilard," Wigner remembered. "With typical directness, he sought out Einstein himself, shook his hand and introduced him to Leo Szilard. . . . Szilard felt that he was already someone important; so, he reasoned, all scientists would benefit from his acquaintance. He did them a favor by presenting himself."

"I went to him," Szilard recalled, "and said that I would like to tell him about something I had been doing. He said, 'Well what have you been doing?' And I told him what I had done. And Einstein said, 'That's impossible. This is something that cannot be done.' And I said, 'Well, yes, but I did it.' " As other, more deferential students passed and nodded politely, it took Szilard only a few minutes to convince the father of modern physics that his Ph.D. dissertation was groundbreaking.

Szilard was soon walking with Einstein after class. Einstein enjoyed the younger man's unorthodox thinking on every imaginable subject. Neither man cared much for the formal courtesies of German academic life. Both loved to seize on problems others had tried and failed to unknot. Both were the sort of men who, when engaged in conversation, would walk through traffic. Both found the highest joy in life, not in human interaction, but, as Einstein put it, "in the flight from the 'I' and the 'We,' to the 'It' of science." Both were Jews of Mitteleuropa, nourished on big ideas and high hopes in the dawn of the age of the Rational Man.

But where Szilard was brusque, impatient, and aggressive in pursuit of his goals, Einstein was almost saintly in his reserves of patience and self-effacement. Einstein and Szilard shared not only a passion for physics, but also an inventive quirkiness. Since boyhood, Szilard had been inventing things of varying degrees of utility. (His nephew John recalled a beach blanket with its own carrying case.) In time, Einstein and Szilard would file eight joint patents for a refrigerator pump they had designed.

It was a friendship that would lead to those two trips to Einstein's Long Island summer cottage.

※

THE HEAD of Paramount Pictures, Adolph Zukor—though himself Hungarian—was not about to let the Warner brothers turn Michael Curtiz into their own Cecil B. DeMille. Zukor quickly bought the rights to Curtiz's blockbuster, *Moon of Israel*, not for distribution, but for Paramount's vault. Thus was Curtiz initiated into the world of Hollywood hardball.

There was much else for Curtiz to get used to in Los Angeles. What did the young man lately from Budapest's noisy boulevards make of the soft pink avenues of Beverly Hills, or Santa Monica's stretch of pale sand? And of Hollywood itself, garish and growing as fast as the Budapest of Curtiz's youth. Between 1910 and 1920, Hollywood—a part of Los Angeles— expanded from five thousand to eighty thousand residents, most all of them linked one way or another to the movies. There was no Ring Road to tie it all together, no cafés to exchange gossip and ideas. Even in the 1920s, the car was king and the telephone the essential means of communication in Los Angeles. Social life was prearranged and formal, and centered inside fantasy mansions behind crew-cut shrubbery. With its balmy Mediterranean climate and a sense of unreality, Los Angeles was undoubtedly disorienting to a Central European.

The Hollywood work ethic, however, was just right for Curtiz. Ambition and drive were fundamental here, just as they had been in Budapest. Hollywood was probably the best place on earth for self-invention, an art Curtiz had already mastered. From poor Jewish boy he had recast himself into a suave continental director. Now he threw himself into his third act. He was working for one of the toughest shops in town, Warner Brothers, the only major family concern in Hollywood. Warners was a famously hard-driving studio where the bottom line ruled, and the director was not indulged as auteur. Warners put the thirty-eight-year-old film magician to the test. And, as always, Curtiz performed.

"When I reach Hollywood," he recalled, "I come out to the studio on the streetcar. Under my arm was the story outline of *Noah's Ark*. The man I am to report to is on the massage table in his office, having his stomach bounced. I ask him when do I start *Noah's Ark*, and he said, 'We have decided not to do that. Leave your script on the massage table. You will make *Third Degree*.' So first I am to make a criminal picture. European criminology is entirely different from Yankee one. I don't know what to do. But I know my entire career depends on it. First I have translation made of the script so I can read it. Next somebody tells me to see the sheriff of Los Angeles County. . . . So for ten days I live with him in jail. I am up every morning at four o'clock studying fingerprint, eating with detectives, going to morning line-up."

With an instinct for the box office and a gargantuan appetite for work, the pace and pressure of Warners suited Curtiz. In the words of actor Peter Lorre, Curtiz not only "ate films, but excreted them." There was no subject he could not handle, but sometimes Curtiz the Ring Road entertainer got carried away. Warners producer Hal Wallis "ran some scenes [from *The Third Degree*] one night and was amazed to discover . . . acrobats, clowns, and high-wire walkers, scenes that hadn't been in the script. We hadn't planned for the scenes and they increased our budget enormously. When I asked Curtiz for an explanation, he said, 'I felt something extra was needed,' " Wallis recalled. "We kept the scenes in. Having spent so much money, I guess we had no alternative but to do so."

Curtiz was just as apt to leave out scenes that were in the script. That was the Curtiz credo: once the camera rolled, the director ruled. With his flaring temper and fierce will, he usually got his way.

Impressed by his drive and range, Warners raised both the quality of Curtiz's scripts and his salary. It did him no harm that he had married one of Hollywood's most respected screenwriters, Bess Meredyth. Her son, John Meredyth Lucas, recalled how this event transpired. "Bessky," Curtiz turned to his future wife, "I like very much we should be married, but I am a Jew." "I know," Meredyth answered. "Is not matter?" asked the astonished Hungarian.

"Mike was convinced America was the greatest country in the world," his stepson remembered. "He hired a teacher who would come to the house at night, sometimes go with him to the studio, working with Mike on the set between takes. He learned American history, the theory of government, the list of presidents and would ask us to test him at the dinner table. He knew far more than any of us did about the history and the running of the country."

Who better to translate the immigrant nation's yearning for respectability and glamour than an exile who clung to America with the passion of the dispossessed? Few could spin more alluring middle-class dreams, or turn mediocre material into convincing escapism. With only a handful of actors, he could create the illusion of massive crowd scenes. "Line up on opposite sides and run at each other," he barked at the extras. "You'll see soch a mess!"

By 1928, Curtiz had sufficiently proven himself to finally draw Warners' epic *Noah's Ark*. For Noah's great flood scene, he ordered up a tank containing 500,000 tons of water, which was then released on a vast set of Babylon. At his command, several hundred extras and stuntmen thrashed in the water, many nearly drowning. For Curtiz, when it came to making movies, the human cost was secondary.

In Hollywood, the Hungarian was fast earning a reputation as an autocrat who dismissed actors unwilling to work through the lunch hour as "actor bums." Take an aspirin, he suggested when a screen idol complained of hunger pains. Since his own days as a failed actor, Curtiz regarded actors as mere tools in the director's hands.

BY THE late 1920s, the once hungry youth from the Ring Road occupied a Beverly Hills fantasy mansion and was a polo-playing member of the Hollywood elite. Curtiz's household included a butler, cook, chauffeur, and maid. At least once a week, Mr. and Mrs. Curtiz received film royals in their paneled, black and white marble-floored entrance hall, in front of the stained glass windows Curtiz had brought over from Vienna's St. Stephen's Cathedral. The Darryl Zanucks, Jack Warners, Hal Wallises, and the woman they all feared, gossip columnist Louella Parsons, enjoyed Curtiz's hospitality.

Curtiz's real home, however, was the cavernous soundstage inside the Warners lot. Mike, as he was universally known, was generally the first to arrive on the set, letting himself in with his own key. The studio was a sacred place. Curtiz came to work in a coat and tie, or in ascot and impeccably tailored jodhpurs. This was his realm, a place he could transform into a jungle or a pirate's ship just as seamlessly as Mihaly Kaminer/Kertesz had morphed into Mike Curtiz. Here, under blazing lights, he was in charge, his restless spirit temporarily focused.

Life was simply raw material for movies. "I see scenes in drive-in restaurants or bars I can use. Once in a little bar, I see a sailor. All the time is flipping a coin. Finally he jumps up and talks to his sweetheart on the telephone. It was easy to see in his mind. He and his sweetheart have quarreled. He leave it to that coin whether he call her or no. I later use that scene in a film." And so, to the enduring pleasure of moviegoers, he would transport the café atmosphere of Budapest to Rick's place in Casablanca.

Beneath the surface, there were banked fires. In December 1929, Curtiz reappeared in Budapest—but only on the screen of the Pushkin Cinema, introducing his latest film, *Noah's Ark*, with a remarkable, carefully nuanced comment. "Ladies and Gentlemen," Curtiz began in English, before switching to Hungarian. "Oh, excuse me. I just realized I'm back home. . . . It's been ten years since this man who stands before you today was swept from his home to distant shores. I wonder," he asked the Budapest audience from the screen, "if there is anyone among you who remembers the youth whose ambitions and restless blood led him to strange places, and who in the wide world is known by the strange-sounding name, Michael Curtiz. But inside, and emotionally, I am still the old Kertesz Mihaly. Perhaps old friends of mine, my brothers, my sister and my mother are in the audience." Indeed, his mother was in the audience, seeing her son for the first time in years.

✕

I N T H E mid-1920s in Berlin, Wigner and Szilard made room in the front row of von Laue's famed physics seminar for the youngest prodigy from Budapest. It did not take long for John von Neumann to rouse the dormant world of German mathematics. Suddenly, he seemed to be everywhere. Zurich, Berlin, Hamburg, all the great university towns competed for his lectures. Delivered without notes, von Neumann interlaced them with private jokes for his small, elite audiences.

Von Neumann spent part of his time in Göttingen. The medieval university had exercised such dominance in mathematics and physics that for many years the *Bulletin of the American Mathematical Society* regularly listed the courses of lectures offered there. He collaborated with the legendary David Hilbert, champion of axiomatics in science and mathematics. In 1925, he was present when the quiet university erupted with the news of Heisenberg's breakthrough in quantum theory. Von Neumann translated Heisenberg's ideas into mathematics, publishing three papers on a mathematical framework for quantum theory. His book *Mathematische Grundlagen der Quantenmechanik* established the Hungarian as a groundbreaking mathematician and physicist. He was only twenty years old.

Even among the geniuses at Göttingen, von Neumann was known as "the fastest mind." Legends soon swirled around him. The Hungarian could tell jokes, including puns, simultaneously in three languages, it was rumored. "I imagined him," recalled von Neumann's future assistant Paul Halmos, "with a checklist before him: Mathematics, check, Physics, check . . . always looking around for green fields to conquer." Soon he would also check off nuclear physics, atomic warfare, Game Theory, and, his boldest innovation, the digital computer.

In 1928, still in his twenties, working on quantum theory, John von

Neumann invented a field that would later change strategic thinking and military doctrine, especially in the United States during the Cold War: Game Theory, applying statistical logic to the choice of strategies as in a game. Von Neumann's new field revolutionized economics and defense strategy, creating a discipline that would soon be used to analyze presidential campaigns, business decisions, poker hands, and nuclear stalemates. Game Theory became a serious branch of mathematics in which naked self-interest determines every decision.*

Like Szilard, Wigner, and Teller, von Neumann had seen Budapest unraveling into anarchy and chaos, Red Terror followed by White. In contrast to his fellow Budapest expatriates, who really only enjoyed the company of other scientists, von Neumann was a hedonist who liked parties and worldly pleasures. Using wit and charm, he was able to camouflage his almost supernatural intensity. Once he read something he retained it for life. He drew on a bottomless well of bawdy limericks and historic and literary anecdotes to deflect argument with people he deemed of lesser intelligence—meaning most of humanity.

Von Neumann's polished surface masked pessimism as deep as that of his fellow Hungarians—and from the same source. "It is just as foolish," he used to tell his friends, "to complain that people are selfish and treacherous, as it is to complain that the magnetic field does not increase unless the electric field has a curl. Both are laws of nature." Neither the Nazis nor Europe's collective cowardice seemed to surprise this seemingly jovial man, who "seemed to take a perverse pleasure," his friend the mathematician Stanislaw Ulam recalled, "in the brutality of a civilized people like the ancient Greeks. For him, I think, it threw a certain not too complimentary light on human nature in general." Like Teller and Szilard, von Neumann would ultimately apply his powerful intellect toward political ends.

ON JULY 14, 1928, carrying a backpack full of hiking gear, Edward Teller, age twenty, jumped off a Munich streetcar just as it accelerated. As he hit the road, he was run over by a second streetcar, which severed his right foot above the ankle. For the rest of his life, Teller wore a prosthetic,

---

* During World War II, von Neumann and economist Oskar Morgenstern turned this study into a groundbreaking 1,200-page book, *The Theory of Games and Economic Behavior*.

walked with a limp, at times using a large tree branch as a cane. Despite this accident, Teller considered "my years as a young scientist in Germany . . . the most satisfying." He was, he recalled, "part of a great enterprise."

For a while, physics provided a safe haven from the gathering madness. "Saturated with the delight of having understood atoms," in Teller's words, "none of us realized how great and imminent our current danger was. We managed . . . to ignore the contradictions in German politics, the turmoil of the world finances, the festering aftermath of World War I, and the prophets of racial superiority."

ON THE SURFACE, life in Berlin still crackled with excitement. Szilard, who lived minutes from the Romanische Café on the Kurfürstendamm, still loitered on its terrace—as did Arthur Koestler, as had, a few years earlier, Alexander Korda and Michael Curtiz. Parties at Eva Striker's nearby studio were a magnet for Budapest intellectuals. Here, in several languages, Szilard argued late into the night.

By 1930, Szilard sensed the change in the air. "The occasion was a meeting of economists [in Paris]," he recalled, "who were called together to decide whether Germany could pay war reparations. To the surprise of the world, the president of the German Reichsbank took the position that Germany could not pay any reparations unless she got back her former colonies. This was such a striking statement that it caught my attention, and I concluded that if he believed he could get away with it, things must be rather bad." As usual, Szilard acted on his fear. "I wrote a letter to my bank and transferred every single penny I had out of Germany into Switzerland."

Another astute observer, German diplomat, man of letters, and defender of Weimar's shaky democracy, Count Harry Kessler, agreed with Szilard's forecast. "The country is coming apart," Kessler wrote in 1932, "the struggles between the radical movements [Communists and Nazis] . . . are bitter armed disputes between two ideologies which exclude compromise. . . . While we spent Sunday driving through the lovely countryside, the unbridled, organized Nazi terror has again claimed seventeen dead and nearly two hundred wounded as its victims." Brown-shirted Nazi students prowled the streets looking for "foreign" elements.

For the first time since they left Budapest, the Hungarian Jews felt vulnerable in Germany. Reluctantly, they began to make plans for a second exile. For Edward Teller, "The fears of my childhood—war, destruction and death—were being made reality, but the German people around me were unprotesting." Teller brooded that his best years were ending. "A period of beauty and excitement . . . a refuge for mind and spirit, was being destroyed. I was full of anger and anguish."

Returning to Budapest was not an option. Just look at what was happening to von Neumann. Between 1929 and 1934 this young man, among the greatest mathematicians of the century, was rejected by the country of his birth for three different positions, including membership in the Hungarian Academy of Sciences. That was sign enough for him and his friends.

For the second time in their young lives, the four scientists had to abandon all that was familiar. "I left behind a piece of my connection to literature when I left Germany," Teller recalled. "But, greater loss by far, the unique and wonderful community that was German physics in its golden years was destroyed." Germany never recovered from the loss of these revolutionary intellects. The country never again regained its preeminent position as the most intellectually creative place in Europe. In attempting to destroy the Jews, Germany ultimately would destroy itself.

※

I N 1925, with his family's help, Andor Kertesz scraped together train fare to the city where talent and new ideas still mattered more than bloodlines. When he arrived at Paris's Gare de l'Est on October 8, 1925, his timing was perfect. Reborn as Andre Kertesz, his luck was about to change. Paris, like Berlin, in the 1920s was bursting with new artistic currents: Abstractionism, Constructivism, Dadaism, and Surrealism.

No new arrival is ever quite prepared for the first glimpse of Paris. The low buildings that reveal a streaked sky above the gray rooftops, the bridges in the late afternoon, the majestic Louvre museum and the Notre Dame cathedral bathed in the pale yellow light of dusk thrilled Kertesz.

The city reminded Kertesz of Budapest. Like his native city, Paris was a city of neighborhoods, full of ancient, narrow, cobblestone streets and buildings on a human scale. The smells of the city were also familiar to

Kertesz: burnt coffee, roasting chestnuts, and coal dust hung in the air just like at home. Goatherds still dragged goats through the streets of the Left Bank.

The young man could not have realized that this was but the first stage of a life of exile. For the first time in his life, he was alone. He had to succeed. There was no time to lose: it was his last chance to prove he could make it as a photographer.

Kertesz spoke no French and had never ventured beyond the border of the old Austro-Hungarian Empire. Along with his camera and his peasant's flute, he had, however, the names of a handful of Hungarian artists making their way in Paris.

Kertesz headed to the neighborhood where others from Budapest formed a sort of village tucked inside Paris. Lajos Tihanyi, Gyula Zilzer, and the sculptor Jozsef Csaky lived in the Latin Quarter, the area that borders the Luxembourg Gardens and the Boulevard Montparnasse on the Left Bank, which, then as now, drew a mix of expatriates. Kertesz found a small room in a cheap hotel off the boulevard on the rue Vavin. The neighborhood was home to Ernest Hemingway, Gertrude Stein, Man Ray, Pablo Picasso, and many other future legends. Sylvia Beach's Shakespeare and Co. in the *quartier* had published James Joyce's *Ulysses*, the most exciting and controversial literary event of the era, a few years earlier. Joyce himself was a regular at the same neighborhood restaurant, Michaud's, that Hemingway liked. This was the fabled "Lost Generation," marked by the Great War in which Kertesz himself had lost his innocence.

In Budapest, Kertesz could not even afford to loiter in sidewalk cafés. Now, with no family to retreat to, Kertesz gravitated toward the grand cafés at the intersection of the Boulevards Raspail and Montparnasse. Amid the cacophony of half a dozen languages, the shy and inarticulate Hungarian found a place.

Eager to learn, Kertesz absorbed the swirling artistic currents. Amid writers, poets, and artists, he benefited from being one of the few photographers. Photography was still relatively new and thus inherently interesting to the Parisian avant-garde. His particular sensibility, seemingly artless and experimental, meshed with theirs. Even his lack of verbal facility in French was an asset, proof of his authenticity. Having arrived in Paris a lost soul, Kertesz would not stay lost for long.

His very first picture, taken the morning after his arrival, shows that in Paris he had found his dream subject. The view from his hotel window offered a typical Parisian vista of a dingy wall, shuttered windows broken by a window box of daisies, and a young woman, wistfully looking out. In other hands the scene might be conventional. But Kertesz's eye was fresh, melancholy, and dreamlike.

So he began to peel back Paris, layer by layer. There was much for him to absorb, and much of it, like the Musée du Luxembourg, housing the great Impressionists and Cézannes, was free. Kertesz never considered himself a refugee: he had come of his own free will. In his mind, unlike the next wave that would flee fascism, Kertesz's exile was voluntary. For a man of such fierce pride, this knowledge eased his assimilation into Parisian life.

The center of Kertesz's universe was the Café du Dôme, the Montparnasse refuge of Budapest's exiled intellectuals. Sustained by coffee, rolls, and the unintelligible language they spoke in front of puzzled Parisians, the exiles gave one another emotional support and artistic affirmation. The Dôme had become the Paris version of the beloved Café New York; both were places of pleasure and business for struggling artists. "My photographs were passed from hand to hand in the café," Kertesz recalled, "and more and more people began to recognize me. I was happy to give my work away to my friends."

Among his new friends was one of Hungary's preeminent avant-garde artists, the deaf-mute painter Lajos Tihanyi. Blending Cubism and Expressionism, Tihanyi was a popular and successful Left Bank artist, who drew the shy new arrival into his circle. The agnostic Kertesz felt comfortable enough with Tihanyi to observe Yom Kippur with him. The rooftops and chimneys of Paris fascinated Tihanyi. Soon Kertesz was photographing them. Kertesz's portrait of Tihanyi, blowing a large plume of smoke that suggests his deaf-muteness, is one of his most powerful. Tihanyi's dictum was simple, "The author composes with words, the sculptor with stone and metal, the painter with colors." Kertesz now asked himself, in Tihanyi's spirit, what were the inherent qualities of photography?

The émigrés brought Budapest's whimsical irreverence to Paris. Kertesz's *Satirical Dancer*, posed by his friend, Hungarian dancer Magda

Forstner, captures this spirit. Another Budapest painter, Gyula Zilzer, introduced Kertesz to the Dutch painter Piet Mondrian. One of Kertesz's most famous images from this early period is of Mondrian's vestibule. The precise horizontal and vertical lines of this photograph distill the painter's style. (In 2004, this photograph was sold for $1 million.)

Kertesz's circle of friends soon included the French painter Fernando Leger and American sculptor Alexander Calder. Their impact can be seen in Kertesz's highly abstract compositions and increasingly avant-garde sensibility. In 1926, Kertesz, always interested in documenting himself, sent his family a self-portrait. It shows a self-confident young man, leaning against a balcony railing, an open book and a bowl of flowers in the foreground. The carefully posed portrait conveys the message: I've made it!

Later, Andre Kertesz would refer to Paris as his "best girlfriend." But the reality of exile was more complicated than that selective memory. He missed his sweetheart, Elizabeth. However perfect a subject Paris might be, however lively his Hungarian circle, at night, he was alone. En route to his own emigration to Argentina, his brother Jeno stopped off to see him, and expressed concern. "Loneliness is not for you," Jeno wrote him, "you have to *belong* somewhere."

Though Kertesz continued to break new ground, so far he referred to his triumph as only "moral." He was still not making a living. He changed hotels regularly. But his determination never flagged. He resisted being defined or categorized. "I like all art, if it's good," he insisted. He studied a Mondrian or a Chagall, assimilated them, and responded in his own way. *Meudon* is a dreamlike, surrealist vision where several events are simultaneously unfolding. A train is passing on a viaduct; a man carrying a large package—with an expression of veiled menace—seems to be approaching the photographer. *Meudon* is the work of a mature artist who has absorbed the exploding artistic currents of his age.

While Elizabeth waited to be summoned from Budapest, in 1927, Andre suddenly married a fellow Hungarian, violinist and photographer Rozsi Klein, who lived in one of the hotels where he briefly stayed. Born of emotional need and loneliness, the marriage was not a success, and only deepened his loneliness.

His melancholy affected his work, however, in a positive manner.

Some of his most poignant photographs during this period contrast monumental, aggressively cheerful wall posters with people passing in front of them—foreshadowing some of the greatest photographs that would emerge from America in the Great Depression a few years later, such as Margaret Bourke-White's images of breadlines and Walker Evans's billboard photographs. A stooped, homeless woman studying a poster called *Sécurité* shows a deeper awareness of his new surroundings. Kertesz's portraits—never his favorite genre—also reflect a new depth. "When we parted you were hesitant, lacked self-awareness, little individuality, much imitation," his brother Jeno wrote him in 1926, after seeing some of his work. "It is not the camera any more that takes the picture, but the lens captures what *you* want it to. . . . I don't even know how you did it. Technically [they] are impeccable, and in composition I do not recognize you. . . . It seems you needed a year of torment for the daily bread to become independent and conscious."

Kertesz's commercial breakthrough came in 1927, when he exhibited forty-two photographs at a Left Bank gallery, Au Sacre du Printemps. Featured in the exhibition announcement was a poem dedicated to Kertesz by the Surrealist poet Paul Dermée. Entitled "Brother Seer," it hailed Andre as a "discoverer and inventor . . . whose retinas, with each blink, become virgin again. . . . No rearranging, no posing, no gimmicks, nor fakery. Your technique is as honest, as incorruptible, as your vision. In our home for the blind, Kertesz is a brother seer."

For the first time, Andre Kertesz attracted the attention of a distant world he knew nothing about. The art critic of the *Chicago Tribune* wrote that Kertesz "has an artist's instinct for the exact placing of objects. . . . What makes ordinary objects and scenes take on a fresh value in [Kertesz] photographs."

The exhibit placed Kertesz at the forefront of the Parisian avant-garde. In just over a year, the lost soul who could not find a place in his hometown had scaled the heights of the most rarefied artistic circle in the world. Hungarian photographers seemed to dominate the Berlin and Paris scene. Laszlo Moholy-Nagy, Brassaï, Martin Munkacsi, and, soon, Robert Capa—exiles like Kertesz—were asserting their vision. When *Coronet* magazine published Kertesz's work, it was accompanied by a tongue-in-cheek apologia: "Can we help it if the best photographs seem consistently to be produced by Hungarians?"

Other exhibits and tributes quickly followed. The Salon International d'Art Photographique in October 1927 featured his *Eiffel Tower*. The Salon d'Escalier in 1928 showed more Kertesz photographs than those of any other photographers—more even than the famed Berenice Abbott and Man Ray. The organizer, Lucien Vogel, was also the editor of *Vu* magazine, which now provided a steady and well-paid outlet for Kertesz's work.

The public was interested in being both informed and entertained through the new technology of well-produced magazine photographs. Germany was the real birthplace of the illustrated photography magazine aimed at a middle-class audience. The *Berliner Illustrierte Zeitung*, and, in France, *Vu* and *Regards*, ushered in the age of the mass media. Across the Atlantic, they would soon inspire the birth of *Life* and *Look* magazines. A rich new field was opening up for photographers. Among the most innovative of the new genre was the *Munchner Illustrierte Presse*, edited by another Hungarian, Stefan Lorant, one of the pioneers of the new genre, a classmate of Eugene Wigner and John von Neumann at the Lutheran Gymnasium, and who, like them, had left Budapest in the early 1920s. Lorant's uncle had been the editor of *Erdekes Ujsag*, the publication that gave Kertesz his start.

Influenced by both Mondrian's severe geometry and Tihanyi's quest for purity in art, Kertesz produced his own radically simple, and, subsequently, iconic photograph, *Fork*. "I was successful," Kertesz said, "in rendering the object with the powerful suggestivity of shadow, light and line in the most direct and rich way possible."

Andre Kertesz was finally fulfilled, successfully melding art and commerce. His magazine work earned him a good living. He was now a frequently exhibited and respected artist. When he purchased a Leica in 1928, Kertesz experienced another form of liberation. A lightweight, small camera with fast advancing film, it was the perfect partner for his unfailing eye. He now had an instrument suited to urban life. More than ever, he could capture small, human moments that pass in a flash—unseen by most.

Increasingly, even his magazine work told stories that needed few words. Lucien Vogel and Stefan Lorant held his work in a regard verging on awe and allowed him almost unlimited latitude in shaping a story. In 1929 the *Berliner Illustrierte Zeitung* devoted three pages to Andre

Kertesz's "The House of Silence," a photo essay on the Trappist order of monks in Soligny, France. It was unusual in those days for a magazine to devote three pages to a single photographic essay. Kertesz's photographs do not *illustrate* the story of an order of monks who had taken the vow of silence, they *tell* the story. It is an early example of a series of images used in a photographic essay and marked the high point of Kertesz's editorial freedom.

It must have been satisfying for Kertesz to read in the popular Hungarian newspaper *Pesti Hirlap* that in his own country he was deemed "the head of the new wave of photography . . . his numerous nudes, and landscapes . . . have made his name known and admired by the readers of the most prestigious reviews of Europe and America."

In 1931, after five years of separation, Elizabeth finally joined Andre in Paris. Beyond his or her wildest dreams, he had fulfilled her challenge to make something of himself. The portrait that commemorated the lovers' reunion shows Andre gazing rapturously at his beloved. She, however, is looking straight ahead. Perhaps she had not yet forgiven his abrupt marriage (followed, predictably, by a quick divorce) to Rozsi Klein, and, though they were soon married, perhaps she never would.

In and around the cafés and galleries of the Left Bank the carefully dressed, courtly Hungarian with his Leica and his mangled French, dubbed "Brother Seeing Eye," was now a *personnage*. "Not one of us here," French photographer Pierre Boucher commented at Kertesz's 1934 exhibit opening, "is fit to hold a candle to him." In a field that attracted the young, Kertesz, now forty, was the "Old Master." Henri Cartier-Bresson, a decade and a half his junior, not yet the century's most admired photojournalist, met him on the terrace of the Dôme. Cartier-Bresson considered Kertesz "midway between art and reportage." In an interview with me just months before his death in 2004, Cartier-Bresson declared Kertesz "the poetic source" of his own photography. "Each time Andre Kertesz's shutter clicks," he had famously noted elsewhere, "I feel his heart beating."

Another new arrival to the Hungarian circle at the Dôme was Gyula Halasz—who would soon become Brassaï. Kertesz took the multitalented (sculptor, painter, and photographer) Budapest-trained artist under his wing. "I was not yet a photographer," Brassaï recalled, "and gave no

thought at all to photography and even despised it at that time when . . .
I met Andre Kertesz. . . . Thanks to seeing his pictures and listening to
what he said about them, I discovered how much this 'spiritless and soul-
less mechanism,' this 'technical process,' had enriched man's means of
expression. . . . I was trapped by photography. But the bird catcher was ex-
ceptionally good."

For several months following Kertesz's patient instruction in night photography, Brassaï disappeared from the Dôme. When he reappeared, he
had finished his classic *Paris de Nuit*, one of the seminal books in the history of photography. Unlike Kertesz, Brassaï loved "the inhabitants of the
lower depths, prostitutes, transvestites, fading courtesans and pimps." In
sixty-four portraits he showed both how well he had learned from the
master—and how different was his sensibility. Kertesz was far too reserved
to prowl the brothels and saloons where Brassaï had found his best material. Often on drugs himself, Brassaï gloried in the demimonde. Henry
Miller, the controversial author of *Tropic of Cancer*, wrote his agent, "I
have found my counterpart in dear Halasz [Brassaï]; he is a man of insatiable curiosity, a 'wonderer' like me, who sets out on an exploration with
no other aim but continued investigation."

Within a year of Brassaï's publishing triumph, the fiercely competitive
Kertesz produced his own book, *Paris Vu par André Kertész*. Where Brassaï
is dark, moody, and titillating, Kertesz is quiet and intimate. Kertesz is fascinated by the Seine, which, like the Danube, plays a key role in the city's
life. But the Paris of 1934 is not quite as alluring to Kertesz as it was in 1925.
A subtle but definite shift has come over Kertesz's view of the city. Mystery
has been replaced by melancholy. Indeed, by the mid-1930s, Paris was not
the city that had first thrilled and embraced the young arrival.

WHAT DID Alexander Korda—European to his manicured
fingertips—make of Los Angeles, a city flanked on three sides
by desert? L.A. was a car town and Korda, after one disastrous
experience behind the wheel, gave up driving. True, the climate was
balmy, but for Korda nature was something to be tamed and perfected inside soundstages, not personally experienced.

He had become used to acknowledgment by headwaiters and others that he was a Man of Importance. Now, he was again a stranger in town. Irony, wit, social polish, and curiosity about the world outside "the business" did not cut much ice on the raw western edge of the American continent. Korda, a deliberately courteous, formal man, was now in a culture that valued the casual; he was treated like some stock figure in an Austro-Hungarian operetta. When he greeted Joseph P. Kennedy with a bow, the future president's father was heard to remark, "Who does that guy think he is, some kind of fucking baron or something?" Rudeness, like anti-Semitism, was something Korda pretended he did not notice. Unlike Curtiz, "Crack of dawn at the studio" was not Korda's working style. I can't expect my stars to make love early in the morning, he grumbled, referring to his own aversion to the L.A. work ethic.

Korda's letters to Lajos Biro reveal a man few ever saw: prepared to pay almost any price for success, but at the same time both cynical and lonely. "Since you left there's hardly anybody to talk to," he wrote Biro in the summer of 1928. "Slowly but surely I am being bored to death. . . . I begin to realize that apart from a raise, nothing in the world interests me." Korda felt marooned in paradise. "Something happened to me that is rare these days," he wrote Biro in September of that year, revealing his despair. "After your letter I was in a bright mood all day. . . . You can imagine how bored I am with these truly kind people. . . . It's a terribly empty feeling to be without a single human being to whom I can talk—and who can talk to me. . . . Anyway: the main thing is to get the money together. With money anything else becomes possible."

The tyranny of the studio system, which suited Curtiz, was torment for Korda. He needed his own shop. Money was the ticket to freedom. Late in 1928, he wrote Biro, "Wednesday [payday] is lovely. I'm saving money. And everything else is unimportant. . . . There is not a soul to whom I could say a single word. . . . My life passes as usual. I read in Swift at the beginning of one of the Gulliver chapters: 'Having been condemned by nature and fortune to an active and even more a restless life . . .' And in this accursedly active and even more accursedly restless life, you can imagine in what terrible loneliness I am living. . . . But I have plans: the great dream, the little dream. A motor tour of Europe and life somewhere on the Mediterranean—after all that is the real world, the rest is just colonies."

Whereas in Budapest and Berlin the director was an esteemed *artiste*, in Hollywood the producer was in the cockpit of power. The director was essentially the movie's manager: there to make sure the camera was loaded, the sets and actors prepared, and the whole enterprise smoothly running before he called out, "Action!" Directors were deemed replaceable cogs. Korda wanted real control: to be both director and producer.

As always, Korda worried about his brothers. "Please, my dear Lajos, tell me frankly: what is happening to Zoli?" he wrote Biro, "and if he can't get on over there [in Berlin] please, persuade him to come here. Here he'll learn about *talkies*, special effects, model shots and if later we do something. . . . Please write sometimes. It is always a great joy and consolation to recognize your handwriting on an envelope."

Nine months later Zoltan Korda joined his brother in Hollywood, and, along with their youngest brother, Vincent, the three would eventually form iron personal and professional bonds that would ease the loneliness of their exile.

But at the end of 1929 world events again blocked Korda's way. This time it was the Depression. "He was a paper millionaire until that dreadful day in October, 1929," Jack Warner remembered. "He was on the phone to New York every day, buying and selling. That morning, Korda disappeared from the stage where he had been working and the studio cops vainly searched the whole of the vast lot. Toward the middle of the afternoon I suddenly remembered what he had once called his private office. I hurried to a telephone booth in a remote section of the back lot and there he was, wild eyed, hair askew, slumped against a side panel and mumbling about suicide."

Broke and miserable, Korda had no choice but to endure Hollywood. By 1931, his contempt for the place was reciprocated. The final blow came when Sol Wurtzel, the head of Fox, screened *The Princess and the Plumber*, a film Korda had been assigned to direct. The studio chief turned to his twelve-year-old son. "What'dya think?" "It stinks," the boy replied. Wurtzel turned to Korda. "You heard the kid. You're fired."

It tasted like failure at the time, but Korda could not have learned the lessons of Hollywood anywhere else in the world. Perhaps the most valuable lesson of all had been just how fast a man can fall. Korda left behind not only the ill-fitting culture, but also his equally ill-fitting wife, whom he would soon divorce.

With $20 in his pocket, Korda boarded the New York–bound *Sky Chief*. "I was the only one to see him off as the train pulled out," Austrian director Josef von Sternberg recalled. "A piece of my heart went with him. But," as von Sternberg wrote, "this was not the end of this remarkable man."

WHAT SWEET relief it was to breathe the damp, smog-filled air of Berlin—Korda's next stop in 1930. To conspire over tiny cups of espresso with fellow Hungarians like Lajos Biro, Max Reinhardt, and Gabriel Pascal on one of the Romanische Café's wobbly tables was heaven after Hollywood's sunshine and orange juice. His spirits and his old ambitions revived, Korda, appraising the political landscape, saw that the Nazi wave had not crested. Taking Lajos Biro with him, he moved on to Paris. Life looked brighter from his suite at the Ritz.

With Vincent already living in France, the brothers were soon collaborating on the sort of film they were born to make: Marcel Pagnol's *Marius*. This was Korda at his best: a sweet and ironic saga of a Marseilles café owner's son who abandons his love to seek his fortune. It was simpler and truer than anything Korda had done in Hollywood.

Image and publicity being the oxygen of Korda's ambitions, he asked Brassaï to create the trademark for Korda's new French company. "Sandor Korda is a very nice man," Brassaï wrote his parents from Paris in September 1932. "He has wholeheartedly taken me into his good graces and often invites me to lunch. . . . My idea and photograph were accepted as the trademark for the company: upon the mast of a sailboat a flag inscribed with the word *Production* flutters in the wind followed by five smaller flags bearing the letters K-O-R-D-A which flutter together for a while as the boat's siren wails."

Soon, Korda's banner would flutter above the Thames. It was in England that Korda saw his greatest opportunity to create an empire to rival the one that had recently rejected him. Again, as in 1908 when he grasped that films were the medium of the future, Korda saw a void that he could fill. England had no film moguls, no big movie stars, no studios. Like Hungary, it boasted a rich history ready to be mined, and—unlike Hungary—a language that was spoken on both sides of the Atlantic. Above all, it was Europe! He would take the lessons learned in Hollywood and transplant them to Britain. He knew the secret to independence. He would create a full-blown corporation and a studio of his own. He would show those crude studio pashas. And he would make his brothers his partners—though never equals—and thus reconstitute the scattered family. Korda had circled from Budapest to Vienna to Berlin to Hollywood to Paris. Approaching his fortieth year, he would make London his final stop.

I N 1931, Berlin was still a magnet for Europe's bright and ambitious. In July of that year, when Robert Capa's train pulled into Berlin's Annhalter Station, Capa—still Endre Friedmann—did not yet feel like a refugee. There had been no wrenching goodbyes from his family or the city he loved. Budapest was home and, in better days, he would be back. But Berlin was open, experimental, and it had hustle—things rapidly disappearing from Budapest. Like all educated Hungarians, Capa spoke fluent German. The Deutsche Hochschule für Politik—a respected political science institute—was his official destination. But school was no more appealing in Berlin than it had been in Budapest. For Capa, Berlin's street life held far more interest than the classroom.

In any case, by the end of his first semester in Berlin, his parents could no longer afford to pay his tuition. The world Depression had finally hit Budapest. The nineteen-year-old Capa was on his own, his formal education finished, but going home would have been an admission of failure, the acceptance of a modest future. Capa preferred to try to make it on street smarts and charm—and the help of his fellow Hungarian exiles.

Eva Besnyo, a Budapest friend and neighbor, was already making her way as a photographer in Berlin. "Is photography a good way to make money?" Capa asked her. "It's a calling," she told him, "not a way to make money." Finding a calling was not Capa's top priority. He needed to pay the rent.

Eva introduced him to her boss, Budapest-born Simon Guttman, the founder of Dephot, a photo agency that supplied many of Germany's

newspapers. Guttman hired Capa as a darkroom boy. It was a lowly beginning but at Dephot, Capa joined some of Europe's most innovative photojournalists: Felix Man, Harald Lechenperg, Walter Bosshard, and Umbo.
As he developed their photographs, Capa studied their craft.

At the Romanische Café on the Kurfürstendamm, Guttman usually
picked up the tab for the youngest and hungriest of Berlin's Hungarian
émigré community. Bad news on the street was good news for the
agency—and for Capa. As militants on the left and right clashed with in-
creasing frequency, and the Reichstag was dissolved in June 1932, Dephot
needed more hands. Europe's growth industry, demagoguery and street violence, provided the opening for Capa's career.

Leon Trotsky was responsible for Capa's big break. On November 27,
1932, as the exiled communist faced an excited audience in Copenhagen's Sport Stadium, Guttman sent Capa, the only man he could spare.
Guttman's Leica in hand, he seized his moment. His pictures of the
doomed revolutionary captured the man's charisma and his desperation.
Technically imperfect, Capa's shots nevertheless were given a full-page
layout. It was the first time he saw his byline at the bottom of the page and
he felt the thrill of professional recognition.

But by 1932, Berlin was no safer than Budapest—and it was threaten-
ing to become far more dangerous. Nazis with clubs hanging from their
belts had a new swagger. The doorman at Dephot's offices started wearing
the gray jacket, brown pants, and swastika armband of Hitler's private
army of stormtroopers, the dreaded SA or Sturm Abteilung. Capa's friend
Eva Besnyo packed up for Amsterdam. On January 30, 1933, Adolf Hitler
became chancellor and Capa observed jackbooted storm troopers, blazing torches held high, parade down the Unter den Linden. He knew that
his time in Berlin was up. Capa joined thousands of others in flight at the
same train station where he had arrived, with high hopes, in 1931. With
nowhere else to go, he returned to Budapest.

Budapest, in its own bubble, tried to float above the unpleasant events
at its borders. After the first wave of virulent anti-Semitism that marked
Horthy's early years, Budapest settled into another round of deluded he-
donism. The Numerus Clausus law still kept most young Jews out of universities and state-controlled jobs. But on the Danube Corso and along
Andrassy Boulevard, the city's legendary beauties paraded the latest Paris-

inspired styles. The Prince of Wales had lately discovered Budapest. His frequent visits—accompanied by Mrs. Simpson—gave the town's night-clubs and gaming tables new glamour. Regent Horthy, resplendent in the admiral's uniform he had worn in service to the fallen empire, attended the gala premiere of Greta Garbo's *Grand Hotel* at the Radius Film Palace on the Ring Road. Horthy found Adolf Hitler bombastic and crude. Not so the overtly racist head of Horthy's government, Gyula Gombos, who was too busy to enjoy Budapest's nightlife. Hitler's seizure of power encouraged Hungary's homegrown racists and irredentists like Gombos. So while Winston Churchill, in political exile, vacationed on the French Riviera, Gombos was courting fascists—and tying Hungary's future to their support. The time seemed ripe for Hungary to reclaim the territories lost under the Treaty of Trianon, but he would need help from powerful friends. It was Gombos who coined the term "Rome-Berlin Axis"—at a time when Hitler and Mussolini were still rivals.

The first official Hungarian National Socialist party, the Party of National Will, was only a year and a half away. Two years later, in October 1937, all Hungarian fascist and Nazi organizations would unite under the banner of the much better known and feared Arrow Cross Party. A year later, Parliament passed the first of a series of laws limiting Jews' freedom.

Capa, who had radar for these shifts, had no intention of staying. Paris, the magnet to so many other of his hometown's brightest, seemed like the obvious next stop. And so he scraped together the fare and eventually he, too, arrived at the Gare de l'Est. Capa was in some ways a natural French-man: urbane, sensual, and hedonistic. But in Paris, too, uniformed fascist militias, the Croix-de-Feu, the Solidarité Française, and the Jeunesses Pa-triotes, prowled the streets. As the French franc continued to fall, the job-less lines grew longer and the government confused and helpless. "Sadly, the situation here is getting worse and worse," Capa wrote to his parents. "I will stay in Europe at most one more year." The twenty-year-old resolved, "After that, I will go to the Other Side." He meant the United States.

IN THOSE days, Robert Capa lived on the edge. Home was a room in a seedy hotel in the Latin Quarter; sustenance was stolen food, sugar cubes dissolved in water, and, occasionally, fish he caught in the Seine. His port-folio of photographs was modest, and there were many others looking for work. His camera spent a great deal of time in pawnshops. Writing home in 1934, he apologized for his long silence. "I'm sure you are very angry with me," he wrote his parents, "and I am mad at the world. . . . I do not even have the 1.50 francs" for postage. But he was determined. "I will stay in Paris for two months and will have to work day and night because I must succeed after all this pain and effort."

One advantage Capa had over Andre Kertesz was the way he picked up languages. German had come easily to him. Now, sitting in the Luxembourg Gardens, he applied himself to learning French. "I have learnt French already," he boasted to his family, "and slowly I will learn English, but this is no great trouble." Add to street smarts and language skills an irresistible personality, and Andre—as the future Capa then called himself—was not alone for long.

One day in 1934, on the terrace of the Dôme, Capa met Andre Kertesz. "He was a charming, irresponsible young boy," as Kertesz remembered. "He asked me if I could help him get work, and so I did what I could. I guaranteed for him with the editors . . . that he could do the work." Kertesz introduced Capa to Lucien Vogel, the editor of *Vu* magazine, and urged him to give his young, perpetually broke friend a break.

"That boy," Kertesz later said of Capa, "was like a son to me"—the son Kertesz never had. Kertesz and Capa were temperamentally and artistically far apart, but there was none of the competition that would poison relations between Kertesz and Brassaï. "He was just a darkroom boy. . . . Elizabeth [Kertesz's wife] straightened him out. She made him understand that you must have responsibilities." One day when the three of them were sitting at the Dôme, Capa turned to Kertesz, "Andre, lend me your camera," and snapped Elizabeth and Andre. For the rest of his life, Kertesz kept this framed photograph on his night table.

On the same terrace, Capa met two other photographers who would play decisive roles in his career: Polish-born David Seymour, known as Chim, and Henri Cartier-Bresson. The three would later form Magnum, the world's first photo cooperative. Chim and Capa, two exiled Central European Jews, formed an iron bond that substituted for family. The tall, fair, and aristocratic Cartier-Bresson was from another world. The son of a wealthy Norman family, he had studied at Cambridge University. "It did not occur to me," Cartier-Bresson told me, "that Andre [Capa] was Jewish.

Chim, though not religious at all, carried the burden of being Jewish within him as a kind of sadness."

On February 6, 1934, a Parisian street demonstration turned lethal. Capa was there. Rioters threw marbles under the hooves of the police horses on the Place de la Concorde and tore up iron railings from the Tuileries Gardens to use as javelins. Soon the demonstrators began an orgy of car burning, uprooting of trees, and tearing down lampposts. Holding his Leica aloft, Capa showed little concern for his safety in a sea of angry Parisians. Light was falling and the inexperienced photographer's results were meager. By midnight, both the rioters and the police were exhausted. Fifteen people had been killed and two thousand seriously hurt. A line had been crossed. As the country, determined never again to let Germany violate its territory, constructed a 150-mile barrier of forts and bunkers called the Maginot Line, fascism — of the homegrown variety — entered by the back door.

The assignments still did not come. "Again, nothing has worked out for me," Capa wrote home, "and truly it is difficult for me to smile." It took all his determination to maintain the facade of the bon vivant. "Here it is impossible to find ten francs," he wrote, "and if the man has an empty pocket, it's the end of him." He was homesick. "The Christmas weather is very grey and [my] good mood is in danger." By now Capa was ready to abandon photography. "It was enough for me, and I would now rather suffer with something else. . . . Towards Christmas the homeless are in a bad mood and I cannot find my place."

By 1934, France's unemployment had risen to 300,000. There was a 60 percent increase in business bankruptcies. Capa joined an army of jobless who lined up outside military barracks for scraps of food left by the soldiers. Even in the polyglot Latin Quarter and Montparnasse, foreigners felt less welcome. Right-wing groups such as Action Française stepped up their agitation against the weak Third Republic.

However desperate his own situation, Capa remained concerned about his family. "You must not worry about anything," he counseled his always anxious mother, "now it is time only to think about yourself." But Paris, wrapped in a sullen, self-absorbed mood, was a dry well for a struggling news photographer. "The Devil should take this world," he wrote bitterly. "I shall study only another hour . . . because my stomach is talking."

. . .

IN THE FALL of 1934, Simon Guttman arrived in Paris and again rescued Capa. "Go photograph a pretty girl sitting on a bench," Guttman instructed him. The assignment came not from a newspaper but a Swiss
advertising firm. But it was work—and Capa was desperate. His search
eventually led to a petite redhead wearing a beret and a provocative smile.
Her name was Gerda Pohorylles, and the chemistry between them was in-
stantaneous.

Gerda was fleeing the Nazis and seeking her fortune in Paris. A German Jew of Yugoslav background, she was as high-spirited and quick-
witted as Capa. "They went to the south of France," Kertesz recalled.
"They came back and Capa said to me, 'Never in my life have I been so
happy.' " A 1935 photograph of Gerda and Capa in a Parisian café radiates
the pure joy of two young people who have discovered love. Never again
would Capa look so relaxed, so unselfconscious, so happy. There is not a
trace of the legendary Lothario in Capa's gaze—only amused acknowledgment that he had met his match.

She brought him luck, a new look—and soon a new identity. For Gerda
he was willing to change everything. "Imagine, Mother," he wrote home
in November 1935, "my hair is short, my tie is hanging on my neck, my
shoes are shined and I appear on the scene at seven o'clock. And what is
more surprising, in the evening at nine, I am already home. In one word,
it is the end of the bohemian life. . . . If you look at the photographs, you
will find me quite a handsome boy! . . . I shave every day—and, what is
more important, I have a very beautiful winter coat (Gerda got it for me)."

For the first time since he began his wanderings at eighteen, Capa was
no longer alone. Gerda was his lover and partner. "She picked him up.
She gave him direction," Eva Besnyo recalled. "He had never wanted an
ordinary life and neither did she. She was as free a spirit as Capa." Capa
seemed to relish his new life and its predictable routine. "I run around a
lot all day and at eight o'clock in the evening we arrive home dead tired.
Naturally, we hope that all will work out and that with less work we shall
earn more, but for the time being, it's good as it is." There was still no work
in Paris, however. "Our money is equal to zero," he wrote his mother in
September 1935.

At age twenty-two, Capa already knew how he wanted to live his life.

"One must be strong and move forward, Mother. . . . Life is very miserable," Capa admonished his eternally complaining mother, "but we must accept it as it is." Despite his poverty, he believed in himself. "Cornell [his younger brother] should learn photography," he wrote his mother late in 1935, with astonishing self-confidence and foresight, "because in the end I shall make it, and then I shall be able to help him."

"Gerda is taking pictures and I am making enlargements, and next week I shall again start taking pictures. . . . I have shown my newest pictures to Kertesz . . . and he was very satisfied." No assignments were forthcoming, however.

Born from a combination of brilliance and desperation, Robert Capa officially came into the world on April 8, 1936. "I am working under a new name," he wrote his family. "My name is Robert Capa. It is like being born again, but this time without hurting anybody." Gerda and Capa had the notion that a rich and famous (and fictional) American character, a photographer whose name combined two reigning celebrities, actor Robert Taylor and director Frank Capra, would get more work than Andre Friedmann—who was getting none. Amazingly, it worked. "I invented Capa," he later said, "a famous American photographer who came over to Europe and didn't want to bore French editors because they didn't pay enough. . . . So I just moved in with my little Leica, took some pictures and wrote Bob Capa on them . . . for double prices."

Gerda, too, reinvented herself, shedding Pohorylles for the dramatic Gerda Taro, with equal success. She sold the "American" photographer's pictures at three times his former rate. Conceived as two glamorous but imaginary photographers, Capa and Taro, the couple started making a living. With a new look and a new name, all Capa needed was a big story.

✴

OSWALD VEBLEN, a celebrated Princeton University mathematics professor, was looking for some of Europe's brightest minds in the late 1920s. Veblen offered more than an American safe haven as enticement to refugees. Armed with a multimillion-dollar grant to establish a world-class center for science and mathematics, Veblen had created a gabled neo-gothic sanctuary that "mathematicians would be loath to leave," in Princeton, New Jersey, near the university. It would become world-famous as the Institute for Advanced Study, the home of Einstein, and many other geniuses. The offices had carved wooden paneling, hidden files, and blackboards that opened like altars. Each lavatory had a reading light, of particular appeal to von Neumann, who, since childhood, was in the habit of taking two books with him on such trips. After Einstein signed on in 1933, the Austro-Hungarian (born in Brno, today the Czech Republic) mathematician Kurt Gödel and German physicist-mathematician Hermann Weyl followed him. English was spoken in many accents at the institute, which rapidly became the new Göttingen.

Looking for star power in the younger generation, Veblen fixed his sights on John von Neumann. But Veblen was hesitant to invite a lone member of this exotic Hungarian tribe, so he added Eugene Wigner. "Promising as I might be," Wigner noted, "it was clear to me that Princeton thought of me mainly as 'the companion of Jancsi von Neumann.' "

Following an eleven-day journey, the two young scientists arrived in New York in January 1930. "Jancsi felt at home in America from the first day," Wigner recalled. "We agreed that we should try to become somewhat American . . . that he would now call himself 'Johnny' von Neumann and I would be 'Eugene' Wigner." Johnny never looked back. "Here are sane people," he told his more skeptical companion, "less formal and traditional than the Europeans, and a bit more commercial. But a great deal more sensible." America's expansiveness and faith in science as the key to progress perfectly meshed with von Neumann's own. Being a Jew did not seem to be an impediment here. Von Neumann felt that, "If civilization was to survive," his daughter Marina von Neumann Whitman remembered, "it would be in America. Nineteen nineteen was an indelible memory for him. He was well aware of what was happening to Jews in Hungary. The Numerus Clausus law. He relaxed in Hungarian. He joked in Hungarian. But he felt that Europe was hopeless."

FEW OF his fellow exiles adapted to America with von Neumann's speed. "No other people," Sandor Marai, the great Hungarian writer forced into an American exile in the late 1940s, later observed, "still living in Europe [are] as stifled by loneliness as the Hungarians . . . left tragically on their own between East and West. The consciousness that being Hungarian meant the same as being lonely, that the Hungarian language was incomprehensible and unrelated to other languages . . . there was something benumbing about this."

Wigner was homesick. He resented the fact that after six months Karl Compton, chairman of Princeton's Physics Department, still could not tell Johnny and Eugene apart. He complained that "the town had no coffeehouses where scholars and their students went for lively extended conversation." He was disappointed in the absence of a sense of community, and what he regarded as the low academic level as compared to Europe. "Princeton's physics was then quite rudimentary. Its students were considered among the best in America . . . but American prodigies who entered had received far less extra teaching from gifted teachers than they would have in Hungary. So we at Princeton had to teach what ought to have been absorbed in high school or in a coffeehouse. Coming straight from the cultivated physics environment of Berlin, I often felt in Princeton that I was talking baby talk."

Stanislaw Ulam, the Warsaw-born physicist, was also surprised "how little people [in Princeton] talked to each other compared with the endless hours in the coffeehouses . . . [in Europe] where the mathematicians were genuinely interested in each other's work." Even von Neumann missed the cafés and dreamed of opening one himself. "But Johnny," his American colleagues objected, "the citizens of Princeton wouldn't know what to do with a café!" Never mind, he replied. He wanted to convert Americans to the pleasures of Budapest café life. "We'll recruit a few of our European colleagues. They'll sit in my café every afternoon for a few days, just to show you how it's done."

With his wealth and charm, von Neumann was never an ordinary refugee. Before leaving Budapest, he requested from Princeton proof of permanent employment (which he received, with a salary of $10,000 a year) so he might bring "various objects of silver, etc.," with him. He and his Budapest-born wife, Marietta, were soon throwing weekly parties in their elegant new home. When Ulam called on von Neumann, he found him "ensconced in a large and impressive house. A black servant let me in." Even Princeton's solitary high priest of science, Albert Einstein, came to at least one, and probably more, von Neumann parties. Witty and entertaining, Johnny was the perfect host. But some of his guests noticed that when they no longer held his attention, he would disappear to work on a problem—his real form of relaxation.

After 1933, von Neumann did not feel it was safe to work in Europe. He had terminated his position in Berlin but continued to return to Budapest. "There is not much happening here," he wrote Veblen from Budapest, in that anguished spring of 1933. "Except that people are beginning to be extremely proud in Hungary about the ability of this country to run its revolutions and counterrevolutions in a much smoother and more civilized way than Germany. The news from Germany is bad: you have probably read that [Richard] Courant, [Max] Born, have lost their chairs, and James Franck gave it up voluntarily. . . . It seems that the purification of universities has until now only reached Frankfurt, Göttingen, Marburg, Jena, Halle, Kiel, Königsberg—the other twenty will certainly follow."

Beneath the debonair surface, Johnny von Neumann was capable of imagining the unimaginable. In 1934, writing in Hungarian to a Budapest physicist, Rudolf Ortvay, he matter-of-factly (but with great clairvoyance) forecast the annihilation of Europe's Jews. "It's naive," he wrote, "to think that the war will help the Jews who are stranded in Europe. There are only two likely outcomes, one of them [their destruction] we need not speak of. But the second one is equally hopeless. There will be utter chaos in the conquered lands. . . . There will be such misery that it is impossible to envision a stable situation [for surviving Jews] ever emerging."

Von Neumann continued to spend his summers in Budapest. When his marriage to Marietta, the mother of his only child, Marina, broke down in 1938, he returned to his hometown where he found a new Hungarian bride, Klara Dan. Von Neumann invited Ulam to join him on what he assumed would be his farewell trip home. "Johnny showed me Budapest," Ulam recalled, "a beautiful city. After dinner at his house where I met his parents we went to nightclubs and discussed mathematics!"

Before leaving, von Neumann had some debts to pay. "Johnny also took me to a pleasant mountain resort," Ulam recalled, "to visit his former professors Leopold Fejer and Frederick Riesz, who were both pioneer researchers in the theory of Fourier series. . . . Fejer had been Johnny's teacher. Riesz was one of the most elegant mathematical writers in the world, known for his precise, concise and clear expositions. . . . Of course," Ulam noted, "the talk also concerned the world situation and the likelihood of war."

Taking his leave of von Neumann, Ulam's Warsaw-bound train snaked through the Carpathian Mountains. He recalled an earlier conversation with his Hungarian friend. "Johnny used to say that all the famous Jewish scientists, artists, and writers who emigrated from Hungary around the time of the First World War came, either directly or indirectly, from these little Carpathian communities, moving up to Budapest as their material conditions improved. . . . Their names abound in the annals of mathematics and physics today. Johnny used to say that it was a coincidence of some cultural factors which he could not make precise: an external pressure on the whole society of this part of Central Europe, a feeling of extreme insecurity . . . and the necessity to produce the unusual or else face extinction." It is striking that, well before the Holocaust, a privileged, successful youth from one of Europe's centers of civilization could contemplate the extinction of his kind.

HAPPY to be back in Europe from Palestine, Koestler arrived in Paris in 1930 as correspondent for the Ullstein papers. Like that of his fellow exiles, the center of Koestler's universe was the Boulevard Montparnasse and its Café Dôme. He was reunited with Eva Striker, his childhood friend, who was about to play a critical role in his life. The slim, darkly beautiful ceramicist and the short, intense Koestler were soon romantically involved. "We often went to dark little nightspots and sat for hours in the Café Dôme," Eva recalled more than seventy years later. "We also went to fine restaurants, because he liked to put on airs and to eat well. Once I sat in such a restaurant for several hours under the disapproving eyes of the waiter, while Arthur, having noticed he was absolutely flat broke, drove from friend to friend until he found one who could lend him the funds to ransom the hostage."

In 1930 it was still possible for two exiled Hungarian Jews to enjoy the timeless beauty of the French countryside. "At Easter," Eva recalled, "we went to Brittany . . . the lighthouse, the sea, were so enticing that we spent the night on two dining tables covered with white damask linen, in order to see the sunrise. The exquisite views inspired us and we bought post-cards." A few years later, Eva recalled, "when I was living in the U.S., during the war, the newspapers asked people to send views of the coastline of Brittany to the War Department [planning the invasion of France]. I sent all but one of these postcards."

IN BERLIN, later that year, Arthur Koestler glimpsed his next utopia. As Ullstein's science editor, Koestler's career was soaring. The twenty-five-year-old now sat behind a big desk with two telephones, had a secretary, several mistresses, and colleagues who addressed him as *Herr Redakteur.* "My income was . . . not far from the maximum that a German journalist could earn." For the first time, his life was full and exciting. "One day [journalism] carried you to the court of Arab kings, the next into a Paris brothel, one day you chased after a vanished Russian general, the next you became absorbed in space travel and the structure of atoms."

Koestler had already survived a succession of earthquakes. "I had sung 'God Bless the Magyar,' and had seen the defeat of my country," he wrote. "I had cheered Karolyi's Democratic Republic and had seen it collapse; I had identified myself with the Commune of the Hundred Days and seen it swept away. I had lived in a communal settlement [in Palestine] and sold lemonade and operated a press agency. I had been a tramp and had half starved to death. I had seen my family go to the dogs. I had run off to help build the New Jerusalem and had come back disillusioned. I had spent countless nights in the company of whores and in brothels; and had gained sufficient insight into French politics to disgust me forever."

Eva had also moved to Berlin, and, though her romance with Arthur had cooled, their friendship had not. Eva's studio, next door to the Romanische Café, soon became the meeting place of Budapest expatriates, who, she recalled years later, believed they were personally in charge of solving the world's social and economic problems. "Leo Szilard believed in H. G. Wells's idea that the best minds of the world should be put in charge of its affairs." Despite his professional success, Eva recalled, "Arthur was the most unhappy of all of us." As well as the hungriest for a new faith.

He still tried to keep faith with Weimar's shaky republic. "We were Central Europeans, steeped in German culture, supporters of Weimar democracy," he wrote. Koestler's employers were Jews, but by 1930 even they had begun to lay off Jewish staff. "We covertly watched each other," Koestler remembered, "wondering whose turn would come next."

BERLIN'S unofficial theme song, "Time is money, seien Sie mein," was heard nightly at the Blue Bird cabaret. In trendy Berlin, all things Russian were suddenly the rage. "There were Russian entertainers in restaurants and nightclubs," Eva recalled, "and the chorus of Don Cossacks brought strange sounds, costumes, and colors to Berlin."

Only the communists seemed to grasp the danger of Hitler's growing legions. "Active resistance against the Nazis," Koestler observed, "seemed only possible by throwing one's lot either with the Socialists or the Communists. A comparison of their past records, their vigor and determination eliminated the first." The second he associated with his thrilling march alongside the workers of Budapest. Stalin had not yet begun his reign of terror; he was still the pipe-smoking, benign Uncle Joe.

Koestler made contact with German Communist Party members, who told him just what he wanted to hear. "We are prepared to stand up to Hitler." Koestler's new friends spouted dazzling statistics of the New Utopia. Cities were rising from czarist wastelands. As Koestler read voraciously about the Communist Party, his deeply rooted sympathy for the underdog, and his discomfort with his parents' bourgeois values, found a perfect outlet. "By the time I had finished with Engels . . . and Lenin, something had clicked in my brain and I was shaken by a mental explosion," he wrote later. At last, "an answer to every question; doubts and conflicts are a matter of the tortured past."

In December 1931, Arthur Koestler made a fateful decision. He joined the Communist Party. As in Vienna, in 1926, when he embraced Zionism, he again burned his bridges. Leaving journalism for the twilight world of the underground was a dangerous break with the past. He was abandoning more than the fashionable Berlin of literary cafés and editorial offices—and friends who would not join him on this journey. "I gave up my flat in the expensive district of Neu Westend," he wrote, "and moved into an apartment house on Bonner Platz known as the Red Block, for most of the tenants were penniless writers and artists of radical views." But he found what he sought. "I was no longer alone. . . . I had found the warm comradeship that I had been thirsting for."

Fired from his job, Koestler now spent his days and nights in the parts of Berlin that respectable people only read about in the crime sheets. "During that long, stifling summer of 1932," he wrote, "the main battle-fields were the smoky little taverns of the working class districts. Some of these served as meeting places for the Nazis, some as meeting places for us. To enter the wrong pub, was to venture into the enemy's lines. . . . A gang of [Nazis] would drive slowly past the tavern, firing through the glass panes, then vanish at break-neck speed." Though Koestler him-self was not a Party hit man, his little red Fiat, "the last relic of my bour-geois past," was "borrowed by comrades whom I had never seen before and returned a few hours later with no questions asked and no explana-tions offered."

At the end of July 1932, the Party yielded to Koestler's plea to be sent to Russia. He was to write propaganda pieces and a book about the Soviet Union. If he had been excited by his trip to Palestine a few years earlier, the prospect of landing in the heart of the boldest social experiment on earth must have been thrilling. The enormity and the sheer *mystery* of the Soviet landmass would have intimidated most Central Europeans. Arthur Koestler was elated.

As HIS train twisted across the Ukraine, a different Soviet Union un-rolled before Koestler's eyes. Fed by the rosy images of the People's Par-adise, Koestler was at first unwilling to believe his eyes. "At every station there was a crowd of peasants in rags," he wrote, "offering icons and linen in exchange for a loaf of bread." The women lifted their babies up to Koestler, "infants pitiful and terrifying with limbs like sticks, puffed bel-lies, big cadaverous heads lolling on thin necks." He had arrived for the great famine of 1932–33, largely provoked by Stalin's draconian policies of forced collectivization.

But Koestler rationalized the nightmare, classifying "everything that shocked me as the 'heritage of the past' and everything I liked as the 'seeds of the future.' " By setting up this automatic screening machine in his mind, "it was still possible in 1932 for a European to live in Russia and yet to remain a Communist."

In Kharkov, in northeastern Ukraine, Koestler stayed with Eva Striker, who had recently married and moved to the Soviet Union. Her new hus-band, physicist Alex Weissberg, was a communist. Eva, apolitical, was looking for adventure. She found Arthur a changed man. "He had lost his lightheartedness, his sense of humor, and his amused and amusing personality," she recalled. "As a communist he could not doubt that his was the right way."

Continuing by train across the Soviet Union, Koestler found an unexpected companion. "As I lay on the sheetless bed, enveloped by gloom and stench," Koestler wrote of his stay in Ashkabad, in Central Asia, "counting the familiar stains on the wall which crushed bed bugs leave behind, I heard the sound of a gramophone next door." The record was the popular American hit "My Yiddishe Momma," sung by Sophie Tucker. He went to explore and found Langston Hughes next door. The famous African-American poet was on a paid propaganda trip to the Soviet Union. Hughes's Communist Party–sponsored project, a film about American racism, had suddenly and mysteriously been canceled by Moscow. Lost in the bleak heart of Soviet Central Asia, the Jewish Hungarian and the African-American bonded. Both were sad, Hughes wrote, but "Koestler wore his sadness on his sleeve. . . . He wasn't happy, unless he was doing something useful—if happy then. Even listening to music, Koestler would be thinking about work. . . . Together for weeks we tracked down what was happening in Soviet Asia." And Koestler's deliberate blindness to reality began to lift.

First there was the physical revulsion of a refined and squeamish Central European. In the Central Asian village of Permetyab, Hughes and Koestler participated in the local custom of drinking communal tea from "grimy bowls" passed from hand to hand, with water scooped up from a filthy irrigation canal. Informed by the local doctor that 90 percent of the population had syphilis, "Koestler," according to Hughes, "almost keeled over."

More serious revelations were to come. "By a strange hazard," Koestler wrote, "I stumbled on the first great show trial in Central Asia—a foretaste of things to come." Atta Kurdov was a small-time local official accused of "crimes against the state." "Koestler," Hughes wrote, "was so fascinated by this sleepy-eyed trial in which everyone looked half hypnotized that he stayed until the court closed. He seemed very much upset when he came back to the guesthouse."

Koestler was indeed shaken by his first glimpse of Soviet justice. "The

Judge and the public prosecutor exchanged a few casual, whispered words," he wrote later, when his disillusion was complete. " 'Atta Kurdov looks guilty to me,' " Hughes teased his friend, " 'of what I don't know, but he just looks like a rogue.' . . . Koestler went to his room and I didn't see him any more until the next day, although I thought he might come back to listen to some jazz or to share a hunk of camel sausages with me around midnight. But he didn't come back. The trial disturbed him."

Koestler's description continued:

> Time seemed to have come to a standstill. Some of the defendants now and then shuffled their feet. Then the Judge seemed to come regretfully back to life. He said something to one of the accused. . . . The man got up obediently like a schoolboy, and said that Atta Kurdov had told him that the Russian people wanted to oppress the people of Turkmenistan. As he went on denouncing Atta Kurdov in a flat, impersonal voice, he seemed to vanish as an individual; all that remained of him was a limp puppet without a will of its own, maneuvered by the arch-fiend, Atta Kurdov. The latter was apparently the Trotsky or perhaps the Tito of Turkmenistan. . . . The trial was an exotic and amateurish forerunner of the great show trials in Moscow.

"IT IS A curious fact," Koestler wrote, "that the really important events which alter the whole course of one's destiny usually appear in an insidiously trivial guise." And so, in February 1933, Koestler, back in Kharkov, was in the middle of a poker game when a Soviet friend remarked, "So they have burnt down the Reichstag. I wonder now what they did that for?" Koestler was about to discover that, along with the Reichstag, his former life was in ashes. "During that poker game," Koestler wrote, "I had ceased to be a traveler and had become a political refugee."

It was the end of democracy and legality for Germany. Hitler's terror state was now fully operational. Koestler felt that he had to get back, but before leaving the Soviet Union he had a fateful series of meetings. In Moscow, he was introduced to the high priests of the Party, including Karl Radek and Nikolai Bukharin. "They were all tired men," he wrote. "The higher you got in the hierarchy, the more tired they were . . . the years of conspiracy, prison and exile; the years of the famine and the Civil War. . . . They were indeed, 'dead men on furlough' as Lenin had called them."

Arthur Koestler's mission to the Soviet Union would ultimately turn out to be one of the Party's biggest mistakes. Radek and Bukharin and what Koestler had seen gave him the material that would produce *Darkness at Noon*.

॥

IN THE early 1930s, Leo Szilard was like a man in a snowstorm who knows an avalanche is coming. He was having trouble convincing his colleagues that the Weimar Republic would not survive the Nazi onslaught. Nourished on Goethe, Heine, Schiller, and Beethoven, many of his friends shrugged off his warning; civilized Germans would never stand for anything as crude as Hitler's storm troopers. Szilard disagreed. "What I noticed was that the Germans always took a utilitarian point of view. They asked, 'Well, suppose I would oppose this thinking. . . . I wouldn't do much good, I would lose my influence. Then why should I oppose it?' The moral point of view was completely absent, or very weak. . . . On this basis I reached in 1931 the conclusion that Hitler would get into power, not because the force of the Nazi revolution was so strong, but rather because I thought that there would be no resistance whatsoever."

When, in early 1933, events confirmed Szilard's fears, he was packed and ready. Days after the Reichstag fire, Szilard boarded an almost empty Vienna-bound train at Berlin's Annhalter Station, hiding the last of his bank notes in his underwear. The next day, as panic spread in the German capital, the same train was jammed and its passengers interrogated by Nazi guards at the Austrian border. "Non-Aryans" were turned back, their belongings stolen. "This just shows you," Szilard noted wryly, "that if you want to succeed in this world, you just have to be one day earlier than most people."

In Vienna, Szilard switched to high gear, mobilizing his family in Budapest, as well as his now endangered colleagues in Germany. "We were convinced," the German physicist Hans Bethe, also fleeing Hitler in 1933, recalled, "that Szilard could be in two places at once." In London, Szilard prodded the chemist and Zionist leader Chaim Weitzman and Harold Laski, a prominent Labour MP and professor of political science, to help Jewish scientists find jobs. With the collaboration of Sir William Beveridge, the director of the London School of Economics, Szilard helped launch the Academic Assistance Council, which placed 2,500 refugee scholars by the outbreak of the war. This activity suited Szilard's temperament, for he always found it easier to solve the problems of others than to solve his own problems. Indeed, in the summer of 1933 Leo Szilard was among the unemployed—a condition that would have historic consequences.

Szilard's mind, the only laboratory he seemed to need, was on overdrive during that summer. Soaking for hours in the bathtub of the Imperial Hotel on Russell Square, or walking the streets of Bloomsbury, he was working on a problem that had defied physicists. One day, as a traffic light turned from red to green on Southampton Row, Szilard suddenly had what some historians have called a Eureka moment in the history of nuclear physics. If a neutron is shot into an atom, Szilard thought, and more than one neutron is produced, a chain reaction, releasing vast amounts of energy, could be the result. In a flash, he saw that a nuclear chain reaction could also mean an explosion. He remembered H. G. Wells's science fiction novel *The World Set Free*, which envisioned a cataclysmic world war with planes dropping atom bombs on Paris, London, and New York.

"The forecast of the writers," Szilard wrote Sir Hugo Hirst, the founder of British General Electric, "may prove to be more accurate than the forecast of the scientists. The physicists have conclusive arguments as to why we cannot create at present new sources of energy. . . . I am not so sure whether they do not miss the point."

As he had since his childhood reading of *The Tragedy of Man*, Szilard saw his destiny as saving mankind from extermination. But, impatient and buzzing with new ideas, he had trouble convincing others. Lord Ernest Rutherford, the eminent head of Cambridge's Cavendish Laboratory, threw him out of his office for talking "moonshine." Atoms will not be liberated in our lifetime, Rutherford and most other physicists maintained.

V ON NEUMANN watched Europe's implosion from Princeton. "I do not believe that global war is avoidable," he wrote Rudolf Ortvay in Budapest, "and I do not believe that the twin arguments that 'it is unnecessary' and that '[war] does not solve problems' get to the heart of the matter. The whole thing is a pathological process and war is an inevitable part of that process. Emotionally, [war] is also 'necessary.' . . . It will bring the acute problems closer to a solution . . . [and] diminish Europe's global moral and intellectual influence, which is deserved. May God grant that I should be wrong."

Von Neumann's prediction was reasoned and accurate, but eerily detached. Several months later he again wrote Ortvay, asserting that, from a historical perspective, war is not always a bad thing. "It is true that many things were lost as a result of the Roman conquest of Greece, but looking at this with the eye of someone living in 150 B.C., that process wasn't all that sad. At any rate, it prolonged by some 350 years the existence of the Greek way of life in the world. In many respects, it even improved it." To observe his continent on the brink of genocidal war with the "eye of someone living in 150 B.C." was a remarkable feat of emotional sublimation.

※

W E ARE scraping along," Andre Kertesz, still in Paris, wrote his brother Imre in Budapest in 1935. "Morally I succeed, but we better not talk about the material rewards." As always, Kertesz preferred to leave unpleasant things unspoken. But the publications, which had provided him a platform and steady income, were looking for different material now. Kertesz's quiet, personal world was out of step with the whirlwind of events. In 1936, Lucien Vogel sold his once liberal magazine, *Vu*, to a right-wing consortium. Other liberal editors were packing for one-way trips to New York. Imre, with a sharper sense of the gathering danger for Jews, encouraged his brother to emigrate. Andre had already received an offer from the Keystone Picture Agency to establish a New York fashion studio. But he hesitated, and began the paperwork for French citizenship.

By the time Kertesz's request for French citizenship was approved, he had accepted Keystone's offer. Later, he claimed it was meant to be only a "sabbatical year." So certain was he of his return that he left his negatives in a friend's care. Perhaps for that reason, Kertesz did not heed the advice of Ernie Prince, the general manager of Keystone, that he study English and "fashion photography, leaf through the American *Vogue* and *Harper's Bazaar*."

If his timing in Paris in 1925 had been pitch-perfect, it was almost the

opposite in New York in 1936. It did not seem so at first. New York was al-
ready challenging Paris as the cultural capital of the world. Many of
Kertesz's Parisian circle—including Mondrian, Moholy-Nagy, Tihanyi,
André Breton, Marc Chagall, Stefan Lorant, Fernand Leger, and Martin
Munkacsi were already in Manhattan. New York was the publishing and
media capital of the world, the headquarters of *Time, Life* (whose first
issue came out November 23, 1936), *Fortune, Vogue, The New Yorker,* and
Harper's Bazaar. Most of his fellow émigrés felt lucky to be there. Kertesz
felt marooned.

What dazzles so many new arrivals in New York disoriented Andre
Kertesz. Nearly everything disturbed this reticent man. The immensity
and anonymity of the city made him feel small and unprotected. Where
were the cafés where kindred spirits could congregate and collaborate?
He saw nothing but coffee shops where people rushed through inedible
meals. Fearful of the traffic that roared through Manhattan's canyons,
Kertesz did not at first explore New York the way he had Paris. He had
never mastered French, but he had made his way in Paris on courtesy and
charm. In New York, he felt a deaf-mute. Andor had smoothly morphed
into Andre, but there was no chance of Andre becoming Andrew.

The day after he and Elizabeth arrived in New York on the SS *Washington* in 1936, he made, typically, a self-portrait, one that seems to foreshadow his coming alienation. Standing in front of an open New York
window, Kertesz has a firm grip on his camera, clinging, as it were, to his
identity and survival. Unlike the elegant, relaxed young man of his Paris
self-portraits, his sleeves are rolled up; he is taut with energy and determination, observing the city with a wary expression.

With his now prickly personality, Kertesz could not engage in the essential editor-photographer give-and-take. His reticence and formal European manners prevented him from joining in the easy newsroom banter
or camaraderie forged in bars and on the road. Stymied in his interaction
with both editors and colleagues, Kertesz felt increasingly isolated. A bred-
in-the-bone European, the forty-two-year-old was neither willing nor able
to adjust to his new environment.

THERE WERE two major categories of photographers in America: news
and documentary photographers, or society photographers who provided

material for the style and fashion magazines. Neither appealed to Kertesz. His ideal was photojournalism as an expression of what the man behind the lens feels about the world he is observing. This was a much smaller field, dominated by a handful of photographers, among them Margaret Bourke-White, Walker Evans, and Berenice Abbott. Kertesz was a reporter of the human condition, not the tumultuous historical events that obsessed men like Capa. His interests did not appeal to American magazine editors in the 1930s and 1940s. Kertesz rapidly earned a reputation as irascible and difficult to deal with. He was a fiercely independent artist in a business that valued team spirit. He assumed he would dazzle New York the way he had Paris. Instead, he discovered that, in middle age, he had to prove himself all over again.

His photograph *Lost Cloud*, a delicate tuft of white floating past the behemoth of Rockefeller Center, expresses his feelings of helplessness and a longing for what he can't have. Kertesz always had a taste for the incongruous and the unexpected, but not for brutality. The menace in *Arm and Ventilator*, showing a seemingly cut-off limb, is new.

Kertesz was cut off not only from Europe, but also from his beloved brother Jeno, who was in Argentina. The mounting anxieties of his older brother, Imre, still in Budapest, heightened his anxiety. "It is difficult to live here," Imre wrote in April 1938, following Hitler's annexation of Austria, "when the earth shakes under one's feet. . . . What the immediate future brings we don't know but there is no promise of anything good. . . . They are debating the Jewish Law [severely limiting the number of Jews in professions]." In September, Imre wrote again, "Human lives are reduced to zero on this contemptible, vile continent, smeared with a thin veneer of culture." Jews, his brother told Andre, "have been reduced to an isolated new subspecies."

In 1939, *Life* magazine, the ultimate showcase for a photojournalist, finally commissioned Kertesz to do a story on New York's harbors. He attacked the assignment with the appetite of the famished, photographing the ports from every imaginable angle. He flew in a dirigible over Manhattan; he circled the men who worked the city's harbors in a tugboat. In August 1939, he submitted over two hundred photographs to *Life*. They used none. Partly, it was again a matter of poor timing. In September, the United Kingdom and France declared war on Germany and, perhaps for security reasons, Kertesz's story was killed. But forever after, he bitterly recounted how *Life's* editor told him that his pictures "talked too much." Rejection felt deeply personal. Photography was Kertesz's only language. His work was who he was. His 1939 photograph *Melancholic Tulip* captures his mood at the outbreak of world war.

Each rejection fueled his alienation from America. But where could he turn? His brother Imre's letters were constant reminders of "how right it was for the two of you to leave Europe." Budapest was too dangerous and Paris had fallen; the swastika fluttered over the Eiffel Tower in 1940.

A RTHUR KOESTLER arrived in Vienna in 1933, a few weeks after the poker game in Kharkov when he had simultaneously learned of the Reichstag fire and his own new status as refugee. He was as "excited as a school boy" to be done with his bleak, disappointing Soviet journey and to be back in Central Europe. He did not, however, find his old continent, which had vanished like Atlantis. His friends and comrades in Berlin had disappeared into jails, camps, or were in hiding. Berlin was no place for a homeless Jew, a communist one at that. But where could he go? At twenty-seven, Koestler was without a country, without a job, and, since the Nazis had seized his apartment and its contents, without possessions. Koestler was at a loss.

Koestler was clear about one thing: far worse was coming. "For us [refugees], the . . . future intentions of this new regime," he wrote, "were not a matter of speculation . . . but an intimate . . . reality." Koestler observed the West's suicidal path, and felt helpless to prevent it. "Nobody likes people," he wrote, "who run about the streets yelling, 'Get ready, get ready, the day of wrath is at hand.'"

As Germany sank into the abyss, Koestler headed toward the familiar landscape of Central Europe. Though it was still five years before the Viennese welcomed Hitler with open arms and roses, Koestler, like Szilard, smelled foul weather. "The old waiters in the cafés still addressed their old clients as 'Herr Doktor' but the warm familiarity had gone, there was an indefinable estrangement and aloofness, as if everybody were holding something back." At his old university the signs of change were even more alarming. "The dominant types were now burly louts in leather shorts and white knitted knee stockings. With stupid and provocative stares, they trampled over the mosaic pavement of the *alma mater*. . . . White stockings and leather shorts were the unofficial uniform of the Austrian Nazis." Worst of all, the "lovely, lively, sophisticated, flirtatious girl students of Vienna" had been replaced by a new type: "the dowdy, sweaty, pigtailed Gretchen . . . intended as a political badge, the counterpart of the bare knees of the young men."

So Koestler returned to Budapest, the capital of a merely semifascist state, and briefly rejoined the remnants of Budapest café society. The pleasure of speaking his mother tongue, inhaling the Danube's familiar, pungent aroma, and retracing the tracks of his youth briefly cheered him. "After a year spent in the grim human desert of Russia," he wrote, "I was suddenly thrown upon the bosom of a cozy, incestuous family. . . . For me it was a perfect escapist holiday."

Observing cataclysmic events from a safe distance was not Koestler's way, however. So after some months in Budapest, he moved to Paris. This was not the Paris of his earlier sojourn, when he and Eva Striker lived their bohemian escapade. Part of a swelling and unwelcome mass, "I now became homeless in the literal sense of the word: unable to pay my rent even in the cheap Belleville hotel." He clung to the life raft of his shaken faith in communism. "When my faith began to falter," he wrote, "Hitler gave it a new, immensely powerful impulse."

In Paris he signed on with Willy Muenzenberg, the head of the West European branch of Comintern—the Communist International propaganda apparatus.

⁂

I T   W A S   in Spain that Robert Capa, the fantasy, became the reality.

The Spanish Civil War was the first full-scale explosion between the forces that had been on a collision course since 1919. On Sunday, July 19, 1936, a right-wing military insurrection tried to overthrow the elected Spanish government. The left-wing Spanish Republic aimed at reforms, arousing anxiety among European fascists and high hopes among progressives. Overnight, Spain became a laboratory of the struggle against fascism.

For Capa this war felt personal. He loved Spain. On his first trip in 1935 he had written, "Madrid is charming. The people are show-offs, just like in Budapest." Like Hungarians, Spaniards were proud and passionate, Capa's sort of people. Now those charming show-offs faced a fascist coup. General Francisco Franco was a Spanish version of Admiral Horthy, and the Spanish Falangists played the role of the anti-Semites who had once beaten up Capa in Budapest, and, wearing different uniforms in Berlin, had forced him into his second exile.

Lucien Vogel, the editor who had done so much to promote Andre Kertesz's work in *Vu*, now gave Capa his big chance. In early August, Vogel flew Capa, Gerda, and a group of journalists to Barcelona. What neither Capa nor any other journalist could know was that the Spanish Civil War was never going to be a fair fight.* While Franco's Falangists had both military and technical support from Germany and Italy, the Loyalists were backed by idealistic anti-fascists (among them communists) whose support was mostly moral and only haphazardly military.

FROM the moment Robert Capa began to squeeze his Leica's shutter in Barcelona, a new brand of photojournalism was born. He was a partisan reporter. Powerful emotions, not technical perfection, infused his Spanish coverage. His gift was to portray the whole by focusing on a telling detail. His photographs are not about battle: they are about the *people* whose lives are forever changed by combat. His lens seeks out the faces of men, women, and children, the old and the infants, transformed in a heartbeat into targets of terror and guns. Capa's lens wraps these faces in a dignity seldom seen in war victims. He loves and supports his subjects.

On September 5, 1936, Capa and Gerda were in the village of Cerro Muriano, eight miles outside Córdoba. There, on a hillside, he photographed the terrible scene that would become a symbol for the age, and change Capa's life. *The Falling Soldier*—the *Guernica* † of war photographs—is a timeless image of war and doomed resistance. Capa snapped the precise moment a militia man, in a white shirt with sleeves

---

* At the post–World War II Nuremberg War Crimes Tribunal, Hermann Göring, founder of the Gestapo and commander of the Luftwaffe, admitted that the Nazis had used Spain to test their deadliest weapons. "It was a pity," Göring told the court, "but we could not do otherwise, as we had nowhere else to try out our machines."

† The famed Picasso mural depicting Franco's 1937 massacre of the civilian population of the Basque village of Guernica.

rolled up, is hit by machine gun fire. He is falling backward to his death, his rifle slipping from his grip. The world had never seen such a picture, a soldier at the instant of his death.

The Falling Soldier first appeared in *Vu* magazine on September 23, 1936, followed by *Paris Soir* and *Regards.* The following July, *Life* devoted an entire page to Capa's photograph. *The Falling Soldier* turned Robert Capa himself into an icon, and remains one of the most famous war photographs ever taken.

For years, controversy swirled around the photograph. Did Capa stage the extraordinary moment? Questions that were raised about how Capa could have gotten that close have been answered by now, and seem to have lost their relevance with the years. Eventually, the identification of the man as Federico Borrell García, killed on September 5, 1936, in Cerro Muriano, ended most of the controversy.

ONE of the first issues of the new illustrated *Picture Post* ran a portfolio of Capa's Spanish Civil War photographs in December 1938. On its cover was the handsome photographer, seen in profile, holding a camera that seems fused to his face. The caption reads: "The Greatest War Photographer in the World: Robert Capa." The Hungarian-born editor of *Picture Post*, Stefan Lorant, who had helped launch Andre Kertesz, now wrote of Capa, "In the following pages you see a series of pictures of the Spanish War. Regular readers of *Picture Post* know that we don't lightly praise the work we publish. We present these pictures as simply the finest pictures of front-line action ever taken. They are the work of Robert Capa. Capa is a Hungarian by birth, but being small and dark he is often taken for a Spaniard. He likes working in Spain better than anywhere else in the world. He is a passionate democrat, and he lives to take photographs."

Thus was Capa's legend enhanced by a fellow Hungarian. Anointed "The Greatest War Photographer in the World," Capa's fortunes took a spectacular turn. In the sudden blaze of fame, he could not foresee the burden of such an accolade. Capa, at twenty-five, was virtually condemned to life on war's front lines. "*The Falling Soldier* gave Bob such a reputation," *Life* photo editor John Morris noted in 2005. "He was competing with himself after that."

For a man without a country, fame conferred privileges. With his short and memorable name, his dark, exotic looks more recognized than any other photojournalist's, he was now someone people talked about. Increasingly, his presence—in a room, in a city, in a war—became part of the story. He was young and spoke an eccentric blend of Hungarian, French, and mangled English that his colleagues dubbed "Capanese." Wherever his pictures were printed, they were given prominent display. From Displaced Person, he had become International Celebrity.

Capa always admonished photojournalists not to cover a war they didn't care about. Like Andre Kertesz in World War I, Capa photographed soldiers engaged in ordinary tasks—playing chess—writing letters home, reading in the sun. Unlike Kertesz, however, Capa focused on faces. His camera conveys an astonishing intimacy with his subjects, as though they were longtime friends, holding nothing back. There is more heart than composition in these portraits. He said his secret was to "like people, and let them know it."

Some of Capa's most powerful images were not at the front, but of the people behind the battle lines. His portraits of the people of Madrid and other Spanish cities living under the rain of Franco's bombs seized the world's attention. The children he photographed, thin, their eyes enlarged by hunger and terror, seem as old as their mothers. One of his most famous photos, a mother and daughter running in a Bilbao street, the little girl's coat misbuttoned in the rush, the mother's eyes fixed on the skies, drives home Capa's message. This was a new kind of war, a war without a front. Franco was terrorizing civilians from the air. Early in the war, *Life*—with five million readers billed as "America's most powerful editorial force"—leaned toward Franco. Capa's pictures revealed a different story.

Perhaps seeing death in such abundance played a part in Capa's proposal of marriage to Gerda. But she was just coming into her own as a photographer. Her photos from Spain bore the stamp "Photo Taro." Journalists and soldiers found her energy, her passion for the Republicans, and her perfect features irresistible. "La Pequeña Rubia," "the little blonde," they called her at the front. Admired and desired by all, she had everything to look forward to. She turned down Capa's proposal. Though still partners, for her the great passion was over. For him it never would be over.

On Sunday, July 25, 1937, Gerda drove from Madrid to the front at Brunete. She was determined to cover a major Republican offensive—the bloodiest battle since the outbreak of the Civil War. Overhead she heard the roar of Franco's planes, like giant birds of prey. As bombs exploded around her, Gerda snapped away. More planes dove in her direction. The Republican forces began to scatter in hasty retreat past Gerda and her companion, journalist Ted Allan. Still, she waited for the perfect shot. When a car carrying the wounded approached, she finally hopped on the running board. "Tonight we'll have a farewell party in Madrid," she shouted to her companion. "I've bought some champagne." Just then, a Republican tank careened in their direction out of control. The tank crushed Gerda. She was still conscious when an ambulance delivered her to a nearby Jesuit school that served as a field hospital. "Please send a cable to Capa and one to my editor in Paris," she asked. Irene Spiegel, the American nurse on duty, remembered her clearly. "She was very beautiful . . . and she was not afraid."

In Paris the next day, Capa picked up *l'Humanité*. "A French journalist," the paper announced, "is reported to have been killed during a combat near Brunete." It was unimaginable. Gerda, his love, the most alive girl he had ever known—dead. A phone call from Louis Aragon, her editor at *Ce Soir*, confirmed the news.

The death of the young and the beautiful is always good copy and Capa's loss became a very public event. *Ce Soir* canonized Gerda as a symbol of Republican resistance. *Life* said she was "probably the first woman photographer ever to be killed in action." By the time Gerda's coffin arrived at Paris's Gare d'Austerlitz, much of the city was ready with a hero's welcome. The funeral at Père Lachaise cemetery took place on what would have been Gerda's twenty-sixth birthday. Robert Capa, fearless under fire, lost his composure at the sight of her coffin. As Gerda's father recited the Kaddish, Capa had to be supported by Louis Aragon. Pain at his loss was compounded by guilt. He had taught her photography, he had taken her to Spain. He had left her there when he returned to Paris.

The streets and the cafés of their Parisian neighborhood were too full of memories now. He fled to Amsterdam, where his childhood friend Eva Besnyo tried to console him. "He escaped into drink," she recalled, many years later. "He was not reachable. I think something also died in him."

Capa's awful year was not yet over. He returned to Spain to witness Franco's forces crush the Republicans. His emotions at being back in the war, which had killed his great love, can only be imagined. But the battle of Teruel was too important for Capa to miss. The Republicans assaulted the walled Franco stronghold in December, hoping to stop the insurgents' push to the sea. Capa was with a group of *dinamiteros* who blasted their passage with grenades. His companion on this journey, Ernest Hemingway, would turn the deadly battle for Teruel into *For Whom the Bell Tolls*, one of the greatest war novels.

After a short-lived Republican victory, Franco's forces reclaimed Teruel. By Easter, Franco had reached the Mediterranean. By April, he had cut Republican Spain in two. By then, Hitler had been greeted by cheering crowds in Vienna, his dream of *Anschluss* realized. On March 12, 1938, Hitler marched into Vienna where jubilant Austrians mobbed him as he declared that the country of his birth no longer existed. Henceforth, it was Ostmark, a province of Germany. Without firing a shot, the führer had added seven million new subjects to his reich. Capa's homeland now shared a border with the Third Reich.

Capa had no reason to stay in Europe—and every reason to get away. He was now twice a legend: as the World's Greatest War Photographer, and the grieving lover of the tragic "Pequeña Rubia." Once, Spain was going to be "the tomb of fascism." Instead, Capa witnessed the crushing defeat of the first proxy war against Hitler. He was only twenty-four, but he had absorbed a lifetime of loss.

T HE FACT that Britain's first ever international film hit was an all-Hungarian production—produced and directed by Alexander Korda, sets by Vincent Korda, and screenplay by Lajos Biro—did not diminish Britain's pride at beating Hollywood at its own game. *The Private Life of Henry VIII* was such a huge hit in 1933 that, for the rest of his life, Alexander Korda, too, would compete with himself. With this film, everything came together for Korda. Filmed in five weeks for a paltry £50,000 (according to Alex, at least), it grossed half a million pounds in its first world run. Well over half a century later, *The Private Life of Henry VIII* turns up on cable channels at odd hours—and, with Charles Laughton's unforgettable, scenery-chewing performance as Henry, it remains an irresistible romp.

Henry VIII was suffused with Korda's love of history with a human, ironic face. "It's a boy!" the monarch whoops at his hunting party, like any clerk receiving the good news. "There's no delicacy, nowadays," Henry grumbles, tearing into a capon and famously tossing the bones over his shoulder. Korda transformed the monarch into a henpecked husband. "Don't you shout at me," Anne of Cleves warns Henry, "just because I'm your wife!" When Henry approaches the marriage bed of his least attractive wife mumbling, "The things I do for England," audiences the world over roared, and still do. Alexander Korda was established as Britain's leading director/producer.

"Everyone wanted to know Korda," British director Michael Powell observed, "and Korda knew everybody." Korda built his dream studio, a private Xanadu tucked away in the Buckinghamshire village of Denham. Financed by the Prudential Insurance Company, the London Film Studio sprawled over 165 acres, boasting seven soundstages, two film theaters, and eighteen cutting rooms. From an antique and art-filled office suitable for receiving prime ministers and maharajas, Korda presided over a staff of more than two thousand. Everything about Korda—from the magic of his name, the suit that seemed molded to his tall frame, his handmade shoes—radiated nonchalant wealth and position, and was as meticulously staged as any other Korda production.

For three years Korda reigned from the proud tower of his dreams. London's greatest actors—Laurence Olivier, Ralph Richardson, Leslie Howard, Valerie Hobson, and Vivien Leigh—formed his personal repertory theater, while so many Hungarians found jobs at Denham that the River Colne on which it was located was referred to as the Danube.

Korda's genius was with people. "An enormous personality," director David Lean recalled. "Fifteen minutes with him was worth two days with anyone else. . . . He could take any subject and talk on it for twenty minutes." Actor Ralph Richardson called him the most magnetic person he had ever met. "I would go see Alex with a problem," Sir Ralph recalled, "with a furious speech about what I wanted and what I'd do if I didn't get it. And all the time he'd be staring at my feet. When I finished, he'd say, 'Where did you get those marvelous shoes? I'd give anything to have shoes like those.' And I would retire defeated."

Though he had a fine, light touch as a director, Korda said directing was like going down into the mines, something to be gotten over as fast as possible. Laurence Olivier recalled a scene where he had "done the worst acting of my life," only to hear Korda call out: "Okay, cut. Next shot!" "Alex, you must be mad!" Olivier protested. "Can't I have another take?" Whereupon Korda coolly replied, "Larry, my dear boy, you know nothing about making pictures. Sometimes there must be bad acting. Next shot."

Great Britain's first movie mogul never did fully master the English language. Left to themselves, the Korda brothers spoke Hungarian and reverted to their childhood names, Lacikam, Vincikem, and Zolikam. Salami appeared from under the silver chafing dish in the Georgian dining room, and soon the three brothers were back in the Turkeve of their childhood, arguing—and ultimately yielding to the eldest's implacable will.

In the 1930s, Korda decided it was time to end his nomadic, hotel-centered existence, and settled into a mansion on Avenue Road where he received the great figures of the day; the writers H. G. Wells and Graham Greene, Lawrence of Arabia, and Winston Churchill.

One of Korda's most appealing qualities was that his largesse matched his ambition. "Korda [was] one of the most generous men I ever met," the legendary Josef von Sternberg recalled. Once when von Sternberg— director of *The Blue Angel* and *Morocco*—was hospitalized in London, instead of flowers Alex brought "an important large bronze [of a woman] by Aristide Maillol to my rooms, with a charming note which said that he thought I could deal with women better than he could."

It was more than Korda's fabled powers of persuasion that kept the money flowing. British financiers got a kick out of premieres under the bright lights of Korda's Hollywood-on-the-Thames. They were proud to be associated with *The Scarlet Pimpernel, The Rise of Catherine the Great,* and *Rembrandt*: finely crafted costume dramas, with Korda's sardonic touch. Competing with Hollywood on the international market was, however, beyond even Korda's reach. Fast-paced action films like Michael Curtiz's *The Charge of the Light Brigade* and *The Adventures of Robin Hood* were world hits, from Burbank to Budapest, in a way that Korda's British costume dramas were not.

But Korda's personality was big. Five years after being fired by Fox, he returned to Hollywood in September 1935, and, flanked by the film world's most iconic figures, Charlie Chaplin, Douglas Fairbanks, and

Mary Pickford, he became a full partner in United Artists. Still, his feelings for Hollywood never warmed.

Michael Curtiz's stepson, John Meredyth Lucas, remembered a three-day train journey on the *Super Chief* from Los Angeles to Chicago with the two Hungarian directors. "Korda had been urging Mike to come to England with him, making him fabulous offers and expounding on the wonders of English life. Each evening we three would have dinner served in Mike's drawing room. Korda would go on about the great opportunities and freedom for a director working in England . . . [and] denigrate the harsh commercialism of Hollywood, and the uncouth American audience."

But Curtiz was not buying. " 'I stay on my home,' [Curtiz] declared. 'I am American. . . . The English is terrible phony.' " The two old Budapest rivals were puzzled by Lucas's amusement. "It took me a while to explain the humor of two Hungarians patriotically refighting the American Revolution."

Korda had good reason to prefer his Hollywood-on-the-Thames; after all, it preferred him, and treated him the way he most wanted. Returning to London from Hollywood in October 1935, Korda's Rolls-Royce glided into the Savoy's driveway. Alighting in his signature homburg, brandishing a tycoon-size cigar, the mogul beamed toward the blinding flash and pop of dozens of photographers. *Variety* carried this breathless account: "Largest gathering of newspapermen ever assembled for anything but a national event, crowded into a large ballroom to get the low-down from Alex Korda on his return from America."

SINCE HIS earliest days as a Budapest film director, Korda had understood the unique power of a radiant, beautiful face on a large silver screen. In 1938, he proved his genius as a talent-spotter and star-maker when he presented a little-known British stage actress to David Selznick, who was conducting a widely publicized search for the actress who would play the central role in what promised to be the biggest film ever, *Gone With the Wind*. "The lucky Hungarian has fallen onto something," Selznick wrote his business partner, Jock Whitney, after meeting Vivien Leigh, "and we're going to make a fortune for him." And so Scarlett O'Hara was chosen, and Korda was handsomely rewarded.

But Korda's London Film Company's debt already exceeded $4 million. "The fact that we have lost a great deal of money through our association with K[orda] must be faced," began an internal memo of the Prudential Insurance Company. "K's engaging personality and charm of manner *must be resisted*," the memo continued. "His financial sense is non-existent and his promises (even when sincere) worthless."

And so, in early 1939, Alexander Korda lost his dream palace, which became a part of Pinewood Studios. "All I have left," Korda bitterly told a visitor, "are a few shares and some old films which are equally worthless."

But for the relentless and resilient Alexander Korda, "a few shares and some old films" were enough to start anew. In Hollywood, he had learned that defeat could be transformed into triumph. It was all a matter of marketing.

On March 20, 1939, Korda announced the creation of Alexander Korda Film Productions. One would never have known from his press release that Korda's dream of running his own world-class studio had crumbled. "The films of the new company will be presented by London Film Productions [Korda's former studio] and distributed throughout the world by United Artists, of which Mr. Korda is one of the owner members." One more time, he had returned from the dead.

Later that year, Alex fulfilled another fantasy. In a simple ceremony in Antibes, he married the actress Merle Oberon, one of the world's most glamorous women. Groomed for stardom by her new husband, in some ways she was as much a Korda creation as London Films. His wedding present to Merle was a necklace once worn by Marie Antoinette.

KORDA was a man who was radioactive with ideas—some brilliant. One of his most inspired resulted in the most powerful (and enduring) anti-Hitler film of the period, Charlie Chaplin's *The Great Dictator*. "Alexander Korda," Chaplin recalled in his memoirs, "in 1937 had suggested I should do a Hitler story based on mistaken identity, Hitler having the same moustache as the tramp: I could play both characters, he said. I did not think too much about the idea then." But Chaplin eventually changed his mind. *The Great Dictator*, with its unforgettable satire of Hitler, was released in 1940 to packed movie houses. By that time, however, it was seen less as satire than a chilling, if belated, wake-up call, especially to Americans who were still out of the war.

Like all the Hungarians who had found refuge in the West, Korda himself needed no wake-up call. He knew that if the Nazis crossed the English Channel, he would be on the Gestapo's list. "I think another war will kill me," the forty-six-year-old producer-director lamented. "The Holocaust," Michael Korda noted, "was no more than he expected to happen."

N O L E S S than Capa, Arthur Koestler's life and career were transformed by the Spanish Civil War. Two months after Franco's right-wing coup d'etat in 1936, Koestler arrived in Madrid, to "cover" the civil war for two publications. His real employer was still the Party. But even had he been an objective journalist, the battle of Madrid, which lasted from October 24 until November 20, 1936, claiming over a thousand civilian lives and wounding three thousand more, would likely have turned him into a partisan—much as it did Capa, Hemingway, George Orwell, and others. "Anyone who . . . lived through the hell of Madrid," Koestler wrote, "with his eyes, his nerves, his heart, his stomach—and then pretends to be objective is a liar." If the world remains unmoved, he wrote, "It is time for Western civilization to say good night."

Koestler understood that a historic line had been crossed in Madrid. Hitler in 1933 had inaugurated the modern police state. Franco in 1936 launched the age of "total war and total fear."

With the fascists ascendant, Koestler was as much a marked man in Spain as he had been in Germany. He found refuge in the Mediterranean coastal town of Malaga, at the home of the British consul, Sir Peter Chalmers-Mitchell, a resident since 1934. Koestler knew Franco's troops were closing in on Malaga, and knew as well that he had been revealed as a communist. Yet he stayed on in the Englishman's beautiful, terraced garden overlooking the sea, paralyzed. "I still had one last impulse to flee," he wrote, but "down below in the town all was chaos and uncertainty and the garden here basked so peacefully in the sun—it seemed highly improbable that things of a disorderly nature could ever happen in this well-kept garden."

But things of a disorderly nature did happen in that beautiful garden—and soon throughout the continent in a state of similar denial. Neither Sir Peter's Union Jack snapping in the breeze, nor the garden's heavy iron gate stopped Franco's thugs. As Koestler scrambled upstairs to inject himself with a poison-filled syringe, a militiaman barked "Hands up!" Raising his hands, while the fascists pressed their revolvers into his neck and ribs and bound his hands behind his back with wire, Koestler waited to be shot.

But instead, Koestler experienced the slow psychological unraveling of a prisoner awaiting execution—an experience that would shape his writing. During ninety-five days of solitary confinement in Seville's Central Prison, he bore daily witness to the beating and execution of his fellow inmates, "in the expectation of sharing their fate." It was during those days and nights, "standing in the recessed window of cell 40," that he conducted his "dialogue with death" and experienced a spiritual crisis which would lead to his final break with the Communist Party and provide critical material for *Darkness at Noon*.

One by one, Koestler's fellow prisoners, members of the Loyalist militia whom he had come to know in the exercise yard, vanished. Koestler had bonded with one in particular, a peasant named Nicolás to whom he would dedicate his prison memoir, *Dialogue with Death*. "Let us hope," he wrote of Nicolás's execution, "it was all over swiftly and that they did not make you suffer too much . . . little Andalusian peasant . . . one of the poor and humble. . . . That is why they shot you; because you had the impudence to wish to learn to read. You and a few million like you, who seized your old firearms to defend the new order, which might perhaps some day have taught you to read . . . *Ecce Homo, Anno Domini, 1937*."

Waiting his turn, Koestler wrote, "I had actually no fear of the moment of execution, I only feared the fear which would precede that moment." Instead, he became the focus of an international protest organized by left-wing and communist intellectuals. To his own surprise, Koestler was exchanged for a fascist hostage held by the Spanish Loyalists.

While Koestler rotted in jail as a communist, Stalin's Great Terror entered its most brutal phase. The Revolution, which had already cost millions of lives with famine, deportations, and the forced transfer of entire populations, now turned on the revolutionaries themselves. In late 1937, eight top-ranking generals of the Red Army were secretly tried and shot. The grotesque judicial charade of the Moscow trial of the "Anti-Soviet Bloc of Rightists and Trotskyites" was well under way. Koestler knew many of these old Bolsheviks, some had been Moscow comrades. When, one by one, they confessed to a list of fantastic and mostly invented crimes against the state, he understood that not only they, but also the Revolution itself had been betrayed. "We knew the truth," he wrote. "Day after day the leaders of the Revolution and our own comrades in Russia were being shot as spies, or vanished without a trace." But Koestler still swallowed his outrage; Hitler trumped Stalin as the world's most dangerous man.

"Closing time was approaching for Europe," Koestler wrote in 1937. "One by one, the doors of the countries of one's youth were being shut in one's face." Once again, he returned to Central Europe, this time to see his father, who was in Belgrade. "I saw my father [who] had read in the news of my arrest and presumed execution in Malaga. He had fallen off his chair in a faint, and had spent the next two hours in a telephone booth, warning all my mother's relatives and friends to keep the news hidden from her. . . . The last time I saw my father he was waving farewell through the window of the night train from Belgrade to Budapest."

Koestler made his first public appearance after Spain in Paris, facing several hundred mostly communist refugee intellectuals gathered in the Place Saint Germain. "No movement," he told the grim-faced audience, "no party nor person can claim the privilege of infallibility. . . . It is as foolish to appease the enemy as it is to persecute the friend who pursues the same end as you by a different road." Koestler closed with a quote from Thomas Mann: "In the long run, a harmful truth is better than a useful lie." The communists in his audience sat stony-faced, with their arms folded.

Koestler had become the enemy. "They walked past [me]," he recalled, "as if I were the invisible man." It was the beginning of his new isolation, the end of "the warming, reassuring feeling of a collective solidarity . . . the coherence and intimacy of a small family."

Unwilling to wait for the Party to punish him for heresy, Koestler struck first. "I worked on my letter of resignation all night," he wrote. Dated April 22, 1938, it is brief. "After long and thorough reflection, I have decided to resign from the German Communist Party. . . . I am not taking this step with any hostile intent and I am not thinking of joining any oppositional or splinter group . . . and I continue as before to regard the existence of the Soviet Union as a decisively positive factor."

The next day he delivered the letter to the Party. He then wrote a longer version that he gave to one of his mentors, Egon Kisch, a well-known Czech German communist, in which he laid out his agonized struggle. "The Moscow trials," he wrote with typically clear vision, "do not appear to be isolated incidents . . . only the crassest and most glaring manifestation of a sickness that embraces the entire movement. . . . I gambled my bourgeois livelihood and lost in order to serve the Party."

The loneliness the thirty-three-year-old now experienced was akin to that which follows the end of a hopeless but obsessive love affair. But he was free, and could turn an unblinking gaze on seven hopeful, delusional years as a member of the Communist Party.

EVA STRIKER dealt another fatal blow to any remaining delusions. The apolitical Eva had been arrested in Kharkov in May 1936 and charged with plotting to assassinate Stalin. Taken first to the infamous Lubyanka Prison in Moscow and then shipped to a Leningrad jail, Eva spent sixteen months in solitary confinement. A clever interrogator had tricked her into signing a confession of guilt. They had "evidence," he told her: two pistols, found hidden in her sewing machine. Back in her cell, Eva went to work on her wrists with a piece of wire, but her suicide attempt failed. In late summer 1938 she was suddenly freed and expelled from the Soviet Union, but her husband, Alex Weissberg, still languished in a Soviet cell. Following the Nazi-Soviet pact, the Soviets turned Weissberg over to the Gestapo. With help from the underground, Weissberg managed to escape to Sweden in 1939.

Eva meanwhile had fled to London, where Arthur came to visit her. More than sixty years later, Eva recalled the "many hours I spent with Arthur telling him the details of my imprisonment." She recounted the six and a half paces it took to cross her cell, which she remembered as "number four." She told him of the message scratched between the lines of a prison library book by another inmate, "I am dying for the Czar and the Fatherland." She told Arthur how prisoners communicated with each other in the Lubyanka: the technique of knocking the alphabet on prison pipes. "The first word I learned," she told me, "in order to establish contact with another person was 'who?' " She also told Koestler of the fate of one of her interrogators who refused to use force to get her to sign a false confession; he ended up before a firing squad. Koestler would work

many of these details of Eva's Soviet prison life into the book he began
in 1938.

✵

MICHAEL CURTIZ escaped from Europe's turbulence into
work. He was unstoppable in the 1930s. Master of the swash-
buckler, a blend of high adventure, romance, and comedy, he
launched a handsome playboy named Errol Flynn into stardom, although they were destined to have an epic clash, even as they made memorable films. The dashing Tasmanian was everything the director
despised: undisciplined, careless, in Curtiz-speak an "actor bum." To
annoy him, Curtiz called him "Earl Flint" and, behind his back, said he
was "a terrific anti-talent." Bound in mutual loathing, Curtiz and Flynn
nevertheless crafted nineteen box office hits, including *The Charge of the
Light Brigade, The Adventures of Robin Hood,* and *The Sea Hawk.*

Captain Blood, their first major film, was shot on location in the coves
of Laguna Beach. It retains the vitality of two men at the top of their game.
All of Curtiz's signature visual innovations are on display: the camera that
almost never stands still, the use of light and shadow to heighten tension,
high shots that look down on the hero—the bravura camera work that had
sent Jack Warner to Berlin to recruit Curtiz a decade earlier. "Be like a
tiger on the camera," Curtiz commanded his actors, "fight for the success
from the picture!" Even the "anti-talent" Flynn responded.

With *Captain Blood,* Curtiz ignited the career of English actress Olivia
de Havilland. More than five decades later, at her home in Paris, this extraordinary film legend—the last survivor of the *Gone With the Wind*
cast—remembered her first glimpse of the Hungarian director. "He was
tall and good-looking and always alone," she told me. "People did not approach him if they did not have to. He was there first thing in the morning
when I arrived on the set. And still there at night when I left. He had a
brusque, military style and treated you as if he didn't like you. But," she
noted, "he didn't need language to let you know what he wanted. He
could act it out for you."

As the heroine in many of the Errol Flynn films, she often felt caught in
the crossfire between the director and the actor. "There was so much ten-

sion between Mike and Errol. Mike felt he could get a better performance out of Errol if he was rough with him. Once, when we were looking at the first rushes together, Mike said, in front of Errol, 'He looks like such a pansy.' How Errol kept from slugging him I don't know. But Mike did get some great performances out of him, all energy, speed, and action."

But even this disciplined actress could not always bear up under Curtiz's bullying. In July 18, 1939, during the filming of *The Lady and the Knight* (later titled *The Private Lives of Elizabeth and Essex*), de Havilland wrote an angry letter to Jack Warner: "I arrived at the studio at 6:45 and shot a number of reaction shots beginning at 9. The morning passed, the afternoon passed and finally at 5:30 with my nose shiny, my makeup worn off, my vitality gone, and my tummy doing nip-ups . . . [Curtiz] wanted to get this charming scene over in a hurry—and then *bang!* He said something very tactless, and to my horror I found myself shaking from head to foot with nerves and unable to open my mouth for fear of crying. . . . He had said the same kind of thing a few days before to [Bette Davis] who had gone home with tears streaming down her face."

"When I see a lazy man or a don't care girl," Curtiz said, dismissing his critics, "it makes me tough. I am very critical of actors, but if I find a real actor, I am first to appreciate it." His work was his life and he was punishing to those who regarded film as less than a calling.

In the Warners commissary and in the actors' watering holes, stories of Curtiz's brutal perfectionism competed with gems about his flagrant womanizing and his propensity for mangling English. "Next time I send a dumb son of a bitch to get a Coke," he once scolded a sluggish assistant, "I go myself." David Niven, Flynn's co-star in *The Charge of the Light Brigade*, described another legendary Curtiz moment. "High on a rostrum [Curtiz] decided that the right moment had come to order the arrival on the scene of a hundred head of riderless chargers. 'Okay,' Curtiz yelled into a megaphone, 'Bring on the empty horses!' Flynn and I doubled up with laughter." Niven later titled one of his Hollywood memoirs *Bring on the Empty Horses*.

Neither actors nor producers knew much about Curtiz's history. He preferred his past, his demons, and his insecurities to stay private. Sometimes even his wife was confused about the most basic facts of his history. "What the hell is this date, Mike?" she exclaimed, seeing Curtiz's date of birth in his passport. "You're two years older than me, but this makes you ten years younger!" Curtiz shrugged. "Why you don't lie like I am?"

Once in a while, he inadvertently revealed himself. "I work because I don't want to be kicked out," he told a reporter in the 1940s. "The only way you can stay on top is keep on smiling. . . . You feeling lousy and they ask you how you feel. You say OK, fine, just fine. Everything is wonderful." Beneath the ruthless film tyrant was a man who understood that his best shield was success at the box office. "In Europe, if an actor or a director establish himself," Curtiz noted, "he live forever. Here, if he doesn't make dough, they kick him out." As long as he was a top money-spinner at Warners, Curtiz felt safe.

But Hollywood would never be home. Even friendships were ruled by the bottom line. "There is one thing we have to watch with Mike," Curtiz's closest non-Hungarian friend, producer Hal Wallis, wrote to Jack Warner during the 1937 shooting of *Robin Hood.* "In his enthusiasm to make great shots and composition and utilize the great production values in this picture, he is of course, more likely to go overboard than anyone else. . . . I did not try to stop Mike yesterday when he was on the crane and making establishing shots . . . but I do object to wasting time and money."

HOLLYWOOD'S Hungarian community—among them, Curtiz, Korda, Adolph Zukor, Peter Lorre, Paul Lukas, and Bela Lugosi—tried to recapture their lost world in Miki Dora's Little Hungary on the Sunset Strip. Dora maintained the Café New York's tradition of feeding starving artists. For the so-called HHs—Hungry Hungarians—a breakfast of leftovers was free. Or they gathered in Curtiz's dining room where his Hungarian cook produced vast amounts of paprika-laced dishes and savored the pleasure of speaking in a language that amounted to a secret code. Paramount's Zukor also clung to this guilty pleasure. His son Eugene described his parents' Saturday nights when, he remembered, "English would yield to a rich, salty Hungarian." The closeness of the Hungarians, and the strange route that had brought so many European refugees to Hollywood, was captured in a famous anecdote, told by the great director Otto Preminger, who was himself an Austrian refugee. He recalled a dinner party at mogul Darryl Zanuck's mansion, where a tight circle of expatriates was speaking

Hungarian. "Come on," Preminger protested, "we're in America now. So talk German."

B Y the late 1930s, the tightening noose around Hungary's Jews was the talk of parts of émigré Hollywood. Many, including Curtiz, had family trapped in Europe. On September 29, 1938, in a meeting in Munich, British prime minister Neville Chamberlain and French premier Edouard Daladier consented to the partition of Czechoslovakia. Chamberlain famously declared "Peace in our time," but soon Hitler's troops were on the march again, shortly to occupy the Sudetenland, given to Hitler at Munich, Bohemia, and Moravia, which he occupied in March 1939. "Munich" became synonymous with betrayal and Chamberlain with appeasement.

Curtiz asked Jack Warner, planning a trip to Budapest in 1938, to contact his mother and brothers and help them get exit visas. Warner obliged and a small woman dressed in black who spoke not a word of English soon joined Curtiz's household. His mother, an observant Jew, spent the rest of her life with her son. He could not rescue his only sister, Margit, her husband, and three children, all of whom would be deported to Auschwitz. Only Margit and one of her children survived.

Nineteen thirty-eight was a terrible year for much of the world but a stellar one for Michael Curtiz, Hollywood magician. He directed Warners' three biggest hits: *The Adventures of Robin Hood, Four Daughters,* and *Angels with Dirty Faces.* Even the seasoned James Cagney, however, remarked on the Hungarian director's ruthlessness. In *Angels with Dirty Faces,* Curtiz pressed Cagney to stay in a window as real bullets were fired around his head. "Nobody is going to hurt you," Curtiz assured him. Cagney refused. "I got out of the scene," he recalled, "and . . . the professional machine gunner fired the shots. One of the bullets hit the steel edge of the window, was deflected and went right through the wall where my head had been." Curtiz's reputation as someone prepared to risk lives for the sake of a shot became part of Hollywood lore. "Flirting with real bullets," Cagney asserted, "was ridiculous."

But Curtiz was now one of the Hollywood grandees, living on a princely 165 acres in the San Fernando Valley, with a polo field and a skeet shooting range connected to his mansion by a mile-long driveway.

I N T H E late 1930s, "the front" for Capa was still Spain. He recorded the flight of refugees before the unstoppable fascist advance. Himself a seasoned refugee of seven years, Capa wrote this caption to accompany his pictures: "I have seen hundreds of thousands flee thus, in two countries. . . . And I am afraid to think that hundreds of thousands of others who are still living in undisturbed peace in other countries will one day meet with the same fate." He closed prophetically: "That is the direction the world we wanted to live in has been going."

Chance and circumstance had led Robert Capa to photography. Now, there was no stopping his legend. On January 31, 1939, *Life* editor Wilson Hicks wrote Capa, "I know your modesty will not lessen when I tell you that you are the No. 1 war photographer today." A few years earlier, such an endorsement from the world's most powerful editor would have lifted the hungry refugee off the ground, but now it meant much less.

Capa revealed his real state of mind only to his family. "I am very tired and would like to go to the mountains . . . the morale is bad [in Paris] and I don't know what lies ahead. . . . I see no one and have not even been to the Dôme. . . . I have some ideas for a book and an exhibition, but I shall write about everything, including my time in Barcelona, in the next letter. At the moment, I am in no mood to think back." His father's death in Budapest that summer, followed by the Hitler-Stalin nonaggression pact in August 1939, guaranteeing war, made up Capa's mind to abandon Europe for the city rapidly becoming the new, real world capital.

CAPA'S CAPACITY for self-renewal—always his greatest asset—was never more apparent than when he arrived in New York, in October 1939. *Life* photo editor John Morris recalled seeing him at Rockefeller Center, ice-skating. "His idea of skating was to hang on to the prettiest girl in sight, and let her do the work. He made it once around the rink, and then took her down with him in a spectacular spill—much to the delight of all of us *Life*rs watching."

Though his mother and brother, Cornell, were now living in New York, Capa himself did not really feel at home in Manhattan. He played poker with Hemingway, Steinbeck, and John Huston, but they were not

Gerda, nor Chim. They were not *family*. He revered Andre Kertesz, who was also in New York, but Andre was a father figure, a mentor, not a brother. Capa missed Paris, where he had spent his formative years. He barely ever photographed New York. He missed the cafés and he hated cars.

Capa's closest American friends were expatriates like the writer Martha Gellhorn, who was married to Ernest Hemingway. Their bond had been forged in the Spanish Civil War. "I was sure you were getting along all right," she wrote him from Cuba, "because you always do and you always will. . . . I really want to see you badly. The war looks awful. And doesn't Spain stand out as a miraculous country, where the people fought for almost three years. Now, no one fights for more than two weeks. I think probably Europe is rotten from the inside. And the Germans are like black magic, everyone is frightened of them before they even begin. I love you very much, as you know."

Once America had entered the war, Robert Capa's own country was again on the wrong side, he was an enemy alien, waiting for permanent resident papers, forbidden to use his camera or to travel more than ten miles from New York without a permit. Capa was miserable when he thought he might not be able to cover the biggest story of his life.

PART THREE

DARKNESS

The possibility of nuclear weapons in the wrong hands seemed increasingly plausible to Leo Szilard. Niels Bohr, who was half-Jewish, arrived in New York on January 16, 1939, en route to Princeton for a term in residence at the Institute for Advanced Study. The news he brought was alarming and confirmed Szilard's worst fear. In Berlin, physicists Otto Hahn and Fritz Strassman had split the uranium nucleus. This breakthrough achievement came at the Kaiser Wilhelm Institute for Physics, where Szilard, Wigner, and Teller had worked a decade earlier. "[We] knew well the excellence of the [German] physicists," Teller noted, "who were likely to be considering . . . questions about fission." Szilard understood instantly that nuclear fission would soon be controlled, and used for man's own purpose. To Szilard, Teller, Wigner, and von Neumann, the distance from Hahn and Strassman's laboratory in Dahlem to Hitler's high command was very short.

Szilard was at Princeton, staying with Wigner, during Bohr's visit to the university. "It seemed to us urgent to set up experiments which would show whether in fact neutrons are emitted in the fission process of uranium . . . [and that] this fact should be kept secret from the Germans." Szilard had just canceled his 1935 patent on chain reaction. No one had expressed interest in financing his experiment. On January 26, 1939, in light of the news from Berlin, he wired the British Admiralty, the keeper of his patent, an urgent cable: "Kindly disregard my recent letter."

The Hungarians understood that Germany would soon occupy Belgium, whose colony, the Belgian Congo, was the world's principal source of uranium. Not many scientists working in the United States at the time had connected those dots, not even J. Robert Oppenheimer, the brilliant and charismatic American physicist who would become director of the Manhattan Project. Whenever Teller, Szilard, or Wigner broached the subject of Hitler's growing danger to their friend, then teaching at the University of California at Berkeley, "[Oppenheimer] brushed [us] off," Wigner recalled. "He wanted to discuss physics."

Even with the Germans apparently embarked on the search for a military application for atomic fission, Szilard could not get Washington's attention. In his cramped room at the Hotel King's Crown near Columbia University in New York, Szilard pursued his obsession, almost alone. "I still had no position at Columbia; my three months [of laboratory privileges] were up, but there were no experiments going on . . . and all I had to do was to think." So, borrowing some money and equipment, he went to work frantically in his lab, bombarding uranium with neutrons to find whether fission would produce additional neutrons.

In early March, as Teller was "attempting . . . to make Mozart sound like Mozart, the telephone rang. It was Szilard calling from New York. He spoke to me in Hungarian and he said only one thing, 'I have found the neutrons.' When I returned to the piano I knew that the world might change in a radical manner. The prospect of harnessing nuclear energy seemed chillingly real."

Leo Szilard knew he needed the attention of Washington—specifically, President Roosevelt. And so, the young Hungarians set out on their two drives to Einstein to get him to sign those letters, the first to the Belgian ambassador in Washington, and the second, the famous letter to President Roosevelt.

It is altogether fitting that three Jewish scientists of Budapest's Golden Age brought the atom bomb to the attention of the American president. They knew, better than their American colleagues, what was at stake. Unlike the Americans, they combined technical knowledge and political sophistication born out of their unique experiences.

By late September, Szilard had not yet heard any reaction to his letter to FDR. He contacted Alexander Sachs, a noted economist and friend of the president "who knew his way around." Finally, on October 11, the president saw Sachs, read the letter, and promised action. Two weeks later, Szilard, Teller, and Wigner were summoned by Sachs to a strategy breakfast at the Carlton Hotel. Later the same day at the Commerce Department, they were introduced to the Director of the National Bureau of Standards, Lyman J. Briggs, at the first meeting of the Advisory Committee on Uranium, the first of many committees named something other than their real purpose—to launch America's first nuclear weapons program.

In addition to the three Hungarians and Sachs, Colonel Keith R. Adamson and Commander Gilbert C. Hoover, weapons experts from the Army and Navy, attended the Commerce Department meeting. Szilard urged the formation of a permanent committee of the physicists and the government. "The colonels kept rather aloof," Wigner recalled. "I had the feeling that these soldiers and government men were just like the others I had approached: they smiled, but they never expected to see a working atomic bomb in this world."

"How much money do you need?" Colonel Adamson asked the Hungarians. Caught off guard by this question, Teller said about $2,000 to buy some graphite, and some lab equipment for experiments. "Perhaps $6,000 in all." "There was a little unhappy pause from the military men," Wigner recalled, "and then Col. Adamson said, 'Gentlemen, armaments are not what decides war and makes history. Wars are won through the morale of the civilian population.' Teller, Szilard and I did not believe that statement at all," Wigner wrote. "I got a bit angry and spoke up, almost for the first time. 'If that is true,' I said, 'then perhaps we should cut the Army budget 30 percent and spread that wonderful morale through the civilian population.' Adamson flushed. Apparently he did not consider the dismantling of any military service a good idea. He slapped the table angrily with his hand and said, 'How much money do you say you need?' We got our $6,000."

"After the meeting," Teller remembered, "Szilard nearly murdered me for the modesty of my request, and Wigner, in his gentle way, seemed ready to assist him." Another six months passed before the next meeting of the Uranium Committee. "Precious months passed," Wigner said. "Getting the U.S. Government to see the value of fission felt like swimming in syrup." For the entire year following the Hungarians' drive to Einstein's Long Island cottage, Szilard wrote with undisguised dismay, "not a single experiment was under way in the United States" aimed at exploring the possibilities of a chain reaction in uranium.

THE NAZI war machine seemed invincible that fall and winter. Without bothering to declare war, Germany invaded Belgium, raising the Hungarians' concern still higher. Though its scope was not precisely known to the outside world, the methodical destruction of Jewish communities in Austria, Czechoslovakia, and Poland was well under way. On

June 14, 1940, German troops entered an almost deserted, totally unprotected Paris, and the following day the unthinkable happened: the swastika flew from the Eiffel Tower. But the Hungarians still heard nothing from Washington. "I had assumed," Szilard recalled, "that once we had demonstrated that in the fission of uranium neutrons are emitted, there would be no difficulty in getting people interested. But I was wrong."

Part of the reason was that American scientists did not share the Hungarians' anxiety. "I still think war is going to be avoided," Ernest Lawrence, Nobel Prize–winning physicist and inventor of the cyclotron, had written his parents three days before Hitler invaded Poland. And Oppenheimer, an American Jew educated in Göttingen, remained firmly opposed to U.S. intervention in the European struggle.

There was a different mood among the exiled scientists—"a terrible anxiety about the fate of all those whom we had left behind—family and friends," as Stanislaw Ulam recalled. "When France collapsed in the spring of 1940, the situation became so dark and seemingly hopeless that despair gripped all the European émigrés on this side of the ocean." Ulam voiced the exiles' deepest insecurity, which not even the safety of distance had eased. "There was the added worry that should German ideas prevail along with their military successes, life in America would become quite different, and xenophobia and anti-Semitism might grow here too."

This fear was less paranoid than it might appear today. Anti-Semitism was unquestionably present in American life, and the Jewish émigrés were especially conscious of it. In the 1920s, before J. Robert Oppenheimer entered college at Harvard, its president, A. Lawrence Lowell, had called for a quota for Jews.

Now, a second alarm bell arrived, this one from Britain. With London's famed MAUD Report (which stood for Military Applications of Uranium Disintegration),* the process begun by the Hungarians and Einstein accelerated. The MAUD Report contained dramatic information: two Ger-

---

* MAUD also turned out to have been coined from a name that appeared in a telegram Niels Bohr sent to a British colleague that included a mysterious request to check on the status of "Maud Ray Kent." The assumption was that Bohr was communicating in code, and all sorts of anagrams were tried by British intelligence. What Bohr meant was one Maud Ray, who lived in Kent and who had been the Bohrs' housekeeper when they lived in England. Thus MAUD.

man refugee scientists, Otto Frisch and Rudolf Peierls, had determined that a bomb made from plutonium or uranium might be small enough to be carried and dropped by existing aircraft.

The Roosevelt administration suddenly switched into high gear. In June 1941, MIT professor Vannevar Bush was appointed to head the Office of Scientific Research and Development, which reported to a high-level group that included Secretary of War Henry Stimson, Army Chief of Staff George C. Marshall, and Harvard's president, James Bryant Conant. It was to report to the White House and was originally supposed to deal with the development of radar and other military projects. Only after October 1941, following the arrival of the MAUD Report during the summer, did the OSRD get FDR's green light to focus on the bomb. Finally, Szilard's message, now almost two years old, that the side that developed an atomic bomb first might well win the war, was heeded. The S-1 Committee (the latest euphemism for the bomb project) had a budget of $100 million, a distinct improvement over the Hungarians' original $6,000. To direct the effort, S-1's head, Major General Leslie R. Groves, chose Oppenheimer. The search for the best and brightest to join the most ambitious military scientific project of all time—soon to be known as the Manhattan Project—was under way.

When the Nobel Prize–winning American physicist Arthur Compton recruited Wigner in September 1941, he found the Hungarian "almost in tears," as he "urged me . . . to help get the atomic weapons program rolling. His lively fear that the Nazis would make the bomb first was the more impressive because from his life in Europe he knew them so well," Compton wrote later.

In addition to Wigner, Compton recruited Teller and Szilard to the Metallurgical Laboratory at the University of Chicago, to work with the great Italian émigré physicist Enrico Fermi. One of a string of secret army laboratories and factories that formed the Manhattan Project, the Met Lab—whose name referred to the metallurgy plutonium and uranium separation—was devoted to creating the first controlled nuclear chain reaction. "Compton," Wigner related, "told me very little about my future duties. He did not have to. It was enough to know that we would try to create a nuclear chain reaction. I had waited years to hear that from a government official."

Occupying Eckhart Hall, the university's physics and mathematics departments, Wigner headed a group charged with designing a nuclear reactor. Wigner lived in "constant fear that with one small error the Germans might beat us to the atomic bomb." In a near paranoid state when it came to the Germans, Wigner feared fascism *could* happen here. "An American security force wanted my fingerprints," he recalled. "I refused to give it to them. A fingerprint record might someday fall into the hands of the Nazis. I had no doubt that if the Germans won the war they would swiftly begin rounding up everyone in the Manhattan Project for execution. And the roundup would go easier with fingerprints. Thoughts of being murdered focus your mind wonderfully. So there was a warmth in the Met Lab, but also a fear: a warmth of human relations and a fear of losing the race."

Security was elusive in a community of fiercely independent—and somewhat absentminded—scientists. Physicist Ralph Lapp recalled going for a shoeshine on Chicago's 57th Street. "The boot black looked at the soles of my shoes—black from the graphite we were using in our chain reaction experiments. 'Oh, so you work over there,' he said, gesturing toward Met Lab." When Enrico Fermi and Eugene Wigner visited the Hanford, Washington, nuclear reactor, they were told that for the sake of security they must assume the aliases Farmer and Wagner. Stopped by a guard and asked to identify himself, Wigner hesitated before he remembered his official alias, Wagner. Suspicious, the guard barred Wigner's way, whereupon Fermi came to the rescue with, "His name is Wagner, as surely as mine is Farmer."

✻

EVERY ONE of Arthur Koestler's life experiences—from his first communist march in Budapest, his stay in Palestine, his life in the Berlin underground, his dispiriting journey across the Soviet Union, to his ninety-five days as a prisoner awaiting execution in the Seville jail—all those moments of excitement, terror, fear, yearning, and emptiness—were poured, in one way or another, into his masterpiece, *Darkness at Noon*. Koestler was only thirty-three when he wrote it, but *Darkness at Noon* feels like an old man's tale.

Many scholars have analyzed and deconstructed the fate of Rubashov, Koestler's Soviet antihero. A timeless account of man's capacity for cruelty to his fellow man and his equal talent for self-delusion in search of utopia, *Darkness at Noon* transcends borders and ideologies. Its message can resonate in strange and unexpected ways. In 1998, during President Bill Clinton's impeachment hearings in the Monica Lewinsky affair, the president reportedly remarked to his confidant, Sidney Blumenthal, "I feel like the character in the novel *Darkness at Noon*."

"Once the opening scene was written," Koestler wrote, "I did not have to search for plot and incident; they were waiting among the stored memories of seven years. . . . A multitude of harrowing episodes. . . . I did not worry about what would happen next . . . I just waited for it to happen." When he began, news from Moscow "kept coming in about the arrest of virtually all my friends and comrades . . . who had sought refuge in the Soviet Union."

Western intellectuals and fellow travelers either averted their gaze or were confounded. Few in America or Europe understood the Soviet system better than Koestler. *Darkness at Noon* is the story of the first half of the century, in which the old institutions—social, economic, and spiritual—have broken down. Communism—like fascism—promised answers to every question, every emotional need. Koestler, along with millions of others, had inhaled their false promises. Without ever naming Russia or Stalin, who is referred to as "No. 1," *Darkness at Noon* is firmly planted in the Soviet Union of Stalin's Great Purge of 1936 to 1938. Unlike George Orwell's *Animal Farm*, a fable set in a barnyard, or the futuristic *1984*, *Darkness at Noon* has the feeling of lived events.

The intensity of *Darkness at Noon* stems from its autobiographical character. This is the story of Koestler's own conversion to a cause that offered community and family to a man who had lost both—only to have that faith turn lethal. For his searing portrait of Rubashov's final days, Koestler mined his ninety-five days in a Spanish prison.

Rubashov, the Old Bolshevik hero whose physical appearance—the pince-nez, the wispy beard, and incisive intellect—is a blend of Trotsky, Radek, and Bukharin, is both symbolic and real. For a man who had dedicated his life to the Party, Koestler makes clear, it was natural to deny it nothing, not even his life, if it were required. In simple, spare but searing prose, Koestler describes a lifetime of brainwashing and the effects of sleep deprivation, which precedes Rubashov's confession.

Exhausted, the condemned hero of the Revolution makes a last feeble effort to save himself. "How can it serve the Party that her members have to grovel in the dust before all the world? I have pleaded guilty to having pursued a false and objectively harmful policy. Isn't that enough for you?" His interrogator, Gletkin, turns Rubashov's words against him. "It is necessary to hammer every sentence into the masses by repetition and simplification," he tells Rubashov. "What is presented as right must shine like gold; what is presented as wrong must be black as pitch. . . . Your testimony at the trial will be the last service you can do the Party." And so Rubashov complies, confesses to crimes he did not commit, and is shot.

(*Darkness at Noon* remains one of the most remarkable documents of the failed God called communism. For my family, it was eerily prescient; a decade later, in Budapest, life almost precisely followed art, and both of my parents covered it as reporters for the Associated Press and United Press. After Yugoslavia's break with Moscow in 1949, Stalin insisted on a few carefully selected show trials in other Soviet satellites to discourage anyone else thinking of following Yugoslavia's Josip Broz Tito. In Hungary, Stalin chose Laszlo Rajk, minister of the interior, an early communist hero, as sacrifice. Rajk signed a trumped-up confession in exchange for a promise that he and his wife and infant son would be spared. Rajk's confession was swiftly followed by his execution. His widow, Julia, was jailed and his son, also named Laszlo, was placed in an orphanage under an assumed name. Later, he became a leader of the movement that brought democracy to Hungary in 1989. Today, he is one of Hungary's leading architects and a good friend. In 1989, the records of his father's interrogation by his old comrade-in-arms Janos Kadar, later the vehicle of the brutal Soviet crushing of the Freedom Fighters, became public. [Kadar was the godfather of Rajk's son.] And those records could have been the text of *Darkness at Noon*. Without realizing it, Koestler had in effect imagined a scene from his own country's future.)

As EUROPE edged toward war in the summer of 1939, Koestler, as a Hungarian Jew, faced more than a publishing deadline. He was determined to finish the book before trying to save himself. In a small French village in the valley of the Vesubie, fifty miles from Monaco, as the surrounding villages of the Alpes Maritimes filled up with French soldiers awaiting orders, Koestler wrote as if his life depended on it, thinking that it might. On August 24, 1939, Koestler read in the local paper that the previous day the foreign ministers Joachim von Ribbentrop and Vyacheslav Molotov had signed the treaty of nonaggression between Germany and the Soviet Union. Stalin's green light to attack Poland extinguished Koestler's last scrap of faith in the Soviet Union. "We did not recoil from betraying our friends and compromising with our enemies," he wrote in *Darkness at Noon*.

His book was unfinished, but Koestler had run out of time. Packing his ancient Ford, he headed for Paris. What followed was a journey worthy of a Michael Curtiz film. En route, Koestler and his girlfriend, Daphne Hardy, learned that the Wehrmacht had rolled into Poland, and that the French government had ordered general mobilization. On the road from Avignon to Paris, Koestler passed tanks, armored cars, and trucks carrying soldiers to the Italian frontier. Outside Paris, on September 3, Koestler learned that Britain and France, after demanding a cease-fire and withdrawal from Poland, had declared war on Germany. Choking traffic, cars, taxis, donkey- and horse-drawn carts—Parisians in a state of collective panic—clogged the roads, anticipating battle. What Koestler did not then know was that, apart from some leaflet-dropping and a noisy show of force on the border with Germany, France and Britain had done nothing. Months before German tanks cut across French fields, well before German cavalry clattered down the Champs-Elysées under the Führer's proud gaze, before the aged Marshal Henri-Philippe Pétain agreed on June 22, 1940, to a shameful armistice, France turned—not on the real enemy—but on "suspicious foreigners."

When Koestler arrived at his flat in Paris, his concierge warned him he should flee at once, as the police were looking for him.

Koestler now slept with a small packed suitcase under his bed, awaiting arrest. Finally, in the early morning of October 3, 1939, while he was having his morning bath, two policemen arrived. After a few weeks of internment at the Roland-Garros Sport Stadium, under heavy guard, he and five hundred other "undesirable aliens" were hurriedly put on a train, bound for Europe's most frightening destination: "location undisclosed." The next morning, they arrived at Le Vernet, a small station in the foothills of the Pyrenees.

As the prison barber was about to cut his hair, Koestler snatched his

scissors and hacked great chunks of his own black thatch. Better to in-
flict humiliation than accept it. Twice each day for several hours, Koestler
and the others were forced to stand at attention while roll calls were taken.
For four months Koestler submitted to the harsh discipline and meager
rations of Le Vernet. In January 1940, he was abruptly told to pack his
bag. His influential friends in London had acted again, this time persuading French authorities to free him.

Returning to Paris, Koestler scrambled to finish *Darkness at Noon*. But
he never unpacked his suitcase—he knew he would not be safe for long.
"Yet a friendly voodoo seemed to be protecting [*Darkness at Noon*]," he
wrote of those months. "On one occasion in March, when the police
searched my flat, they took away nearly all my files and manuscripts, but
the typescript of *Darkness at Noon* escaped their attention. The top copy
was lying on my desk, where I kept it on the theory of Edgar Allan Poe that
conspicuous objects were least likely to attract suspicion; while on an opposite theory the carbon copy was hidden on the top of the bookshelf. In
the end, I was again arrested and the original German version of the book
was lost. But by that time the English translation had been completed."

Ten days before the Germans reached Paris on June 14, 1940, Koestler
mailed his manuscript to a London publisher and set off on a breathless
flight, which took him to Oran in Algeria, then to Casablanca, Morocco,
and, finally, to neutral Lisbon—a trip that might seem in retrospect to
foreshadow the story line in *Casablanca*. In Lisbon, for two months, he
haunted the British consulate, but failed to obtain a visa. Of course he
turned this ordeal, too, into a book, *Arrival and Departure*. The American
consul in Lisbon helped him gain passage to New York. But Koestler preferred to risk an uncertain future in Europe to exile in America. So he
waited in Portugal.

Eventually, he won a coveted place aboard a Dutch aircraft bound for
England. Landing in the Channel port of Poole without valid papers,
Koestler was promptly arrested as a suspicious alien. Such were the times
that for a Hungarian Jew, the British prison of Pentonville was blessed
sanctuary. Koestler later joked that he would give Pentonville three stars if
he wrote a tourist's guide to European jails. He was in the Pentonville
prison when *Darkness at Noon* was published in December 1940.

Darkness at Noon was the last book Koestler wrote in German before switching to English. Only one thousand copies were sold when it was first published in England. Britain was at war with Germany and unwilling to face the harsh truth about Stalinism. For both Washington and London, Hitler seemed invincible and a far more imminent danger than Stalin.

George Orwell was among the first to call attention to Koestler's work—and its urgent message. "Brilliant as this book is as a novel," Orwell wrote, "and a piece of prison literature, it is probably most valuable as an interpretation of the Moscow 'confessions' by someone with an inner knowledge of totalitarian methods. What was frightening about these trials was not the fact that they happened—for obviously such things are necessary in a totalitarian society—but the eagerness of Western intellectuals to justify them."

Kingsley Martin, the editor of the *New Statesman*, called *Darkness at Noon* "one of the few books written in this epoch which will survive it." A few years later, Michael Foot, leftist intellectual and future leader of the Labour Party (from 1980 to 1983), pronounced Koestler "the greatest foreign novelist since Joseph Conrad who has paid us the compliment of writing in the English language."

Upon its American publication, in May 1941, the *New York Times* wrote that *Darkness at Noon* "does more to clear up the mystery of what has happened in Soviet Russia and, ultimately, what underlay the Soviet-Nazi pact" than any prior publication. Later that week, the *Times* went further. "Here is a splendid novel, an effective explanation of the riddle of the Moscow treason trials . . . written with such dramatic power, with such warmth of feeling and with such persuasive simplicity that it is as absorbing as melodrama."

But in 1941, not all Americans were ready to face the facts about Stalinist terror. "[Koestler] is unfair to Russia," Malcolm Cowley wrote in *The New Republic* that summer. "Writing in the bitterness of personal disillusionment, and in the conviction that Stalin had become Hitler's faithful ally, he makes points and presses home accusations which, I imagine, he would now like to withdraw." In a later issue, Cowley asserted that Koestler "fails to consider the possibility . . . that an actual plot against Stalin came close to being successful. . . . Moreover, [Koestler] makes the worse mistake . . . of using statistical arguments. Rubashov says to one of the examiners 'We deliberately let die of starvation about five million people to do forced labor in the Arctic regions and the jungles of the East. In the interests of the coming generations we have laid such terrible privations on the present one that its average span is shortened by a quarter.' " These assertions, *The New Republic* maintained, "may or may not be factually true."

It would take a few more years for Koestler's assertions to be proven "factually true," but *Darkness at Noon* was nevertheless an American bestseller in 1941—the third most popular fiction book of the year. Koestler knew it was his most important work. "It is the only good one," he wrote Eva in 1946. He also knew that in time, Stalinism's true face would be exposed, and that *Darkness at Noon* would come into its own. Today, in a post-communist world, its warning of totalitarian thought control and the ruthless use of power to change society lives on as a universal message, no longer tethered to a single political movement.

During the summer of 1943, at the secret city of Los Alamos, where the scientists raced to develop the atomic bomb, Edward Teller read *Darkness at Noon*. It had an electrifying effect on him. "I had been interested in communism since my original negative experiences with it as an eleven-year-old in Hungary," Teller wrote in his memoirs. "I don't believe I have ever been more fascinated with a book than I was with *Darkness at Noon.* . . . *Darkness at Noon* brought together and crystallized the objections to the methods of control used by Russian communism, which had been forming and accumulating in my mind for fifteen years."

ON SUNDAY MORNING, September 3, 1939, the shrill wail of the war's first air raid warning pierced through London's early morning sky, bringing the nightmare home to Alexander Korda. "We had all gathered in one of the big concrete coal bunkers [at Denham Studios]," director Michael Powell remembered, "to listen to [Neville Chamberlain's] broadcast [admitting the failure of his policy of appeasement and announcing a state of war between Great Britain and Germany]. . . . Alex and his brothers were there, and Merle, who was holding Alex's hand and crying. Alex was smoking one of his Coronas, as usual, and he took a deep breath and sent a perfect smoke ring into the air." For Korda, like Curtiz, the war against the Nazis was personal—and it presented an opportunity.

Winston Churchill returned to office, as first lord of the admiralty in 1939, before becoming prime minister in May 1940. He was the man of the hour, and Korda called on him. The two shared a deep love of history, especially British history, a flair for showmanship, and a taste for cigars and brandy. Now they had a common enemy. The Hungarian offered Churchill all the resources at his command in waging a propaganda war against Hitler. Afterward, "Alex summoned a meeting of all his principal contract people," Michael Powell recalled. "He explained his personal agreement with Churchill and how it affected us all. Britain was preparing for war. Denham was already a classified area. Now came our orders. When war was declared, filming on *The Thief of Baghdad* would stop. The next day everybody at Denham would start working on a feature propaganda film which Alex had promised Churchill would be ready in one month. . . . All he asked of us was that we would go with heart, mind and soul into making his new picture, and work with whomever we were assigned to."

The Lion Has Wings was Korda's first engagement in his personal war against the Nazis. His wartime sacrifice entailed returning to "bloody California." Ten years after his spectacular Hollywood flameout, Korda was back as Winston Churchill's personal emissary in the campaign to bring America into the war.

It was Churchill who suggested the story of Lord Nelson and the Battle of Trafalgar as a subject for a Korda film. But it was Korda who persuaded Laurence Olivier, the world's most admired actor, and Vivien Leigh, fresh from her blazing success as Scarlett O'Hara, to play Nelson and his mistress, Emma Hamilton.

"Propaganda," Korda told Olivier, "can be a bitter medicine. It needs sugar coating—and *That Hamilton Woman* is a very thick sugar coating indeed." There was nothing sugary, however, in the message beneath the frosting. In the opening scene, Captain Hardy, Nelson's deputy, attacks those countries that are "neutral against England and so scared of Bonaparte they daren't lift a finger for the people brave enough to fight him."

When Laurence Olivier, as Nelson, addresses the Admiralty, he is speaking Churchill's words, via Alexander Korda. Nelson is not referring, of course, to Bonaparte when he says: "Napoleon can never be master of the world until he has smashed us up—and believe me gentlemen, he means to be master of the world. You cannot make peace with dictators. You have to destroy them. Wipe them out! Gentlemen, I implore you—speak to the Prime Minister before it is too late. Do not ratify this peace!"

When *That Hamilton Woman* came out, America was still neutral; its message was clear. A Senate committee sent a subpoena to Korda instructing him to testify on December 12, 1941, on whether he was "inciting the American public to war." Five days before he was scheduled to appear, Pearl Harbor was attacked. The testimony was canceled.

That Hamilton Woman was brilliant propaganda. It was also vintage Korda, a lavish peek behind a historic event, suitably improved from the literal truth. The film was a labor of love for Korda, who produced, directed, and financed it—in five weeks. Vincent Korda's astonishing eighteenth-century armada for the re-creation of the Battle of Trafalgar was so lifelike that Vivien Leigh became seasick during the filming. "The Nelson film is nearly over," Leigh wrote on November 4, 1941. "We have rushed through it because apparently after Thursday there is no more money!— Alex's usual predicament." Perhaps because Europe's fate was a personal matter for him, *That Hamilton Woman* has more genuine emotional content—and less ironic detachment—than other Korda films. Alex said making it made him feel twenty years younger. Churchill wept when he saw it.

On September 23, 1942, in top hat and cutaways, the man born Sandor Kellner in Turkeve, Hungary, with a radiant Merle Oberon on his arm, strode up the driveway of Buckingham Palace. A short while later he emerged Sir Alexander Korda, Knight of the Realm. For a Hungarian, a Jew, a refugee, and a member of the movie industry, this was an astonishing honor, beyond even the wildest dreams of Sandor Kellner during the long nights on the Great Plain.

David Selznick, Korda's Hollywood rival, grasped the knighthood's significance: "The stature it has given the whole business," Selznick wrote, "and the dignity it has given to the profession of producing, is doubly significant first because it comes in the midst of war, second because it comes from Winston Churchill. . . . Everyone in the business should feel deeply indebted to Korda because his efforts, which have been conducted quietly and without fanfare or publicity have won this honor which should be accepted as an honor to us all."

But Korda's moment of grace did not satisfy him for long. From Hollywood, he had written to Lajos Biro that, like Gulliver, he was condemned to eternal restlessness. Early in 1945, Korda, age fifty-two, suffered his first heart attack—in a very public place, collapsing during dinner at Romanoff's restaurant, in full view of many Hollywood luminaries. In June of the same year, his marriage to Merle Oberon ended in divorce.

He recovered, but there was a new sadness in the man. The actress Joan Fontaine (sister of Olivia de Havilland) remembered dining with Korda sometime after his collapse. "Over an excellent glass of Château Lafite [Alex] warned me. 'No matter what, Joan, aim for the impossible. If you accomplish all your ambitions, there is nothing left.' Puzzled, I asked the silver-haired producer what he meant. Holding his glass up to the light, he sighed. 'I was a poor boy in Hungary when I conceived my dream. . . . I wanted to belong to the most important nation, to become rich, respected, marry the most beautiful woman, be world famous. . . . I've done all those things. I became a British subject, I founded my own film company, I owned a yacht, Winston Churchill is my close friend, I married Merle, I was knighted. . . . Now . . . now I've no more dreams left.' "

Korda had used himself up. By the 1940s, he was a prematurely old man who could not change his habits. Pale and haggard, Korda no longer quite filled his beautiful suits. An intellectual who dreamed of reading the Greek classics in the original, who quoted Boswell and Baudelaire, Korda's addiction to power ran just as deep. Control was security for a man who had experienced a lifetime of insecurity. When he acquired the ultimate rich man's toy, his yacht, *Elsewhere*, he used it not so much for escape, but as a tool of power. Winston Churchill and the writer Graham Greene were his preferred sailing companions, but there was almost always the less congenial presence of a David Selznick or a Sam Goldwyn on board.

On one thing they all agreed: there was no one else quite like Korda. Graham Greene described Korda in *Loser Takes All*: "There was something grand about him, with his mane of white hair, his musician's head. Where other men collected pictures to escape death duties, he collected for pleasure. For a month at a time he would disappear in his yacht with a cargo of writers and actresses and oddments—a hypnotist, a man who had invented a new rose, or discovered something about the endocrine glands."

KORDA was determined to revive his prewar stature as Britain's preeminent film mogul. An incorrigible gambler, he bought back London Films from the Prudential Insurance Company. From King George VI's former residence overlooking Hyde Park, at No. 145 Piccadilly, Korda breathed new life into the company he had founded—and driven into the ground. Michael Korda remembered his uncle playing host to No. 145's former residents, Their Majesties King and Queen Elizabeth. "Alex was so polished, so gracious," Korda recalled, "as if he had been raised in a palace himself. He made their majesties feel perfectly at ease."

What a role: a country boy—a Hungarian Jew—convincingly playing the British lord. He was most in his element, however, with other Hungarians. Not only his brothers, but dozens of other Hungarians were on his payroll, performing mysterious services. "The hangers-on would be asked to handle transfers of money all over the world," Michael Korda remembered. "Everywhere I went people would say, 'Ah yes, I knew your uncle,' in mysterious ways which left much unexplained."

With the breakup of his marriage to Merle Oberon, Korda gave up on domesticity, and resumed his old custom of hotel-living, this time in a suite at Claridge's in London. From there he attempted to revive his empire. Powell remembered how Korda gathered the best of London around him. "We were asked to dinner not once but often to the fabulous penthouse apartment at the top of Claridge's where Alex lived and entertained. There were always interesting people at those parties," Powell wrote. "As for myself, I loved Alex the way I loved the film business. I loved him for his glamour, his good taste, his shrewdness, for the audacity and sheer fun that he got out of manipulating men and millions."

Few of Korda's guests could see past the glamour of his life into a certain sadness and emptiness. Paul Tabori, a Hungarian-born author working on a Korda biography, received a call from Alex's secretary. "I'd take my pajamas [to the interview] if I were you." Indeed, at around 3:00 A.M., Alex suggested Tabori spend the night, "so we can talk some more in the morning." Tabori sensed that Korda was lonely. Speaking the language of his youth was consolation.

✻

CURTIZ was skeet-shooting with Hal Wallis on the morning of December 7, 1941, when his stepson raced down the long driveway, breathlessly shouting, "Pearl Harbor!" Curtiz and Wallis rushed inside and turned on the radio. The war that would catapult Michael Curtiz to the front rank of America's directors had begun.

Casablanca, half a century later, is still the most popular, the most familiar, the most discussed, and the most dissected romantic film in history. It transformed Humphrey Bogart's screen persona, launched Ingrid Bergman as an international star, and made Curtiz himself something more than the studio's bankable director.

On the surface, not much happens during *Casablanca*'s 102 minutes. The story line of a mysterious American nightclub owner, Rick Blaine, who has washed ashore in Morocco, reuniting with, and giving up his lost love, Ilsa, to her husband, a Nazi resistance fighter, named Victor Laszlo, is almost as well known as *Romeo and Juliet*. The tale is improbable and glosses over both logic and historical facts. Most of the action takes place inside Rick's café. Only two sequences are shot out-of-doors. The circumstances of the production could not have been much more chaotic and there are many legends surrounding the movie. But it is clear that Jack Warner wanted George Raft for the lead. Fortunately, Hal Wallis and Curtiz did not agree. "I have discussed this with Mike [Curtiz]," Wallis wrote Warner, "and we both feel that [Raft] should *not* be in the picture. Bogart is ideal for it and it is being written for him."

Neither Curtiz nor the actors had a complete script: it was being written and rewritten as the cameras rolled. "Every day we were shooting off the cuff," Ingrid Bergman remembered. "Every day they were handing out the dialogue and we were trying to make some sense of it. . . . Every morning we said, 'Well, who are we? What are we doing here?' And Michael Curtiz would say, 'We're not quite sure, but let's get through this scene and we'll let you know tomorrow.' " Curtiz didn't know where the plot was heading either. When Bergman asked Curtiz who she was supposed to be in love with, Rick or Laszlo, Curtiz could only answer, "Just play it, well . . . in between." "Humphrey Bogart was mad," Bergman wrote, "so he retired to his trailer." An exchange between Rick and Ilsa mirrors the film's dilemma.

ILSA: Can I tell you a story?
RICK: Has it got a wow finish?
ILSA: I don't know the finish yet.

At that point in the filming, neither did the director or his stars. *Casablanca* is testament to Curtiz's mantra: "Don't worry what's logical, I make it go so fast no one notices."

What transformed this piece of black and white celluloid, shot on Warners' back lot, into an enduring classic? Long after the theater lights come on, the lushly visual world Curtiz created in a very small space lingers. "Curtiz has an instinctual visual sense," Paul Henreid (Laszlo in the film) noted. "It's quite different from the way actors visualize. Every now and again he would stop the camera and say, 'There's something wrong here. I don't know what it is.' And by and by he'd realize what it was and we'd begin the scene again."

As usual, Curtiz was under relentless pressure from the studio to stay on budget and on deadline. "These are turbulent days," Jack Warner wrote Curtiz, "and I know you will finish *Casablanca* in top seven weeks. I am depending on you to be the old Curtiz I know you to be, and I am positive you are going to make a great picture."

From the minute the Nazi plane circles over the neon *Rick's* sign like a bird of prey, until the final moments in the fog-shrouded airport where Rick and Ilsa part, and Rick and the corrupt Vichy police chief, Louis (Claude Rains), begin their beautiful friendship, *Casablanca* has a tension that never lets up. Curtiz never allows our attention to wander, though he frequently manipulates our mood from fear to humor. All the precepts about making movies Curtiz laid down thirty years earlier in Budapest reach their fullness here. There is nothing extraneous to the plot, no overacting, and extreme close-ups of the stars—especially a luminous Bergman—draw us in, no matter how often we have seen the movie.

Begun in 1885, the Gothic-Baroque Parliament, on the Pest side of the Danube, expressed the emerging capital's grand aspirations.

Young Arthur Koestler and his parents on vacation on the Dalmatian coast in 1911, the time of plenty.

Sleeping Boy. In 1912, eighteen-year-old Andre Kertesz already showed his sense of composition and intimacy.

2

3

Regent Nicholas Horthy, decorated for service to the Austro-Hungarian Empire, brought right-wing order to Hungary and ended its Golden Age.

The Kellners of Turkeve in 1903, with the future Sir Alexander Korda gazing boldly and mischievously into the camera.

Kertesz photographed the *Young Swimmer* while in physical therapy from a war wound in 1917, well before Bauhaus and the Surrealists popularized reflections and distortions.

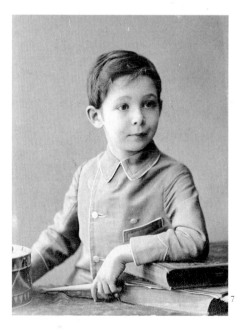

Leo Szilard at age five, an intense, coddled child of whom much was expected.

Though the young John von Neumann's teachers could not keep up with him, they guided and encouraged him to fulfill his breathtaking gifts, including the ability to divide two eight-digit numbers in his head, at age six.

Kertesz's *Long March*, a geometrically perfect composition with a lone soldier casting a sad, backward glance.

"The Greatest War Photographer in the World—Robert Capa," the cover of the new illustrated *Picture Post* anointed him in December 1938.

10

11

Langston Hughes and Arthur Koestler, picking cotton in Turkmenistan during their shared Soviet journey in 1932.

Arthur Koestler engaging in the only activity that temporarily calmed his agitated spirit, in 1952.

12

13

Kertesz's 1921 *Blind Musician* blends rigorous composition and emotional power.

14

15

Leo Szilard, casting a worried and skeptical gaze at the Oxford countryside, in the spring of 1936. He saw the storm approaching but could not get the world's attention.

Edward Teller, a research associate at the University of Göttingen in the 1930s, a time he called his happiest.

Michael Curtiz, with cigarette, at the Ufa studio in Berlin in the mid-1920s, as coiled as a wrestler ready to pounce.

Gerda Taro and Robert Capa in a Parisian café in 1935, radiant in love, just before they reinvented themselves.

Capa's *Falling Soldier* (September 5, 1936), capturing the moment when a Spanish militiaman was hit by machine-gun fire, his rifle slipping from his grip, became a symbol for the age and changed Capa's life.

In *Chartres* (August 8, 1945), Capa shows jeering townspeople taunting one of their neighbors who has had a child with a German soldier. Capa makes us feel for her, not the mob.

The newly knighted Sir Alexander Korda and Lady Korda (Merle Oberon) leaving Buckingham Palace on September 22, 1942.

Korda and his favorite yachting companion, writer Graham Greene, aboard the *Elsewhere* around 1950.

Kertesz shot this picture, *Elizabeth and I*, in a Montparnasse café in 1931. It radiates the photographer's joy at being reunited with his Budapest sweetheart and soon-to-be wife after many years of separation.

23

D-Day, June 6, 1944. Capa on Omaha Beach. Steven Spielberg would faithfully recreate this photograph in *Saving Private Ryan*.

24

A serious Capa prepares to parachute into Germany with the American forces gathered in Arras, France, on March 24, 1945.

Capa records an American MP searching a captured German SS officer in Normandy, June-July 1944.

Ingrid Bergman at the
height of her love affair
with Capa, in bombed
out Berlin in 1945.
"He said this was going
to be his scoop," she
wrote, "Ingrid Bergman
in a bathtub."
Unfortunately, Capa's
film was destroyed, but
the scene, also pho-
tographed by one of his
colleagues, has been
preserved.

26

Curtiz directed his two costars, Bergman and Humphrey Bogart, in *Casablanca*, which
would earn him an Academy Award for Best Director. The movie won
the Academy Award for Best Picture.

John von Neumann and J. Robert Oppenheimer on June 10, 1952, standing before von Neumann's early computer at the Institute for Advanced Study. It was the fastest computing machine of its day, but some of Johnny's friends maintained it was not as fast as its creator, the acknowledged midwife of the modern computer.

28

In 1963, President Lyndon B. Johnson awarded Oppenheimer the Fermi Prize, the occasion for the reunion between the estranged Teller and Oppenheimer. Oppenheimer smiles at the man who testified against him in 1954, but his wife, Kitty, is stone-faced and unforgiving.

29

Two old friends from Budapest, Edward Teller and Eugene Wigner *(left)*, the most quiet of the four Hungarian scientists, at a meeting of the American Association for the Advancement of Science, in Washington, D.C., December 27, 1965. Wigner would always defend his controversial friend Edward.

30

Eleanor Roosevelt and Leo Szilard, natural allies on many issues, at a 1961 Washington seminar.

31

Washington Square Park, by Andre Kertesz, 1954.

Curtiz's use of light and shadow to create tension, his groundbreaking use of newsreel footage of refugees on the run and the Wehrmacht on the march, lift a clever, often ironic script to far greater heights. It is the most soulful of all his films. Curtiz insisted on the heartbreaking Parisian flashback sequence of Rick and Ilsa's romantic interlude in the weeks prior to the Nazi occupation, which others feared would slow down the narrative. Other memorable Curtiz devices are Ilsa knocking over the champagne glass with which she and Rick have just toasted each other, and the Paris rain blurring the ink on her note telling Rick they will never see each other again.

Curtiz filled Rick's café with the sort of Central European refugees who crowded his dining room—indeed some of the very actors he entertained at his own home. Curtiz's old Budapest friends, with their own memories of the Café New York, Peter Lorre and S. Z. Sakall, playing the unctuous crook and the rotund headwaiter, turn small roles into gems. Tension is etched on the refugees' faces, yet they are carefully, even elegantly dressed, as Curtiz and Korda always were, particularly in the toughest times. The elderly couple, even as they excitedly practice English, convey an undercurrent of longing and loss. It took someone close to the refugee experience to portray so sharply the poignancy of their situation. In *Casablanca* even the comic scenes are poignant. (There is little question most of the many memorable lines in *Casablanca* are the work of the Epstein brothers, Julius and Philip; the *look* of the film, however, is pure Curtiz.)

History, too, played its part in *Casablanca*'s near mystical power. At the first public screening, the audience was not wildly enthusiastic. So the team of writers under the Epsteins crafted yet another ending, this one showing Rick and Louis as refugees aboard a freighter, later dropped. Then, in November 1942, the Allies landed in the real Casablanca, shortly followed by the summit conference of Churchill, Roosevelt, and Stalin. Casablanca—and *Casablanca*—were suddenly on the map.

The film was nominated for eight Academy Awards, winning three, including Best Picture, and Curtiz finally won Best Director. In accepting it, he came up with yet another memorable Curtizism. "So many times I have a speech ready, but no dice. Always a bridesmaid, never a mother. Now I win, I have no speech." After *Casablanca*, even Bogart, who never had much personal rapport with Curtiz, picked him as one of the five directors he most wanted to work with.

• • •

THE SAME YEAR, 1942, Curtiz directed the most patriotic of his films, *Yankee Doodle Dandy*, which earned an Oscar for James Cagney. The biography of the superpatriotic showman George M. Cohan survives as an uneven masterpiece. Cohan had turned down many attempts to film his life, but in the 1940s, as he was dying of cancer, he agreed that Cagney, an old song and dance man himself, should play him. The combination of Cagney and Curtiz, two tough guys handling potentially maudlin material, was inspired.

Yankee Doodle Dandy was Curtiz's personal tribute to his adopted country at war. As usual, Curtiz drove his actors, as he drove himself, to exhaustion. The title dance number will live forever as one of the most stirring patriotic scenes ever filmed. In it, Cagney is simply breathtaking. Yet it was not easy. "I was so dog tired," Cagney recalled, "that at one step in the routine I went blank. . . . I told Mike Curtiz that I couldn't think of my own step and that we'd better call it a day." But the director kept pushing, and got a performance that is widely regarded as Cagney's greatest. Watching Cagney's final scene, collapsing in his dying father's arms, the hard-nosed director himself wept. George M. Cohan lived just long enough to see the film and give it his blessing.

In 1945, Curtiz directed the third of his great classics, *Mildred Pierce*. Here Curtiz again claimed new territory, the film noir, and, in the process, rescued Joan Crawford's flagging career with an Oscar-winning performance in the title role. The story of Curtiz's brutal initial treatment of Crawford is the stuff of Hollywood legend. When Crawford appeared on the set in a dress with her trademark football-player-size shoulder pads, Curtiz ripped them out of the dress. "This stinks!" he told her. But Crawford, out of work for several years, endured the abuse. "I didn't care what I wore," she recalled. "I sailed into *Mildred* with all the gusto I'd been saving for three years, not a Crawford mannerism, not a trace of my own personality." When Jack Warner saw a rough cut, he threw a celebratory lunch for Crawford and Curtiz. Curtiz rose to deliver a toast. "When I started the tests for *Mildred Pierce*," he said in his heavily accented English, "I heard my star was very deefeecult. So, I say OK, Crawford, Curtiz will be even more deefeecult. She took it like a trouper." He smiled at Crawford, who was not an "actor bum," and added, "I luff her." Suffering from flu on Oscar night, Crawford asked Curtiz to accept the Best Actress Academy Award on her behalf.

ONE DAY in 1945, a young singer for whom, as she wrote later, acting "had never so much as crossed my mind," was sent by her agent to see Curtiz about a part in a musical film to be called *Romance on the High Seas*. With her marriage breaking up, she was distraught and did not take the audition seriously. But the audition was to produce one of the biggest stars in Hollywood. Her name was Doris Day, and her memories of the audition and the movie that made her a huge and enduring star remain perhaps the most vivid picture of Curtiz and his genius for finding and developing talent:

> Curtiz had his own bungalow on the Warners lot, a tribute to his eminence at the studio. . . . Tall, handsome, expensively tailored, steel gray hair, thick Hungarian accent. "So what you do?" he asked. "You stand up in front of band and you sing? . . . You do that for whole evening? You ever act?"
>
> "No . . . I don't know a thing about acting."
>
> "Would you like to be actress?"
>
> "To tell the truth, Mr. Curtiz, I'm on my way back to New York." Mr. Curtiz patiently listened to all this.
>
> "I see. Well, would you sing for me? . . ."
>
> "Where? Here?"
>
> "Yes, the piano here. I have a man here will play. . . ."
>
> I sang maybe six bars and then broke down completely crying my eyes out, on the verge of hysteria. . . . When I came back, Mr. Curtiz was smiling at me. . . . "I would like to test you for the part," he said. . . . "You're very sensitive girl—to be good actress is to be sensitive. . . . I sometimes like a girl who is not actress. Is less pretend and more heart."

Curtiz chose Doris Day out of over one hundred actresses who auditioned, shooting the test himself. But Curtiz was not just a brilliant talent-spotter; he also made himself Doris's personal guide into the art of acting; and his advice, which she quotes at length in her 1975 memoir, obviously stayed with her for her whole dazzling career (*The Pajama Game*,

The Man Who Knew Too Much, Love Me or Leave Me, Pillow Talk, and
so on).

  "Some people," Curtiz told her, "acting lessons are very good for them.
But I tell you—you have very strong personality. No matter what you play,
it will always be you. The Doris Day will always shine through the part.
This will make you big important star. . . . You take other actors, maybe
better actors, who become the character and lose all of themselves. They
can be fantastic, but big stars, never. . . . Always there is Humphrey Bogart
himself coming through every part he play. So with you. Is you. Is unique.
That's why I don't want you to take acting lessons. . . . You listen to me,
Doris. Is very rare thing. Do not disturb."

I N   T H E late spring of 1943, letters postmarked Washington, D.C.,
rather than Princeton, alerted Stan Ulam to his friend Johnny's new
role. "I have two hours between trains," von Neumann wrote Ulam,
"come meet me at Union Station." When Johnny appeared accompanied
by two muscular security men, Ulam knew von Neumann had left academia for "war work." All von Neumann would say—even to his wife and
daughter—was that he was "headed to the Southwest." The Southwest, of
course, meant Los Alamos, the secret city in the New Mexico desert
where the Manhattan Project was centered. Happiest in the vortex of the
military-industrial complex, he did not need much persuasion to abandon
academia for the top secret world.

  It was only natural that Oppenheimer would recruit von Neumann,
whom he had known since their days in Göttingen. He now needed
Johnny to solve the vast mathematical problems involved in constructing
the atom bomb. Although he would famously wear a three-piece suit and
tie for a mule ride down the Grand Canyon, Johnny was surprisingly in his
element in Los Alamos's wild terrain.

  Set on a seven-thousand-foot-high plateau above the desert, "The Hill,"
as it was called, offered an unaccustomed vista for a Central European.
"Johnny," his colleague Herman Goldstine recalled, "loved looking out so
that you looked practically to forever." Here, among the pine forests, hills,
and streams, he found perhaps the greatest collection of scientific lumi-

naries ever assembled—certainly the greatest ever to work on a single project. (General Groves's view of his brilliant charges was slightly different. "At great expense," he reportedly told Army officers stationed in Los Alamos, "we have gathered on this mesa the largest collection of crackpots ever seen.")

For von Neumann, the chance to match wits with such "crackpots" as Fermi, Hans Bethe, Richard Feynman, Oppenheimer, Teller, and many others was bliss. "[Teller and von Neumann] were talking about things," Ulam recalled, "which I only vaguely understood. There were tremendous long formulae on the blackboard, which scared me. Seeing all these complications of analysis, I was dumbfounded, fearing I would never be able to contribute anything."

Behind the barbed wire and security curtain of Los Alamos, Johnny enjoyed special status. He came and went as he pleased, equally respected by the scientists and the military. When people at Los Alamos heard von Neumann was coming, they would line up all their advanced mathematical problems. "Then, he would arrive," physicist Ralph Lapp remembered, "and systematically topple them over." Eyes shut as if in a trance, Johnny would smile slowly as he zeroed in on the solution. It was not only the speed of his calculations, it was the beauty of the process. "He had a completely sure sense of what was elegant mathematically," Herman Goldstine recalled. "It was never enough for him merely to establish a result; he had to do it with elegance and grace. He would often say to me while we worked on some topic, 'Now here is the elegant way to do this.' "

He needed no more than four hours sleep and mental exercise refreshed him. Lapp was his roommate at Los Alamos. "One night I was awakened by Johnny," he recalled more than half a century later, "he was half-asleep, talking to himself, doing mathematical calculations."

Von Neumann and Teller were a singular pair: von Neumann short, dapper in suit and tie, small feet beautifully and inappropriately shod, moving fast over the stony terrain, and Teller (who still maintained that Hungary's Tatra Mountains were superior to the Rockies), his gait heavy and uneven, his eyebrows rising and falling, oblivious to all, save what was on his mind. In their native tongue, they talked not only of science but literature, the classics, poetry—for the sheer pleasure of exercising their minds.

"When [Teller] could forget his problems," Enrico Fermi's wife, Laura, recalled, "he delighted in simple pleasures. His favorite author was Lewis Carroll and he started to read Carroll's stories and poems to [his son] Paul long before the child could understand them. Edward also composed a rhyming alphabet for Paul, of which the following couplet is a sample:

S stands for secret, you can keep forever
Provided there's no one abroad who is clever."

Even the arrogant Teller was in awe of von Neumann's brain and claimed he understood what Johnny said in some of their conversations only after he had repeated them for the third time. Hans Bethe sometimes wondered whether "a brain like von Neumann's does not indicate a species superior to that of man." General Groves, a deeply suspicious person, trusted Johnny more than he did most of the other scientists and relied on him for advice that went well beyond mathematics and physics to the strategic. Groves, who deemed Szilard too Hungarian and too Jewish, was unaware that von Neumann was himself both.

VON NEUMANN'S truly visionary contribution, however, was the modern computer. In 1943, the Pentagon sent him to England to observe the British military-scientific effort. While there, he met with the eccentric British computer genius Alan Turing, whose pioneering work had helped break the German codes. The visit rekindled von Neumann's longstanding interest in mechanized mathematics. Von Neumann was put off by Turing's overt homosexuality (which eventually would lead to the deliberate destruction, by British officials, of one of the most brilliant careers in modern scientific history). But he was excited by Turing's visionary concept of a "universal machine" for doing mathematics.

After the war, von Neumann told a friend, "I am thinking about something much more important than bombs. I am thinking about computers." In fact, von Neumann's interest in computers predated his interest in bombs. Long before he joined the Manhattan Project, he had been, in his own words, "obscenely obsessed" by the idea of an electronic brain—a computer. He and Rudolf Ortvay had exchanged letters in which they discussed how the computer might mimic the human brain. Von Neumann saw the computer's revolutionary potential far beyond its utility as a high-speed calculator. "Von Neumann was the first person," Goldstine noted, "who understood explicitly that a computer essentially performed logical functions, and that the electrical aspects were ancillary."

Von Neumann conceived the idea of programming, the notion that you could break down a problem into a series of simple steps that could be manipulated as numbers are manipulated. You don't have to change the basic design of the computer, von Neumann insisted, just the instructions you give it. The computer's stored program capacity, which would come to be known as "von Neumann architecture," was the prototype for today's digital computer.

Ahead of anyone else, von Neumann also saw the role the computer could play in defeating Hitler. He knew the mathematical calculations necessary to ensure accuracy for rockets and bombs would require powerful computers, which did not yet exist.

Brilliance and vision were not enough to launch one of the twentieth century's transforming inventions. Von Neumann's ability to manipulate powerful people and institutions — without seeming to be doing so — was a priceless asset in the computer's development. Only a man who was trusted by both scientists and the military could persuade the Institute for Advanced Study and the Army to collaborate on his computer research. "The best way to get something done," he once remarked, "was to propagandize everybody who is a reasonable potential supporter." The word "networker" had not yet been coined, but Johnny was one of its most accomplished practitioners.

Thanks to von Neumann, it was not a corporation like IBM but the Institute for Advanced Study that developed the computer. Perhaps only von Neumann could have persuaded an elite academic center to back an engineering project and then attract the brightest engineers to Princeton and let them flourish. Only a trusted insider could have gotten funding from both the U.S. Navy and the U.S. Army for his computer. Moreover, von Neumann published everything, making his work public. In the crucial early stages, thanks largely to his work, the computer was not a captive of a single company.

Von Neumann brought the first, cumbersome "computer" (an IBM card sorter, which used vacuum tubes) to Los Alamos in the spring of 1944. Feynman, the flamboyant physicist (who would go on to win the

Nobel Prize in physics in 1965), immediately put the machine to work on implosion calculations. This method, in which the outer layer around the plutonium core is faster burning than the inner layer, allows the rest of the shock wave to catch up. Von Neumann did the complicated calculations that enabled the explosives experts at Los Alamos to design shaped blocks of high explosives that acted as lenses to selectively slow down and redirect the shock waves so that they converged on the bomb core. His calculations speeded up the making of the plutonium bomb by at least a year. Without von Neumann's contribution, the U.S. would not have had two bombs ready to use against the Japanese in August 1945.

Joining forces with the team at Philadelphia's Moore School of Electrical Engineering working on the first electronic computer, known as ENIAC, von Neumann soon took the project in a different direction. His 101-page report written in the final winter of the war is still considered "the most important document ever written on computing and computers." But von Neumann was already working on a vastly more advanced version of the ENIAC that, with characteristic irony, he called the MANIAC.

I N MARCH 1943, Robert Capa, duly accredited as a reporter for *Collier's* magazine, sailed to Algeria to cover the U.S. Army's North African campaign. Army life suited Capa. There were few decisions to be made, most were made for you. There was plenty of human warmth, the camaraderie of brothers in arms. Best of all, after almost four years Capa was back in the fight against the fascists.

Capa soon made friends with generals and enlisted men, playing nightly poker with both. He took the same chances as the soldiers, with the camera his only weapon. "He was a good guy to have around," General James M. Gavin of the 82nd Airborne recalled. "His conversation wasn't limited to . . . how to take pictures. He had had a lot of practical combat experience, and he knew more about judging combat troops and how to fight than most." Nothing serious ever seemed to happen to Capa, who turned danger into adventure. Capa was their good-luck charm.

In the Tunisian desert, Capa jumped off the Army jeep he was riding.

"After the previous night's experience," he wrote, "I did not feel inclined to visit the toilet of an Arab cultural institution." Before relieving himself in the open air, he noticed a sign in German, "Achtung! Minen!" It was his first experience with this cruel weapon of war. "I did not dare do anything," he wrote. "I shouted my predicament to my driver. I told him I was standing in the middle of a minefield. He seemed to think the situation very funny. I urged him to drive off and bring back somebody with a mine detector." Several hours later a mine squad rescued Capa. As he did many other acts of reckless courage, Capa turned this into a colorful story.

After five years' absence, Capa returned to Europe in September 1943, the first to photograph the liberation of a major European city. "The first ride through a captured town gives you an initial feeling of elation," he wrote of Naples. "But soon your heart is gripped with pity." As revenge for Italy's surrender to the Allies, the retreating Germans had blown up some hospitals and schools in Naples. Bodies and body parts were strewn on the city's piazzas. Capa photographed a funeral of twenty teenage partisans at a school. The boys had held off the Nazis for fourteen days. The focus of his lens is the children's feet, which hang out of their small coffins. "Those children's feet were my real welcome to Europe, I, who had been born there. More real by far than the welcome of the hysterically cheering crowds I had met along the road, many of them the same that had yelled *Duce!* in an earlier year." Another of his pictures shows the faces of the children's mothers, screaming in mourning. "Those were my truest pictures of victory," Capa wrote. This was his third war, and by now he believed that in war there are only losers.

Capa's courage during the Italian campaign so impressed General Matthew Ridgway that—in an unusual gesture—he wrote *Life* magazine: "Mr. Capa, by reason of his professional competence, genial personality and cheerful sharing of all dangers and hardships has come to be considered a member of the [504th Regiment] Division. The 'All American' Division wishes to express to you its appreciation of his services and to assure you of his welcome, should future assignments again bring us together." *Life* magazine was also lavish in its praise. "You are going great guns, Bob," Hicks telegrammed him. "I salute you again."

In truth, Capa was depressed. "The war is like an actress," he told John Morris, "who is getting old. It is less and less photogenic, and more and more dangerous." But he had to stay. "To come home this winter is impossible," he wrote his anxious mother, reminding her of his still unresolved immigration status. "You know my situation is slightly different from the others and I cannot afford to get home every six months. . . . So I am asking you again for books which are the most important entertainment around here."

Capa dreamed of returning to the Europe of his youth. He fantasized about walking the streets of a free Paris—and maybe even Budapest. In a sense, the whole of his career had been preparation for the invasion of Europe. Capa knew that the war would be won or lost on the beaches of France. For the thirty-year-old photographer, this would be the biggest event of his career.

By late 1943, his attention was fixed on the upcoming campaign, although it was still shrouded in secrecy and many months away. Capa was one of a handful of volunteers for the first, most perilous moments of the Normandy invasion—the assault on Omaha Beach. The Germans defending the beaches had planted metal stakes, mines, and thousands of troops to stop the invasion.

In London, Capa prepared for his life's most dangerous mission by playing poker and having sex. "When he was not touring pubs," his friend and fellow poker player, the writer Irwin Shaw, recalled, "he was the host for intense poker games, during which, in the middle of almost nightly bombings by the Luftwaffe, it was considered very bad form to hesitate before placing a bet or to move away from the table, no matter how close the hits, or how loud the antiaircraft fire." Never one to take anything too seriously—least of all himself—Capa rigged himself out in a new Burberry trench coat, and a silver hip flask, determined to be the "most elegant invader."

The Normandy landing is rarely depicted as a tragedy. But Capa captured its early brush with disaster. "I decided," Capa recalled, "to go in with Company E, in the first wave." Standing with two thousand men in silence on the deck of the USS *Samuel Chase* transport ship in the predawn light, he tried to make out the coast of France. "None of us was at all impatient and we wouldn't have minded standing in the darkness for a very long time."

The Channel crossing was rough and Capa was soaked by the time he transferred from the *Samuel Chase* to a swaying landing barge. As the ramps dropped and the men jumped into the water, the Germans opened fire from a bluff. Many GIs were mowed down before they could return fire. Capa and those still standing dodged machine gun fire from both ends of the beach. Scores of wounded men around him, dragged down by overloaded packs, drowned. The sea around him was red. "The bullets tore holes in the water around me, and I made for the nearest steel obstacle," he recalled later. But corpses barred Capa's way to the shelter of the antitank traps. He repeated the mantra that had calmed him during battle in Spain. "Es una cosa muy seria, Es una cosa muy seria"—this is a very serious business. Staying alive was a full-time job. He spotted a burned-out tank. "Between floating bodies I reached it, paused for a few more pictures and gathered my guts for the last jump to the beach." His body flattened against the sand, his hands trembling, he continued to aim and press the shutter of his Contax camera for ninety minutes. "Poor fellow," a nineteen-year-old motor mechanic recalled, "he was there in the water, holding his cameras up to keep them dry, trying to catch his breath." Out of film and shaking, Capa crawled back into the water and jumped on a landing craft fifty yards out to sea. "I climbed aboard," he recalled, "and started to change my film. I felt a slight shock. . . . I was all covered with feathers. I thought: 'What is this? Is somebody killing chickens?' Then I saw that . . . the feathers were the stuffing from the jackets of the men who were blown up. The skipper was crying because his assistant had been blown all over him."

When the *Samuel Chase* docked on the English coast, Capa thrust his ten rolls of film into the waiting hands of a *Life* courier, changed into dry clothes, and jumped aboard another vessel heading back to the beaches. But Capa's record of courage on Omaha Beach—three thousand men died that day—almost died with them. A young and nervous darkroom technician in London, knowing he had the first photographs of D-Day in his hands, panicked. Instructed to turn up the heat in the darkroom, he did not pay close enough attention and all but eleven of Capa's 106 pictures were ruined.

The surviving sequence, however, has become immortal. Those grainy, slightly out-of-focus photographs capture the danger, drama, and cost of liberating Europe. D-Day will forever be remembered, visualized, by Capa's eleven surviving frames. In a loving homage, Steven Spielberg reproduced them perfectly in the opening sequence of *Saving Private Ryan,* and they have never ceased to have a power over anyone who has seen them.

Capa accepted the crushing loss of the other photographs with grace. He did not want the darkroom technician punished. Only to his family did he express dismay. "I still do not know if my first pictures ever arrived," he wrote home on July 19, 1944, "and I am rather disturbed."

Capa told friends that those who crossed the English Channel on June 6, 1944, ought to celebrate a special Passover of their own. One of his favorite expressions was, "Are you a good Jew?" Meaning, are you a good human being? "Children [of D-Day veterans]," he said, "after finishing a couple of cans of C-rations should ask their father, 'What makes this day different from all other days?' "

After the exhaustion and the disappointment, there was an emotional payoff. Joining General George S. Patton's fast-moving Third Army as it raced toward Paris, Capa recorded the humiliation of Europe's once invincible oppressor. "The old arrogance is gone," he wrote home, "now we are ketching [sic] them and hitting them hard." In Cherbourg, he had savored the capture of General Karl Wilhelm von Schlieben, regional commander. "He was our first high ranking prisoner," Capa wrote, "and I wanted his picture badly. But he turned his back, refused to pose, and told his aide in German that he was bored with the whole idea of American press liberties. In German I replied, 'And I am bored with photographing defeated German generals.' He became furious and turned sharply around at me. I snapped his picture. It couldn't have been better."

ON A relatively quiet day in July, Capa suggested to his companions, Ernest Hemingway and *Life* photo editor John Morris, a trip to the spectacular monastery at Mont St. Michel in Brittany. It had survived the war, as had its famed restaurant La Mère Poulard. "That day I had a taste of how Capa worked," Morris remembered sixty years later. "He literally conquered the village: talked to a young girl, leaned over some chess players, had a smoke with a couple of fishermen. He owned the place. He liked people, and they couldn't help but like him back."

On August 18, Capa took one of the most important photographs of his career. If Cartier-Bresson moved like a fox, avoiding contact with people, if Kertesz saw people as subjects for perfect compositions, Capa's pictures conveyed his affection. That day, he captured an unforgettable street scene in the cathedral town of Chartres that illustrated the tragic and complicated aftermath of the war. Jeering townspeople are taunting one of their neighbors, who has had a child with a German soldier. Her head is shaved, she is alone in the center of the angry crowd. Capa makes us feel for *her*, not the self-righteous mob.

Capa was impatient for the supreme moment of his war: the liberation of Paris. "The night of the 25th [August] we bivouacked under a road sign reading 'Porte D'Orleans—6 kilometres.' It was the best road sign I've ever slept under." The road to Paris was open. Riding in an American jeep, wearing U.S. Army fatigues, Capa arrived in the city the next day. "I felt that this entry into Paris had been made especially for me," he recalled. "I was returning to Paris—the beautiful city where I first learned to eat, drink and love." To his mother he wrote, "Nobody was surprised that I came back, everybody expected that I would be the first one. The Café Dôme has the same waiters, and we had quite a celebration." The "Marseillaise" could be heard from every corner of the city, and for a day or so it felt as if the war had ended. Soon, Capa would return to begin the most publicly celebrated romance of his life.

It is revealing that Capa chose to miss the war's final two chapters: the liberation of the concentration camps and the Battle of Berlin. "From the Rhine to the Oder I took no pictures," he wrote. "The concentration camps were swarming with photographers and every new picture of horror served only to diminish the total effect. Now, for a short day, everyone will see what happened to those poor devils in those camps; tomorrow very few will care what happens to them in the future," he wrote. "The Germans," he noted, "now sullen, now suddenly friendly, didn't interest my camera either."

B Y THE mid-1940s, Arthur Koestler was ready to plant his roots in the one European country that had not betrayed him. With its predominantly gray weather, where reserve was prized more than optimism, Britain suited him perfectly. For Koestler, who described himself as a "typical case-history of a member of the Central-European educated middle class, born in the first years of our century," America was a world too far from his roots.

In 1944, Koestler turned his anger on the United States for its apathy toward the fate of Europe's Jews. "It is the greatest mass-killing in recorded history," he wrote in the *New York Times* in January 1944, "and it goes on daily, hourly, as regularly as the ticking of your watch. . . . But . . . nine out of ten average American citizens, when asked whether they believed that the Nazis commit atrocities, answered that it was all propaganda lies, and that they didn't believe a word of it. . . . And meanwhile the watch goes ticking."

Two months later, on March 19, 1944, Hitler dispatched Adolf Eichmann and his Einsatzkommando to Hungary, to solve the Reich's last remaining "Jewish Problem." Andy Grove, a Budapest youth who, five decades later, co-founded the high-tech giant Intel, described the event. "My mother and I stood on the sidewalk of the Ring Road," Grove wrote in 2001, "watching as the cars and troop carriers filled with soldiers drove by. The German soldiers were neat and wore shiny boots and had a self-confident air about them. The sidewalk was lined with passersby, all watching the procession of soldiers, all looking very serious. . . . There was no sound except for the engine and tire noise from the cars. . . . They set up headquarters a few blocks from our house."

Beating their prior record for speed and efficiency, the Nazis proceeded to expropriate, ghettoize, and round up Hungarian Jews. "At the end of the summer," Grove remembered, "our lives changed in a major way. Jews had to move out of their apartments by a certain date and into special buildings that were designated as houses for Jews. People called them 'Star Houses' because a big yellow Star of David was painted above the entrance of each of these houses. . . . Things were happening to us one after the other. Just when we got used to one thing, another thing happened. We were forbidden to step outside the Jewish house without wearing [a yellow star], just one more of those things to accept numbly and silently."

What gave the murder of Hungary's Jews a particularly cruel edge was that the end of the war was in sight. By summer of 1944, the Allies—who never had the slightest intention of liberating Hungary, which they left to the Red Army—were on the road to Paris. Hungary's Jews had nearly escaped; their mass deportation and slaughter took place with astonishing speed in full view of the world.

A few weeks later, Koestler learned that his aunt Rose and first cousin Margit and her children had perished at Auschwitz. He loved Margit, who had first introduced him to the plight of Hungary's workers during the 1919 Commune. "Six million," Koestler wrote, "is an abstraction; my Aunt Rose and Cousin Margit, gassed like rats, were the reality behind the abstraction. . . . To [the Allies], the holocaust was indeed an abstraction—they had no Aunt Roses to mourn."

Koestler now learned, belatedly, that his father had also died—of heartbreak. "He died in 1940," he wrote, "as I was making my escape from France, when communications with Hungary were broken. . . . [My mother and father] both thought I had fallen into the hands of the Nazis. . . . On the day before he died, my father had asked [my mother] to take my photograph away from his bedside table. 'I can bear it no longer,' he said quietly."

In January 1945 Koestler returned to Palestine—which he now saw as the Jews' last best hope. Accredited to the *Times* of London, he was also on a secret mission for Chaim Weitzman, the president of the Zionist Organization and later of Israel. "Talk to those mad friends of yours," Weitzman asked Koestler, referring to his old comrades from Jabotinsky's Revisionist movement. "Try to convince them that partition [of Palestine into an Arab and Jewish state] is our only chance."

Koestler made contact with the Irgun and Lehi (the Stern Gang), the two underground groups hunted by the British. He made a dangerous journey that involved "my changing cars and travel companion no less than five times until I was safely relayed from my Jerusalem flat to a house in a slummy suburb in Tel Aviv, having no idea where I was. Two unsmiling toughs led me up some steps into a large, pitch dark room, where I was told to sit down. . . . I sensed the presence of another human being—which was Menachem Begin. I asked whether I might light a cigarette, whereupon one of the toughs said I might not, but he would light it for me. . . . The reason for the precaution I learned later: it was rumored that Begin had disguised his features with a beard or plastic surgery. In his memoirs Begin says ironically that I wanted to strike a match to have a glimpse of him out of journalistic curiosity—whereas I was much happier not to know where I was, nor his appearance, in case I should, after all, run into trouble with the police."

Koestler described Begin, the future Israeli prime minister, as "hard, bitter and fanatical." Begin told Koestler he would continue his guerrilla war against the British. After his failure at diplomacy, Koestler returned to London and wrote a novel about the birth, "in the poisoned soil of Jewish and Arab terrorism," of the state of Israel. *Thieves in the Night,* like *Darkness at Noon,* created political ripples and it pleased Koestler when he heard that the members of the 1947 United Nations Palestine Commission had used his book in preparing their recommendations to the world body. The commission concluded—as had Koestler—that the partition of Palestine was the answer to the claims of the two warring sides.

***

WHILE FEVERISHLY working on the weapon meant to stop Hitler, the Hungarian scientists kept a watchful eye on their terrorized homeland where friends and families were still trapped. "While dead and dying Jews were being shoved into the icy Danube," Teller wrote, "I was safe and comfortable in Los Alamos."

Almost exactly six years after the day Edward Teller "entered history as Leo Szilard's chauffeur," the warning contained in Einstein's letter literally exploded. In those six years, the most destructive war in history had claimed around 55 million lives. Centuries of European civilization had been reduced to mountains of rubble. But the killing was not yet done.

The first test of an atomic weapon was scheduled for July 16, 1945, in a flat, scrubby slice of desert known as the Jornada del Muerto—Dead Man's Trail—two hundred miles south of Los Alamos between the Rio Grande River and the Sierra Oscura Mountains. The exact spot would become known in history as Trinity.

"We were all lying on the ground," Teller remembered, "with our backs turned to the explosion. But I had decided to disobey the instruction and instead looked straight at the bomb. I was wearing the welder's glasses that we had been given so that the light from the bomb would not damage our eyes. But because I wanted to face the explosion, I had decided to add some extra protection. I put on dark glasses under the welder's glasses, rubbed some ointment on my face to prevent sunburn from the radiation, and pulled on thick gloves to press the welding glasses to my face to prevent light from entering at the sides. . . .

"For the last five seconds, we all lay there quietly waiting for what seemed an eternity. . . . Then," Teller recalled, "I saw a faint point of light that appeared to divide into three horizontal points. As the question, 'Is this all?' flashed through my mind, I remembered my extra protection. . . . I lifted my right hand to admit a little light under the welder's glasses. It was as if I had pulled open the curtain to a dark room and broad daylight streamed in. . . . A few seconds later we were all standing, gazing open mouthed at the brilliance. Then we heard a loud report. . . . We returned to the buses with hardly a word. We knew the next nuclear explosion would not be an experiment."

Almost all those present later used religious or mythological images to describe what they had seen. Groves's deputy, General Thomas F. Farrell, recalled, "The whole country was lighted by a searing light with an intensity many times that of the midday sun. . . . Thirty seconds after the explosion came first the air blast pressing hard against the people and things, to be followed almost immediately by the strong, sustained, awesome roar which warned of doomsday." Oppenheimer, conflicted, famously recalled a line from the Bhagavad Gita, "I am become Death, the shatterer of worlds." Observing Oppie's ambivalence, von Neumann noted with typical Budapest sarcasm, "Some people profess guilt, to claim credit for the sin."

PERHAPS no man had been more responsible for the ideas that launched the $2 billion enterprise known as the Manhattan Project than Leo Szilard, who had first understood the connection between a nuclear chain reaction and a bomb. Yet by the summer of 1945, as two bombs were being readied for sea transport to Tinian in the northern Marianas, from which they would be dropped on Japan, no one worked harder to stop their use against civilian targets than Szilard. Leo was as political as von Neumann, but his goal was the opposite of Johnny's. On April 30, 1945, the madman who had first frightened Szilard into mobilizing the world had blown his brains out in his Berlin bunker. Szilard saw no further rationale for using the weapon he had helped deliver to the world. He now envisioned and feared a postwar nuclear arms race. As early as 1943, he had begun advocating international controls to prevent such a nuclear arms race.

If General Groves felt at ease around von Neumann, he felt irritation and suspicion toward Szilard. Groves refused to believe that Szilard and Wigner could have drafted Einstein's 1939 letter to FDR. "It was too cleverly written," Groves said, "and indicated a knowledge not only of international affairs but also of what would appeal to President Roosevelt." Therefore, Groves concluded, Alexander Sachs, who was the messenger, was the letter's author. As far as Groves was concerned, Szilard "was completely unprincipled, amoral and immoral." Elsewhere, Groves revealed a deeper prejudice. "I don't like certain Jews, and I don't like certain well-known characteristics of theirs, but I'm not prejudiced." Hoping to discredit Szilard, Groves had FBI agents tail him.

The agents found evidence of a man who did indeed pose a threat—not to the United States, but, on occasion, to himself. The FBI portrait of Leo Szilard's day in Washington is vivid: "The Subject is of Jewish extraction, has a fondness for delicacies and frequently makes purchases in delicatessen stores and eats his breakfast in drug stores . . . speaks in a foreign tongue and associates mostly with people of Jewish extraction. He is inclined to be rather absent minded and eccentric, and will start out a door, turn around and come back, go out on the street without his coat or hat and frequently looks up and down the street as if he were watching for someone or did not know for sure where he wanted to go."

Szilard knew exactly where he was going, he simply enjoyed playing games with the FBI. Together, Szilard and Wigner, who was also under surveillance, managed to deliberately exhaust seven FBI agents as they wandered around Washington, finally settling on a bench by the tennis court of the Wardman Park Hotel, "where both [Wigner and Szilard] pulled off their coats, rolled up their sleeves and talked in a foreign language for some time." If the FBI had known that those daily drugstore breakfasts of Szilard's consisted of liverwurst sandwiches, they might have seen him as an even greater security risk. (Szilard's weakness for certain delicacies was well known to his friends. In a 1937 conversation about the feasibility of the atomic bomb, Szilard also revealed his idea for preserving

. . .

"ONE DOWN!" the driver of a passing jeep yelled to Teller as he walked to his Los Alamos lab. Thus Teller first heard of the destruction of Hiroshima. Three days later, Nagasaki followed. Even Edward Teller was stunned. "The fires raging unopposed, wounds remaining unattended, sick men killing themselves with the exertions of helping their fellows." It was even possible, he wrote, "that the effects of an atomic war will endanger the survival of man."

Genia Peierls, wife of German-born physicist Rudolf Peierls, who, according to Laura Fermi, "always managed to learn what was going on [in Los Alamos] ahead of the other wives," brought the news on the morning of August 7, 1945, to Mrs. Fermi. " 'Our stuff was dropped on Japan!' She stepped into my kitchen and stood there, her brown eyes aglow, palms upward, her red lips parted. 'Our stuff,' that is the phrase she used. Not even then, the morning after Hiroshima, did we, the wives, fully realize that Los Alamos was making atomic bombs."

SHORTLY BEFORE boarding a plane to return to London in August 1945, Arthur Koestler saw a headline in the *Jerusalem Post*: "Hiroshima Destroyed by Atomic Bomb." "That's the end of the war," Koestler commented to a friend, "and it's also the beginning of the end of the world."

ONLY AFTER Hiroshima did Szilard's family learn of his historic role. "Leo went into a deep funk after Hiroshima," his nephew John told me. "He was shattered and drew into himself." Also in the dark was Szilard's future wife and longtime companion, Trude Weiss. In a letter from Leo that she called "an apology," he wrote to her the day after Hiroshima. "Using atomic bombs against Japan is one of the greatest blunders of history. . . . I went out of my way (and very much so) in order to prevent it, but as today's papers show, without success."

Perhaps for the first time in his hyperactive life, Szilard was at a loss. "It is very difficult to see what wise course of action is possible from here on," he told Trude, "maybe it is best to say nothing." Silence was not part of Leo Szilard's DNA, however. As messianic in his way as Teller in his, Szilard pursued an opposite goal from Teller. Teller felt the role of science and scientists was to uncover all of nature's secrets, regardless of the consequences; Szilard, who realized those secrets might be dangerous for humanity, sought to control their consequences, even if it meant not pursuing basic research in certain areas.

ALTHOUGH being Hungarian and Jewish were defining characteristics of all those we are following in this narrative, that is not in and of itself sufficient to predict the politics each man would follow, especially after the seminal public event of their lives, especially for the scientists: Hiroshima and Nagasaki. Von Neumann and Teller would become pillars of the conservative establishment—von Neumann, until his premature death in 1957, and Teller, astonishingly, into the twenty-first century as an emblematic, heroic figure to conservatives. Szilard, on the other hand, became a hero to the liberal arms control and nuclear arms community, founding enduring organizations, lecturing and making television appearances, even writing a best-selling political satire, *The Voice of the Dolphins,* a collection of stories, including the famous title story, in which those intelligent mammals teach humanity a lesson about world peace. Wigner, less political, remained faithful to his Hungarian friends in both camps, and won the Nobel Prize in 1964 for physics—the only one of the four to do so.

They were more political than their American-born colleagues for an obvious reason: they had seen firsthand, at an early age, the effects of communism, fascism, and anti-Semitism. Why, then, did they divide over the greatest issue of their time?

For the answer to this critical question, we need to return to their Budapest childhoods, where subtle but significant early differences would shape their post-Hiroshima political lives.

The politics of Leo Szilard, the eldest, and ultimately the most liberal, were shaped most by the humanistic values of his mother, and the city at its most secure and optimistic. His zeal to save humanity probably came from both his mother and the book *The Tragedy of Man,* which he had memorized as a child. Szilard's passion led him first to his relentless advocacy for building the bomb, and then his fervent efforts to prevent its use and post-Hiroshima development.

From his birth, John von Neumann was the most at ease in, and desirous of being part of, that elusive thing called the Establishment. In his more sophisticated childhood, anti-Semitism, while certainly not absent, was subtle. His brilliance, even compared to the others, was so widely known he easily gained entrée into social and political circles wherever he went. In contrast to Szilard, and more like Teller, he did not feel that scientists were responsible for the consequences of their discoveries. With the beginning of the Cold War, von Neumann's willingness to explore the outer reaches of military use of scientific discoveries—such as his chilling apocalyptic vision in 1955 of harnessing weather changes as an ultimate weapon of war—made him popular in the Pentagon.

The fact that Edward Teller was born a decade after the others is essential to understand the astonishing ferocity with which he advanced his views in the more than half-century he lived after Hiroshima. At a highly impressionable age, the young Teller saw the communists destroy his family's social and economic standing, and then personally experienced the anti-Semitic backlash. Those memories, which never left him, explain almost every major political and scientific act of his career, from his advocacy of the far more powerful nuclear weapon known as the Super to his passion for what became known as the Strategic Defense Initiative, or Star Wars. Teller's impact on President Ronald Reagan and his supporters was enormous. Even the most controversial act of his controversial career, his decision to publicly question the patriotism of J. Robert Oppenheimer, can be seen and understood best through this lens. Finally, he unintentionally left a deep mark on popular culture as the primary model for one of the most famous antiwar movies of all time, *Dr. Strangelove, Or: How I Learned to Stop Worrying and Love the Bomb.* The target of relentless attacks by the left and canonization by the right, Edward Teller occupies a singular place in the history of the Cold War.

I N L I B E R A T E D F R A N C E , the Communist Party, the largest bloc in the legislature, seemed poised for power in 1946. At that very moment, *Darkness at Noon* was published in France—breaking publishing records and severely damaging the French Communist Party's position. General Charles de Gaulle read Koestler's book in one sitting. Four hundred thousand of his countrymen and women bought copies. Many attributed the communists' defeat in the referendum to the impact of Koestler's book. The author, who regarded France as the front line in the war against Soviet influence, was delighted.

Having barely escaped Vichy France five years earlier, Koestler now returned as a conquering literary hero. "I left France with a kick in my pants," Koestler wrote, "and now they receive me like Frank Sinatra." Left Bank intellectuals and the Parisian elite lionized the former "scum of the earth." André Malraux, Jean-Paul Sartre, Simone de Beauvoir, and Albert Camus feted, wined, and dined him. Montparnasse's Coupole and Dôme had once been his haunts; now the inner sanctum of the Parisian *literati* opened its doors, welcoming him to the Café de Flore and Les Deux Magots on the Boulevard Saint Germain.

As always, the black cloud of Koestler's gloom soon rolled back. "To be a lion," he wrote to his future second wife, Mamaine Paget, in October 1946, "is only fun for a very short time . . . or if one is younger . . . I cancelled a big press reception, refused all interviews, radio, etc. and shut myself completely off. . . . Camus is charming but to make real friends one has to start at twenty. I am dining with him tomorrow and with Malraux tonight. . . . I had dinner at the British Embassy which was perfectly ghastly . . . and there was a chain of luncheons and parties given by my four publishers—but none of them the real thing. The gold," he wrote, "has somehow turned to *merde*."

Middle-aged and famous, Koestler continued to rail against the injustices of his age. He was an international figure now, a character from a postwar *film noir*, whose every assertion was punctuated by a pull on a cigarette, and for whom social occasions frequently ended in an alcohol-induced intellectual brawl. "But I don't want to be reasonable," says Joseph, the Koestler stand-in in *Thieves in the Night*, his 1946 novel about Palestine. "I have had enough of being reasonable for two thousand years while the others were not." There was never any danger of Arthur Koestler being reasonable.

PART FOUR

FALSE DAWN

L ike other weary veterans eager for home, the scientists at Los Alamos packed up and streamed off the mesa. In October 1945, Oppenheimer announced his resignation as director of Los Alamos and headed back to the University of California at Berkeley. Teller joined the faculty of the University of Chicago, Wigner became director of research and development at Oak Ridge, Tennessee, the nuclear laboratory where work was under way on uranium separation and plutonium production, von Neumann, characteristically, seemed to be everywhere. In a declaration of "War Work" to the trustees of his primary base at the Institute for Advanced Study, von Neumann listed, among other activities: ballistic research at the Aberdeen Proving Ground, the U.S. Navy Bureau of Ordnance, consultant to Los Alamos on military and explosives, high-speed computer development, and aerodynamics research. Some of his colleagues may have found unseemly the excitement von Neumann got from the thump of the waiting helicopter, but he loved his role in the arena. No one, before or since, occupied the intersection of academia, military, and policy-making more effectively.

Unlike Teller and Szilard, von Neumann was not only emotionally detached but possessed iron self-control. Edward emanated gloom; Johnny's sunny surface masked a similar inner pessimism. While Teller's obvious ambition and intensity frightened people, everybody trusted and liked von Neumann, who, in Goldstine's words, "warmed both hands before the fire of life." Laura Fermi, an active member of the Los Alamos community, marveled that von Neumann "was one of the very few men about whom I have not heard a single critical remark."

But some colleagues thought his fame and celebrity had begun to impair his work. In 1954, von Neumann gave a much anticipated lecture to the International Mathematical Congress, meeting in Amsterdam. After the lecture, a disappointed Freeman Dyson, professor of physics at the Institute for Advanced Study, wrote a colleague, Richard Kadison, that von Neumann had been "expected to produce a list of problems for the second half of the twentieth century." But, Dyson continued, "We . . . were bitterly disappointed. He gave a boring warmed up talk . . . stuff he had done before and was no longer interested in." Kadison agreed that it was "a very poor talk. . . . It occurred to me that [von Neumann] had been dragooned into giving the talk at a time when he was impossibly busy."

Los Alamos continued to lure von Neumann back. Marina von Neumann recalled driving cross-country with her father the first summer after the war. Their destination was the still secret city where Johnny was about to rejoin Teller to help him with the Super. "We had been stopping in motels along the way," his daughter remembered, "the kind with little wooden bungalows and outhouses. Dad needed only three or four hours of sleep a night. I could hear him scribbling and talking to himself much of the night, doing calculations."

Now von Neumann's sights were fixed on the need to ensure America's postwar security. Earlier than anyone else, he had understood the potential of the computer in the development of weaponry. Many scientists were upset that von Neumann had become such a staunch advocate of the military-industrial establishment. "I wanted him to be a mathematician," his assistant Paul Halmos wrote. "He stopped by the mid-1940s. Not because of war but because his interest had changed. He might have had a place as one of the all-time greats of mathematics. He didn't fulfill himself in using his talent. He spread himself too thinly."

Jacob Bronowski, another polymath, bemoaned the loss of von Neumann as a pioneering scientist. "He became more and more engaged in work for private firms, for industry, for government. They were enterprises which brought him to the center of power, but which did not advance either his knowledge or his intimacy with people."

TELLER lacked von Neumann's social skills. But he was single-minded: tenaciously he would fight for the Super, a weapon some did not think technically feasible, and others opposed on political or ethical grounds. This conflict lay behind the titanic struggle, then in its early stages, between Edward Teller and J. Robert Oppenheimer. They were already rubbing each other the wrong way inside the claustrophobic community of Los Alamos. According to Teller, it had begun during a 1942 train trip to California. Oppie had hinted darkly that, after the war, "We will have to do things differently and resist the military." In Teller's account, he was "shocked" by such an unpatriotic hint at what he considered civil disobedience. When Oppenheimer picked another great Los Alamos figure, Hans Bethe, to head Los Alamos's Theoretical Division, Teller took it as a personal rebuff. In fact, for Teller everything was personal. Self-absorbed and moody—his wife, Mici, would sometimes warn the Teller children, "Daddy has black bugs in his head"—he bristled at the need for collaboration and compromise. The Super, the hydrogen or fusion bomb, obsessed Teller. He had realized early on that the atomic bomb would be developed without him and wanted a breakthrough he could call his own. Oppenheimer, focused on building a weapon that would end the war quickly, was not much interested in the Super and had doubts about its feasibility. "God protect us," he famously quipped, "from the enemy without, and the Hungarians within." But he let Teller pursue his quest, deeming it quixotic.

Hans Bethe thought part of the difficulty was that Teller and Oppie were so similar. Both were spurred by burning ambition, both felt themselves superior to others, and, "They were more like artists than scientists." Physicist Freeman Dyson also agreed. "Each of them having achieved his technical objective, wanted more," Dyson told me more than half a century later. "Each of them became convinced that he must have political power to safeguard his creation, to make sure it didn't fall into the wrong hands. In the end, each of them was committed to exercises of the human will in the political as well as the scientific fields." It was probably inevitable that two such ambitious forces of nature would collide—but not in a manner so epic and highly publicized that a half-century later their clash would still be the subject of books, movies, and plays.

Always intense and obsessive, Teller became even more so in Los Alamos. Sometime during the summer of 1944, Oppenheimer summoned a meeting of his top advisers and asked Teller how his work on the Super was proceeding. "I always felt uncomfortable at those gatherings," Teller recalled. "Johnny was in Los Alamos that day, so he also attended. . . . I mentioned that I had found a new difficulty with the original design of the Super . . . but would rather talk about it later. 'No,' Oppie said. 'Talk about it now.'" At that quite reasonable request, Teller stalked out of the room. "Johnny caught my eye on the way out," Teller admitted later, "and raised his eyebrows disapprovingly." It was not the sort of behavior von Neumann would ever indulge in.

※

FOR A decade Capa had shown the world the face of our time: war, which spares no one. He had more than borne witness; he had participated in the cataclysmic events of the century. That seemed enough for one man. Capa was ready to "pack up my war." But the myth had fused with reality. After his spectacular D-Day coverage, he was more than ever "The World's Greatest War Photographer." *Life* gave his story of the liberation of Paris eleven pages. Once again, his images of that historic day provided a definitive record.

After atomic bombs were dropped on Hiroshima and Nagasaki in August, Capa remarked to friends that that was the end of war photography for him. Wars of the future, he said mistakenly, would not be accessible to his kind of close-up photography. But war had defined his entire adult life and he was not sure what to do next. "Maybe it's better not to plan so much," he wrote his family. "It always goes wrong."

Into this indecisive mood stepped perhaps the world's most famous and beautiful movie star. It was on June 6, 1945, one year after D-Day, while Capa and his friend the writer Irwin Shaw were having drinks in the lobby of the Ritz Hotel when Ingrid Bergman walked by. Rather boldly—this was a heady moment to be in Paris—the men sent her a note proposing dinner that very night. To their amazement she accepted. The three dined at Fouquet's, the famous restaurant on the Champs-Elysées. The chemistry between Bergman and Capa was immediate. Bergman was as elated as Capa to be back in Europe. They had much in common. She was not simply the cool Swede who appeared on-screen. Bergman enjoyed his off-color stories and admired Capa's free spirit. "I love your merry mind," he wrote her later. So, *Casablanca*'s incandescent Ilsa fell in love with a Hungarian as glamorous as the fictional Rick, and nearly as famous as Bogart.

They were together in Berlin as she entertained American troops. They walked the rubble-filled streets of the city he had fled twelve years earlier. Sometimes he followed her with his camera. They delighted in each other's company. "Capa found a bathtub in the street," she recalled. "He said this was going to be his scoop; for the first time Ingrid Bergman photographed in a bathtub. I laughed and said OK. And so there I was sitting in a bathtub out in the street, fully clothed."

"He was intensely aware that he had but one short life to live," Bergman wrote in her memoirs, "and that he should not leak it away conforming to a set of standards which did not amuse him." Capa even tried to change Bergman's lifestyle. "You've become an industry," he admonished her, "an institution. You must return to your status as a human being. You've got no time for living." With him, she took the time. "I wanted very much to be with him," she recalled. "He was an adventurous, freedom-loving man. Money didn't mean anything to him, he was terribly generous. Once, in Hyde Park, London, I'll never forget, we passed this old tramp asleep in the grass. And Capa said, 'Let's surprise the old bum when he wakes up by putting a fiver in his hand.' "

Capa followed her to Hollywood, which he hated. He loved Bergman, who was ready to leave her husband, Dr. Aron Petter Lindstrom, for Capa, but he was not ready to give up his freedom, even for Ingrid Bergman. "He told me," she wrote, "I cannot marry you. I cannot tie myself down. If they say 'Korea tomorrow,' and we're married and we have a child, I won't be able to go to Korea. And that's impossible. I'm not the marrying kind." John Morris believes that Capa did not trust himself to keep a commitment. "He was insecure about himself. He didn't trust himself to marry," Morris noted. "But women were madly in love with him." In Capa's mind, according to Morris, Gerda Taro was his only permanent partner.

"He went away," Bergman recalled, "and came back again, he went away, and came back again, but nothing was ever going to change. . . . I understood that."

The Capa-Bergman romance was immortalized by director Alfred Hitchcock, who observed the attraction between his star and the photographer while filming *Notorious* with Bergman. He turned their chemistry and the conflict between a man who loves danger too much to settle down, and a woman who wants him, into one of his most memorable films, *Rear Window*, in which James Stewart plays a *Life* magazine war photographer and Grace Kelly plays an Americanized version of a cool Swedish beauty. In the intense exchange the two have, early in the film, over whether he will ever give up war photography, one can hear the clear echoes of the Capa-Bergman affair.

SHE: Someday you may want to open a studio of your own here . . .

HE: How'd I run it from, say, Pakistan?

SHE: Isn't it time you came home?

HE: Can you see me driving down to fashion salons wearing combat boots and a three-day beard?

SHE: I can see you handsome and successful in a dark blue flannel suit.

HE: Let's stop talking nonsense, shall we?

Their relationship lasted for several years and his effect on her ran deep. "I know the Hungarian influence," she later wrote. "I'll always be grateful for it. I feel sure that it changed much in me." Their romance ended definitively when, in 1949, Ingrid met and, after a notorious affair, married the Italian film director Roberto Rossellini, a man as unconventional and passionate as Capa.

IN SEPTEMBER 1947, Capa was awarded the Medal of Freedom for "exceptional meritorious achievement, which aided the United States in the prosecution of the war against the enemy in Continental Europe from June 6, 1944, to May 8, 1945"—an extraordinary honor for a photographer. On the surface, his life continued to follow the script: skiing with Gene Kelly at Klosters, vacationing with John Huston in Biarritz—and women, always women. He drank too much, though his friends denied he was an alcoholic. "Capa did not drink to get drunk," according to John Morris. "In those days people had two-martini lunches. Hard liquor was part of the male bonding routine. Hemingway's macho man was the ideal." Morris recalled once flying from New York to Chicago with Capa. "He'd had a very long night of drinking and he asked for oxygen. He said it was the best thing for a hangover."

But for all his seeming openness and expansive personality, on subjects near to his heart, he was closed. Just as he never talked about Gerda, he never mentioned his affair with Bergman. Most of his friends learned of it only when Bergman published her memoirs in 1980.

Irwin Shaw, not only a great friend but also a great writer, gave us a vivid description of the complexities of being Robert Capa at this time in his life. "Only in the morning," Shaw wrote in 1947, "as he staggers out of bed does Capa show that the tragedy and sorrow through which he has passed have left their marks on him. His face is gray, his eyes are dull and haunted by the dark dreams of the night; here at last, is the man whose camera has peered at so much death and so much evil, here is a man despairing and in pain, regretful, not stylish, undebonair. Then Capa drinks down a strong bubbling draught, shakes himself, experimentally tries on his afternoon smile, discovers that it works, knows once more that he has the strength to climb the glittering hill of the day, dresses, sets out, nonchalant, carefully lighthearted . . . to the bar of '21' or the Scribe, or the Dorchester, all places where this homeless man can be at home, where he can find his friends and amuse them and where his friends can help him forget the bitter, lonely, friendless hours of the night behind him and the night ahead."

May 22, 1947, saw the birth of Robert Capa's only child: Magnum, the world's first photo cooperative. The place of birth was the members dining room of New York's Museum of Modern Art, and the agency's name honored the bottle of champagne with which the event was toasted. Since the first phase of the Spanish Civil War, Capa had been dreaming about a brotherhood of photographers. "Why be exploited by others?" he asked. "Let's exploit ourselves." Capa's idea that photographers retain ownership of their copyright and negatives was revolutionary. It curbed the power of such media giants as *Time* and *Life*. Magnum would collect and care for the photographer's prints, and guarantee that the photographers were paid each time their photos were used. Persuading the reluctant Cartier-Bresson to be his partner was challenging. But Capa appealed to the aristocratic Frenchman's anticolonialist feelings by proposing Asia as his territory. Cartier-Bresson signed on as a founding partner, along with David Seymour (Chim), and George Rodger. Each partner contributed $400.

Capa groomed the next generation of photographers, future greats such as Marc Riboud and Ernst Haas. In addition to New York, Magnum would have an office in Paris. Maria Eisner, trained in Berlin by Capa's old Hungarian mentor, Simon Guttman, would run it from her apartment. Capa would be Magnum's heart. A man who seemed so reckless at times, even irresponsible, was turning into a forceful manager. "When you do a story," he told Magnum's new recruits, "think of the spirit of all the publications, so that you may then publish your photos everywhere."

He negotiated Magnum contracts with magazines around the world. He came up with big stories. "Capa never ran out of ideas," Magnum photographer Gisele Freund recalled. "One day in October he called us together in the agency's narrow, smoke-filled Paris office. 'With December approaching I suggest a story on Christmas celebrations. John [Morris] will do one in New York, Inge [Morath] in London, Henri [Cartier-Bresson] in Moscow, Gisele in Ecuador, and Chim in Israel.' Capa assumed a paternal role toward Magnum photographers, even gave the women beauty and fashion advice. "He was very supportive of women," Inge Bondi of Magnum's New York office, recalled, "and quick to get the message if his advances were not welcome. He patted me on the fanny once, I responded in kind and he never did it again." Capa told Inge Morath (later Arthur Miller's wife) to buy better clothes, take voice lessons, and shave her arms and legs. "All of which she did," Bondi said, laughing.

Fourteen years after his flight, in 1948, Capa returned to the city where Endre Friedmann was born. But he could not find the Budapest of his memories. A Stalinist puppet, Matyas Rakosi, had brutally eliminated all opposition to the communists. The great boulevards and squares of Capa's neighborhood had been rebaptized Lenin, Stalin, and, most ironically, Freedom Square. Of the elegant string of hotels that had once lined the Danube, only one, the Bristol, remained. The graceful bridges across the Danube had been blown up by the retreating Nazis. Pest's Baroque landmarks had been pulverized by the Allies' bombs. Giant posters of uniformly smiling workers with bulging muscles building a socialist future could not disguise the bomb-scarred buildings. "Budapest," Capa observed sadly, "appeared like a beautiful woman with her teeth knocked out." The new masters, the communists, did not encourage the loitering that had been the city's favorite pastime. Most of the cafés were closed, some replaced by coffee bars where standing customers hurriedly knocked back espressos.

On the once elegant Vaci Street near his old house, Capa found a childhood friend, who had been a furrier before the war. "As only one out of twenty of Hungary's Jews survived the war," Capa wrote, "I was surprised to see that his name was still above the shop and even more surprised to find him alive. His hair was all gone, but he looked the same. Somehow, he was not surprised to see me. He brought out a bottle of Hungarian applejack and we adjourned to the empty shop." Capa, having deliberately avoided photographing the liberation of the camps, now heard the story of the roundup of friends and neighbors, marched to the frozen Danube or sent on death marches to the German frontier. Capa knew that Budapest was no longer his hometown.

THE NEWS from postwar Europe was uniformly depressing. In 1948, Czechoslovak communists, with the support of the Soviet army, carried out a coup that turned Prague into a Soviet satellite. That same year, the Soviets tried to drive the Western Allies out of Berlin by blockading all ground transport to the city. President Truman responded with the successful Berlin Airlift. The Marshall Plan was one year old; NATO was a year away, the Korean War two.

Of the four Budapest scientists, only Szilard saw any reason for optimism. The others feared Stalin as much as they had Hitler, and worried that the West's blindness in the 1930s would be repeated. "Sad to say," Wigner noted, "many [American scientists] seemed quite as blind to [the communists] as were the scientists of 1938 who had blithely ignored the Nazis." It was just a matter of time, the Hungarians felt, before the Soviets recovered sufficiently from the war to challenge American supremacy. Von Neumann, as we have seen, was already contemplating the next war. "I think you will find," he said, "generally speaking among Hungarians, an emotional fear and dislike of Russia. . . . If we are going to risk war while Europe was still a smoldering ruin . . . better to risk it while we have the A-bomb and they don't."

Washington's postwar security plans were based on its exclusive possession of the bomb. Truman did not believe the Soviets were near to achieving a bomb of their own. When Oppenheimer, asked by Truman to predict when the Soviets would have nuclear capacity, avoided a direct answer, Truman answered his own question: "I know. Never!" The joke making the rounds in Washington was that there was no need to fear that the Soviets might surreptitiously slip a suitcase bomb into the United States since they had yet to perfect a suitcase. But in fact these weapons of mass destruction were being developed in great secrecy inside the Soviet Union—and the American intelligence community did not discover them.

Then, on August 29, 1949, as Teller had feared, America's nuclear monopoly ended. Teller and von Neumann were at Los Alamos discussing how to get the still unpopular Super into development when they heard the news. They knew immediately that Stalin's A-bomb would be the biggest gift imaginable in their quest for the Super. The two would play a more important role in the development of the hydrogen bomb than in the birth of the Manhattan Project.

Shortly after hearing the news about the Soviet achievement, Teller called Oppenheimer. "What shall we do? What shall we do?" he asked, excitedly. "Keep your shirt on," Oppie answered coolly. Stunned and furious, Teller left for Washington the next day. The battle lines for an historic confrontation between Oppenheimer and Teller, first glimpsed in their friction in Los Alamos, were becoming clearer and more visible.

Knowing that the political winds were finally behind him, Teller began building a new team to revive the Super project. But this was not the Manhattan Project; without a shooting war, there was no consensus. The new enemy had lately been our wartime ally. Many scientists were exhausted, or conscience-stricken by Hiroshima. The Super was too destructive for most to contemplate. Albert Einstein said he regretted his role in signing the Hungarians' letter to FDR in 1939. When asked what kind of weapons would be used in World War III, he answered he had no idea, but was certain the war after that one would be fought with stones.

When Hans Bethe and Enrico Fermi, two of the most respected scientists in the world, turned down Teller's request to join the Super project, Teller blamed Oppenheimer. In the spring of 1950, Oppenheimer rebuffed Teller once more, saying, "In this matter, I am neutral." Of Oppenheimer's reluctance about the Super, Stanislaw Ulam noted later, "Someone who, having been instrumental in starting a revolution (and the advent of nuclear energy merits this appellation), does not contemplate with pleasure still bigger revolutions to come." But Oppenheimer was not alone. The General Advisory Committee, a committee of scientists and engineers designated to advise the Atomic Energy Commission about scientific and technical issues, also came out against the Super. The universally respected scientist and Harvard University president James B. Conant said the hydrogen bomb would be built "over my dead body."

It was Teller's moment and he fought back. Mobilizing the support of those Los Alamos colleagues, like Ernest Lawrence and Louis Alvarez, who believed in the Super, he brought them to Washington where they now received a friendly reception. Von Neumann also believed America needed to accelerate its weapons programs to stay ahead of Moscow. "With the Russians," he observed, "it is not a question of whether, but when."

With the help of Senator Brien McMahon, chairman of the Joint Committee on Atomic Energy, Teller's group swayed the Joint Chiefs of Staff, who then persuaded the president to press forward with the hydrogen bomb. On January 31, 1950, Truman directed the Atomic Energy Commission to "continue its work on all forms of atomic weapons, including the so-called hydrogen or super-bomb." Oppenheimer, chairing a special panel in December 1950 for the Pentagon on the long-range uses of atomic weapons, continued to raise questions about the Super. Teller, who had told that same panel in March that the country might be in even greater danger than in World War II, felt that Oppenheimer, with his magnetic charm, was the major obstacle between him and the Super.

BUT FOR all his tenacity, Teller's calculations for the Super were wrong on a critical technical point. When Stan Ulam proposed a solution, Teller's ego prevented him from a reasoned examination of Ulam's critique. Only von Neumann could adjudicate between Teller and Ulam. Ulam later acknowledged von Neumann's role: "He hoped one way or another a good scheme would be found, and he never lost heart even when the mathematical results for the original approach were negative." Once convinced by Ulam and the high-level calculations of his own ENIAC computer that Teller's original design was unworkable, von Neumann persuaded Teller that Ulam had indeed solved the problem. One can imagine Johnny and Edward arguing in a mélange of English and Hungarian, technical terms and Budapest argot, until Teller yielded.

In another breakthrough to a thermonuclear design, in January 1951,

Ulam figured out a two-stage process using a fission bomb to provide the energy to set off a fusion stage. The road was thus cleared for the development of the first thermonuclear weapon. Later, sadly, Teller denied Ulam's central role in the breakthrough.

The Super was exploded at Eniwetok atoll, in the South Pacific, on November 1, 1952. One thousand times more powerful than the Hiroshima bomb, incongruously code-named "Mike," the bomb left a crater a half-mile deep and two miles wide. The fireball stretched for three miles. The rift it created within the science community was almost as wide. "Now that you have your H-bomb," Oppenheimer said to Teller sarcastically, "why don't you use it to end the war in Korea?" Offended, Teller stiffly answered, "The use of weapons is none of my business and I will have none of it."

TWO YEARS later, in the spring of 1954, came the event that would forever define Edward Teller in the eyes of many. The confrontation between Teller and Oppenheimer has been dramatized in movies and plays, fictionalized, analyzed, and debated ever since; it remains one of the classic moments of the Cold War. Teller recognized this and spent the rest of his days trying to explain, and sometimes atone for, his action in "the Matter of J. Robert Oppenheimer."

The issue was simple, the stakes enormous: should Oppenheimer's security clearance be continued? On the surface, the answer seemed obvious: Oppenheimer was still a major figure in the development of America's strategic weapons systems, but without a clearance he could not be consulted by the U.S. government on sensitive matters.

The drama began in secret in a run-down government building in April 1954—simultaneous with the highly publicized Army-McCarthy hearings. Even as Senator Joe McCarthy self-destructed on national television, Oppenheimer, his security clearance already suspended by President Dwight D. Eisenhower, was being investigated for a series of charges concerning his loyalty. Eisenhower's priority was to protect his beloved Army against McCarthy. He did not much care about Oppenheimer, and in the words of historian Priscilla J. McMillan, "countenanced a travesty of justice that rankles in the American conscience to this day."

For Edward Teller, the spring of 1954 was an intense and dramatic time. The second American hydrogen bomb—"Bravo"—had been tested in the Pacific, at Bikini atoll. The Russians were continuing tests that were moving toward full thermonuclear capability, as Teller had warned. The French were defeated at Dien Bien Phu by the Vietnamese communists in May. Communist China threatened Taiwan. And Oppenheimer, the embodiment of all Teller's enemies, had become an obsession.

What happened next is so complex that its details lie beyond the scope of this work. But it is reasonable to assume that, without Teller's aggressive, active efforts to destroy his former boss, J. Robert Oppenheimer would have been vindicated and his security clearance restored.

Everything about the hearing was political. Held in private, the venue was as undignified as the temper of the times. Inside the fluorescent glare of a temporary wartime office, the hearings lasted three weeks. Oppenheimer appeared first before the three-man tribunal and testified for twenty hours. Most of his fellow scientists gave him their support, including John von Neumann, who had no great affection for Oppenheimer, but despised what he considered a witch-hunt. Typically, he managed not to alienate either side.

The night before Teller testified, Szilard raced around Washington trying to find his old friend and talk him out of appearing. He failed because the prosecution had sequestered Teller, leaving Szilard to complain to Trude Weiss, "If Teller attacks Oppenheimer, I will have to defend Oppenheimer for the rest of my life."

Teller's testimony was dramatic and its consequences irretrievable. As early as 1950 he had told investigators privately that it was common knowledge that Oppenheimer was far to the left. Now, he was prepared to go further. Working closely with Atomic Energy commissioner Lewis Strauss, Teller prepared a frontal assault.

"I think it would be presumptuous," he told the tribunal, "and wrong on my part if I would try to analyze his motives. . . . I would feel personally more secure if public matters would rest in other hands." The head of the panel, former secretary of the army and special assistant to the president Gordon Gray, asked Teller if national security would be at risk if Oppenheimer regained his security clearance. Teller's answer was a nail in Oppenheimer's coffin, but ultimately in his own as well. While

Oppenheimer would not "knowingly and willingly" endanger the nation, Teller said, "if it is a question of wisdom and judgment, as demonstrated by actions since 1945, then I would say one would be wiser not to grant clearance."

With Teller's slippery but devastating testimony ringing in their ears, Gordon Gray's special panel voted 2–1 against reinstating Oppenheimer's security clearance, with Gray casting the deciding vote. Oppenheimer's public career, one of the greatest in American scientific history, was over. Oppenheimer, who continued as head of the Institute for Advanced Study, was regarded as a victim of an unfair, McCarthy-style plot and vindicated and honored before his death in 1964. But Teller's victory over his adversary, ironically, began what he would call his third exile—an estrangement from the scientific community he cared most about. Thus began the most painful period of his life.

Shortly after the hearings, Teller got a glimpse of his own future. Spotting two old friends, Robert Christy and I. I. Rabi, across a crowded dining room at Los Alamos, he extended a hand. Rabi and Christy did not raise theirs. Shattered, Teller and his loyal, long-suffering wife left Los Alamos the next day. "Twice before," he wrote later, "I had been forced to relinquish the familiar—first my homeland, then Germany, a country where I could speak my second language and was familiar with the culture; and then even the continent of my birth. In my new land everything had been unfamiliar except for the community of theoretical physicists. . . . Now at forty-seven I was again forced into exile." Teller felt rejected by those he most admired. "Apart from my closest family," Teller remembered, "I had absolutely no one except the scientists. . . . I was a criminal, I was worse than isolated." When a reporter asked Teller later how he wished to be remembered, he answered bitterly, "I do not wish to be remembered."

The Hungarians stayed by his side. Leo Szilard, despite their vast political differences, remained in touch. Wigner refused to criticize his controversial friend. "But those friends were far away," Teller noted, "and many others who knew me less well—or not at all—saw me as a villain."

"Edward had been very foolish," his friend, future defense secretary Harold Brown, recalled fifty years later. "He was motivated by a combination of personal animosity and conviction. He really felt that Oppie was wrong, and that it was important to remove him from political influence.

Though Edward never said this in public, he felt there was a 10 percent chance that Oppie was a Soviet spy. His circumstances were sufficient to raise suspicion: his wife, his girlfriend, his close friends were all communists. But I think the commies may have thought of Oppie as too high a risk. A retired KGB general told me much later a decision had been made not to approach him because they knew he would be closely watched."

🎴

IN THE 1950s, as Stalin continued to order the Soviet satellites to stage their own versions of the Moscow purges and show trials, an old communist colleague of Arthur Koestler, Otto Katz, was hauled before a Prague court. Katz, famous for his *bon mot* to Koestler, "We all have inferiority complexes, but yours is a cathedral," was forced to confess his "betrayal" of the Party. "I . . . belong to the gallows," Katz told the Prague court. "The only service I can still render is to serve as a warning example to all who by origin or character are in danger of following the same path to hell . . . the sterner the punishment . . ." whereupon Katz's voice trailed off. Once again, as with Laszlo Rajk, his confession mirrored Rubashov's final "service to the Party" speech. So close were Katz's words to Rubashov's that Koestler read it as a plea to the outside world for help.

But where Katz had been able to mount a public protest against Koestler's Spanish death sentence, Koestler could do nothing for his old comrade. "Not one voice was raised," he bitterly noted, "among the editors, journalists . . . hostesses and film stars who had swarmed round Otto in the romantic, pink days of the 'People's Front.' His last message was like a scribbled S.O.S. in a bottle washed ashore by the sea, and left to bob among the driftwood, unnoticed by the world."

The grotesque pageant of show trials in Prague, Budapest, and other satellite capitals finally swayed many of those who still held out hope for the Soviet Union. They were further vindication of Koestler's prophetic warning in *Darkness at Noon*.

Koestler had had his fill of politics. "When I finished my piece for *The God That Failed* [an anthology by six ex-communist intellectuals, including Ignazio Silone, André Gide, Louis Fischer, and Stephen Spender], I had at last done with writing on political subjects for the rest of my life." He turned to an earlier love, natural science. Though he became a British subject in 1948, and bought a house on one of London's beautiful squares, Koestler felt himself forever "a stranger on the square." For one thing, he was deeply self-conscious about "the torture of my accent." Once, when he asked his friend George Mikes to make a restaurant reservation for him, Mikes asked Koestler why he didn't pick up the phone himself. "What sort of table," Koestler asked, "would we get if I rang up with my accent?"

Still restless, Koestler tried life in America. In the early 1950s, he bought a farm on an island in the Delaware River. Working on his memoirs, he often received John von Neumann, who lived in nearby Princeton. The two products of Budapest's Golden Age reveled in each other's company and intellects, speaking a mixture of Hungarian and accented English. Though they had not known each other before, now they roamed across their common intellectual universe. "Listening to [von Neumann] and Arthur talking," Koestler's third wife, Cynthia, remembered, "I realized with surprise that I had understood next to nothing of a conversation which had lasted all evening in my native tongue."

Historian Arthur M. Schlesinger, Jr., was struck by Koestler's parting comment to a fellow guest, an Italian antifascist who had also been incarcerated during the war, at the end of a cheerful dinner party. "See you in the concentration camp." Koestler made a similar fatalistic reference in a letter to Eva Striker, now a successful ceramicist in New York. "Who would have thought," Koestler wrote her at Christmas 1954, "that we would survive it?"

He could not settle down in America. "Five times a day I am telling myself," he told Schlesinger, "that this is the country where I want to be forever, and five times a day that I would rather be dead than live here." Life in London makes me very happy, he wrote a friend, "and New York makes me very unhappy. I guess I'm just a hopeless European."

In the spring of 1952 he returned to London. "London was only a stone's throw from the continent of Europe, and with my Austro-Hungarian, Franco-British background, I felt foremost a European."

Koestler's interests may have shifted from politics, but his drive and discipline were as relentless as before. "His regime," Elizabeth Jane Howard, a British novelist whom he had romanced, recalled, "was to write all morning . . . people came to see him from all over the world. He adored parties and going out to dine with friends." And women. Always a vain man, Koestler basked in the attention of women drawn by his burning intensity. Compensating for his short stature with electric energy, with his high, intelligent forehead; shock of thick, now graying hair; and, above all, the history he embodied, in late middle age he was still magnetic. As with other passions, with women, too, he sometimes went too far. "Arthur," Martha Gellhorn commanded, loud enough for all the guests at a 1961 London dinner party to hear, "take your hand off my leg."

I N MAY 1948, Arthur Koestler and Robert Capa found a story that excited them: the birth of the state of Israel. Capa and Koestler, though they knew each other only casually, felt equally devastated by the wreckage of Jewish lives in Budapest. Though Koestler's mother, Adele, survived the Arrow Cross terror, she spent the final months of the war in the Budapest ghetto, where thousands died of cold, hunger, and disease. After so much death, now, in Israel, Capa and Koestler could celebrate a birth, and a Jewish one.

On a bright spring day in 1948, driving down the Mediterranean coast to Tel Aviv, Koestler encountered a scene that reminded him of the heady early days of the Spanish Civil War. "The road was teeming with trucks and requisitioned passenger buses packed with singing soldiers," he wrote, "in the open trucks they all stand upright holding on to each other; in the buses they sit on each other's knees with elbows sticking out of the windows and their fists banging the rhythm of the song on the tin plating."

At midnight on May 14, Capa was in Tel Aviv, photographing David Ben-Gurion as he declared the creation of the first Jewish state in nearly two thousand years. But war—not birth—seemed to be Robert Capa's companion. Already random gunfire in the distance punctuated the wail of British regimental bagpipes sounding retreat. The armies of Egypt, Lebanon, Transjordan, Syria, and Saudi Arabia were poised on the new nation's borders. Like the Spanish Civil War, this was a war Capa could believe in, with men and women fighting with the fury of a last stand.

At the shabby seafront Hotel Armon in Tel Aviv, he found his old battlefield companion from Spain, Martha Gellhorn. Divorced from Ernest Hemingway, Gellhorn and Capa, two secular Jews, rejoiced at Israel's birth. For the first time in his life, Capa was in the company of Jews who did not need to camouflage that fact. Everywhere he turned he saw familiar features, expressions, gestures as each day brought more Eastern European survivors of the Holocaust.

Capa stayed long enough to photograph Israel's victory over six Arab armies. By the time civil war threatened to erupt between extremists insisting on an Israel of biblical proportions, and moderate Jews prepared to negotiate land for peace—Capa had packed up. But he had an emotional stake in the region's most unwanted state—and kept coming back. For a while he even contemplated settling in Israel. "Here I am in the Homeland," he began a letter to his mother in 1950. He had so fused into the persona of his invention that even to his mother he now signed his letters, "Capa."

Strolling down the Champs-Elysées with his camel-hair coat flung over his shoulders, a cigarette glued to his lower lip, a beautiful girl on his arm, the Robert Capa of the early 1950s could be mistaken for a playboy. Every celebrity wanted to be photographed by Capa. Decades later, *Washington Post* editor Ben Bradlee recalled a night at the Klosters chalet, Chesa Grischuna. "Our friend Noel Howard appeared with this enchanting woman—almost a child, maybe sixteen. All of us—Irwin Shaw, Peter Viertel, and I—were spellbound. And Capa, of course. But Capa did something about it. He followed her back to Paris, and the next day came back to Klosters with her. He was something," Bradlee said, marveling at the memory. As reckless with other people's property and money as he was with his own, Capa was nearly always broke from high living and gambling debts. At times he dipped into Magnum's till to stay afloat.

To old friends like Eva Besnyo he seemed a lost soul. The woman who had introduced him to photography in Berlin and had consoled him after Gerda's death found she had little in common with this Capa. She thought her old friend luxuriated far too much in his glamorous life. "I visited him in Paris in the early 1950s," she recalled. "Instead of a quiet dinner he took me along to a noisy party. It was a wasted evening for me. I found him very superficial, very much taken up by this life of quick pleasure."

After six years, Capa was bored running Magnum. He flirted with a new career in television and movies, but nothing came of it. "Well, boys," Capa began a New York meeting of Magnum's partners in January 1953, "from now on take your problems to him!" he said, pointing at John Morris, newly named international executive editor of the agency.

Cold War paranoia was Capa's new enemy. In the treacherous McCarthyist climate, his passionate advocacy of the Spanish Republic in the 1930s raised new suspicions. The war that launched Robert Capa the legend now threatened him. In 1953, the State Department revoked the passport of a man who had been awarded the Medal of Freedom, and charged him with having once belonged to the Communist Party. His time covering the left-wing Lincoln Brigade—American volunteers who fought the fascists under the aegis of the Communist International—was at the core of the indictment against him. The anxiety, common to the Budapest generation, stateless and defenseless, returned to haunt Capa, a proud recent American citizen. In an attempt to get his passport back, Capa wrote the State Department a seven-page typed letter. "I have never, in my entire life, in any country where I have ever been, or under any name under which I have been known or any other name, held a card of the Communist Party. . . . I was never with them," he wrote, referring to the Lincoln Brigade, "and as I spoke hardly any English at that time, even the hotel encounters were short and not personal."

Also under investigation was Capa's postwar assignment to the Soviet Union with the novelist John Steinbeck. "During our entire stay in that country we were together every hour of the day, and we even lived in the same room. We had no political meetings with any organizations or persons. On any occasion we were asked about our feeling toward the policy of the United States Government . . . we would refuse to criticize it outside of the United States."

It was an ugly time, a reminder that for all his celebrity, Capa, like Robert Oppenheimer, was still vulnerable. "Hitler, Dollfuss [Engelbert Dollfuss, Austrian chancellor, assassinated by the Nazis in 1934], Paris riots, Spain, China, Normandy," Capa's brother Cornell, since 1946 a New York–based *Life* staff photographer, wrote to him on March 21, 1953, "and the Inquisition 1953 style. . . . You just couldn't miss."

For the first time, the photographer, now forty, had serious medical problems. In May, he slipped a disk while carrying too much equipment. Neither codeine, nor traction, nor liquor took the edge off. "That back of mine," he wrote John Morris in June 1953, "continues to hurt and the third professor [to examine him] found that I had a displaced disk in my vertebrae which inflamed the so-called sciatic nerve and the pain was and is unbearable. . . . This has been definitely the black year."

"Photography is finished," Capa told Marc Riboud, "the future is television." But what else could the World's Greatest War Photographer do? Wars provided work and income. He needed both. He was in debt to Magnum for his medical bills. When an assignment from the Tokyo publisher Mainichi Press came in 1954, it seemed a godsend. A new country, a new challenge. "I am very pleased to be off for two months," he wrote Morris, "and it also will be good for everybody if I am unreachable and not hovering around."

Japan turned into a "photographer's paradise" for Capa. He was greeted like a conquering hero in a photography-mad nation. Snapping children and Buddhist temples, he was having fun with his camera for the first time in years.

But war had a way of finding Capa. The French struggle to hold on to its colonies in Indochina was too close to ignore. *Life* was looking for someone to fill in for its resident photographer, Howard Sochurek, who was going on leave. "See Capa [in Tokyo]," *Life's* managing editor instructed. "He may cover Indo-China while you're gone." For the cash-strapped Capa, the offer was seductive: $2,000 a month and a life insurance policy. "Price subject to considerable upraising," Morris wired Capa in late April, "if becomes hazardous."

Capa did not need persuading. He already had an idea for a story called "Bitter Rice," contrasting the life of Vietnamese peasants along the paddy fields of the Red River delta with that of the French army. Morris had second thoughts and called Capa. "Bob, you don't have to do this," he cautioned. "It's not our war." But Capa had made up his mind. "I didn't take the job from a sense of duty," he wrote from Tokyo in his final letter to Morris on May 1, 1954, "but with real great pleasure. Shooting for me at this moment is much fun and . . . shooting on a very complicated subject down my alley even more so. . . . I am off and will be back here in four weeks and mid-June in Paris if lots of irresistible offers are not stopping me."

In mid-May 1954, after three days in Hanoi, Capa flew to northern Laos to cover the evacuation of the French wounded after their utter defeat in the battle of Dien Bien Phu. It was the turning point in the war. But General René Cogny, the tall, rangy French commander, fought on, even as the French negotiators in Geneva were in the process of agreeing to a settlement that ended the French colonial empire in Southeast Asia. Capa and Cogny hit it off and traveled together to the Red River delta.

"This is going to be a beautiful story," Capa commented, as he set off on May 25, 1954, with two reporters and one of Cogny's senior officers. "I will be on my good behavior today," he promised his companions. "I will not insult my colleagues and not once mention the excellence of my work." The sun was hot, he had a flask of cognac and good company. He was a legend and was treated as such by commanders and fellow journalists. He was back where he wanted to be: at a place of opportunity and danger.

They joined a convoy of French army tanks and jeeps on a mission to evacuate and demolish two forts on the road from Nam Dinh to Thai Binh. If the North Vietnamese communist forces under General Vo Nguyen Giap attacked again, Cogny wanted to avert a Dien Bien Phu–style disaster.

Capa, pursuing his "Bitter Rice" story, photographed peasants plowing rice paddies using water buffalo. The French fired their mortars, tanks, and artillery into Vietminh positions as they made their way. For a man so adept at calculating risk, who had seen so much fire, this seemed like an easy, picturesque war.

By 2:50 in the afternoon, under a fierce sun, Capa was bored. "I'm going up the road a little bit," he told his companions, jumping off the jeep. "Look for me when you get started again." Capa left the dirt road to photograph soldiers advancing through waist-high grass against a darkening horizon. The last photograph of him shows Capa in battle fatigues and combat boots, confidently striding forward, his Contax camera dangling from his neck.

Ten minutes later, the convoy was rocked by an explosion. A Vietnamese soldier ran up to the convoy. "Le photographe est mort," he shouted. Time-Life reporter John Mecklin turned to his colleague Jim Lucas. "This guy is trying to tell us Capa is dead," he said. A second soldier ran up and said, "Maybe not dead, but wounded by mortar. Très grave." The two journalists raced to the field where Capa lay. His left leg had been blown to pieces by a land mine. With his left hand he clutched his camera. He had a grievous chest wound. Mecklin called his name. His lips moved slightly, "like those of a man disturbed in sleep." Mecklin recorded his death at 3:10 P.M. Robert Capa had achieved one final first: he was the first American journalist killed in Vietnam.

A LEXANDER KORDA had one great film left in him. Though he did not direct it, *The Third Man* (1949) is his summa. For some time, Korda had been searching for a way to tell the story of the moral devastation left by the war where it had started, in Central Europe. The fighting was over, Hitler a suicide, and many of his henchmen sat in the Nuremberg dock. Auschwitz and Dachau had at last revealed the scale of the barbarity. What of the survivors? Did the rubble of Berlin, Budapest, and Vienna signify the end of civilization? Korda could not return to Budapest—now under communist rule—but Vienna had experienced the same convulsions as Budapest. A short journey up the Danube, Vienna was almost Budapest.

The friendship and mutual respect between Korda and Graham Greene and director Carol Reed was at the heart of *The Third Man*. "Korda over the dinner table," Greene recalled, "wanted a story written with the background of an occupied city. Berlin? Vienna? Vienna would be a more agreeable city to live in—he recommended Vienna and Sacher's cake." Write a film, Korda urged Greene, about postwar Vienna, under the Four-Power Occupation. The Americans, the British, the French, and the Russians each administered their own sections of the city—a microcosm of the Cold War. Vienna, on the edge of the Soviet East, but desperate to stay in the West, was a perfect laboratory for Europe in twilight.

The most memorable figure in *The Third Man* is, of course, Harry Lime, unforgettably played by Orson Welles. Graham Greene, who knew Korda well, put many of Alex's traits into the character. Harry Lime is, like Alex, a manipulative, magnetic rogue. Unlike Alex, Lime is also cold-blooded. When Lime admonishes his naive American friend, Holly Martins (Joseph Cotten), "The world doesn't make heroes, old man," we are hearing pure Korda. Like Korda, Lime "could fix anything," says Martins. "He fixed my papers for me," Lime's battered lover adds. The look of the film captures postwar Europe: shadowy figures appear and recede into dark passages, pushing wheelbarrows containing their belongings. The Baroque palaces of a vanished civilization are barely visible.

The Third Man, according to film historian Jeanine Basinger, is a postwar bookend to *Casablanca*. As with *Casablanca*, the film is more about atmosphere than a convoluted, implausible plot. Pulp fiction writer Martins joins a chase for Lime, who has been profiteering in toxic penicillin on Vienna's black market. *The Third Man* has no heroes, no idealists, no one willing to pay a price for a noble goal, no love or sacrifice for a cause. Instead of "As Time Goes By," the haunting sound of the zither, the first single-instrument movie score, underscores the despair. Love does not triumph. The film ends with Harry Lime's lover walking past the good-hearted American, who has risked everything for her, without even acknowledging him. Like Korda, she prefers danger to secure boredom.

Korda had traveled far from the witty repartee and lavish sets of *Henry VIII* and *That Hamilton Woman*. Light touches are absent from *The Third Man*. Because Harry Lime is such a captivating villain, *The Third Man* is good entertainment. Lime's most famous lines, though reportedly crafted by Welles himself, were—according to Korda's nephew Michael—pure Korda. "In Italy for thirty years under the Borgias," Lime/Welles says to Martins as they sit at the top of the Prater's Ferris wheel, "they had warfare, terror, murder, bloodshed. They produced Michelangelo, Leonardo, and the Renaissance. In Switzerland, they had brotherly love, five hundred years of democracy, and they produced the cuckoo clock."

The Third Man was produced with Hollywood's financial support but without Hollywood's imprint. Korda was clever enough to keep his co-producer, David Selznick, at arm's length. Selznick had a different movie in mind. He wanted Robert Mitchum, Cary Grant, or David Niven—not Orson Welles—for the role of Lime. But Korda was determined and sent his brother Vincent and nephew Michael on a comic wild-goose chase to locate and literally capture Welles in Italy. Selznick hated the title and preferred *Night in Vienna*. He edited about ten minutes out of the American version. And, true to his Hollywood roots, Selznick abhorred the moral ambiguity and general darkness of *The Third Man*. Yet it is precisely those qualities that still make it compelling decades later. The public understood it, even if Hollywood did not. *The Third Man* was a big hit and made David Selznick a great deal of money. Its success was vindication for Korda. In a stroke he was reestablished as a leader in the British film industry.

BUT KORDA seemed incapable of enjoying life for more than brief intervals. "Sometimes," he said, "I think of retiring but then I go to my desk again and know I cannot. . . . When you have been on the treadmill as long as I have it goes faster and faster and it is not possible to step off." With age and distance from his roots and the brothers he could not keep near, his loneliness deepened.

"Alex was so lonely in his suite at Claridge's," his mistress Christine Norden remembered. Drawn as much as ever to glamour and youth, Korda was destined to be alone. "I loved Alex with all my heart," Norden wrote in her memoirs, "but I was not in love with him. . . . [Alex] told me of a dream he had very often: I was dancing for him on a very lonely beach in white chiffon. We were both laughing and singing Hungarian songs. I would drift further and further away from him, until I seemed to be dancing on the ocean, out out out until I finally danced out of sight. He would wake up in a cold sweat of terror." When Christine, three decades Korda's junior, married a younger man, Korda was once again alone.

In November 1955, his doctors informed the sixty-two-year-old Korda that his heart was growing weaker; he had but months to live. Married again to a much younger woman, Alexa Boycun, he was still often alone. He summoned British journalist David Lewin for a final interview. He offered a summary of his philosophy—unchanged since his first glimpse of the carnival of Budapest's Ring Road. "We are in show business," he said, "and we come from the fairground and the fairground barker. The barkers may have worn checked coats and crude colors," Korda said, perhaps alluding to Ferenc Molnar's Budapest barker, Liliom, "while we are more elegant. But never forget that we are the same. We are in show business—and we should make a good show."

The night before Korda was to be hospitalized for the last time, Lewin asked if he might sneak into the hospital for a final interview. "Don't you know how to get into a hospital?" Alex challenged the Englishman. "You simply phone the props department at Shepperton [Studios] and you ask them for a white coat with a clipboard and a white hat. Then you come and you wear this and they do not stop you. Just ask for Alex Korda and they will show you." Korda's final scheme failed. He died the next day of a massive heart attack.

LIGHT SNOW slicked the steps of St. Martin-in-the-Fields, on Tuesday, January 31, 1956. The choice of the much loved church on Trafalgar Square, in the shadow of Lord Nelson's column, was fitting for Alexander Korda's final performance. One by one, the great icons he had burnished mounted the steps. Laurence Olivier, Ralph Richardson, Vivien Leigh, Charlie Chaplin, Claire Bloom, and scores of others gathered to celebrate the life of one of the age's great showmen. It was, as Alex would have noted, a full house. The greatest actor of the English-speaking world eulogized the man born sixty-three years earlier on the Great Plain of Hungary. "He managed the difficult and rare mixture of artist and businessman with an extraordinary virtuosity," Laurence Olivier said of Korda. "Though he never really mastered the English language, he improved it. . . . We loved him as actors and craftsmen because he loved us, and loved our problems, too. . . . With a backward eye perhaps, to those beginnings from which he became such an international figure, he relished what life had to offer and lived it in a beautiful and enviable style. . . . When his back was against the wall, he was quite magnificent." Olivier closed with a line from *Hamlet*. "Take him for all in all—we shall not look upon his like again."

Korda would have most appreciated Graham Greene's remembrance. "With the death of Korda, fun has gone out of the film industry—yes, one begins to think of it again as just an industry. So long as he was alive the unexpected might always happen—a chance word at the dinner table and a week later it was quite possible that one might wake up in Hong Kong. . . . He has no successor, no one with whom it is possible *not* to talk about films . . . but about painting, poetry, music, anything in the world rather than that 'industry.' "

The barker's gift of drawing a crowd to the spectacle, combined with a passion for history and literature—that was Korda's legacy. He showed the bottom-line moguls that—with the right blend of the high and the low— they could turn history into big box office. From the cafés and cabarets of Budapest, he had carried those lessons to Berlin, Hollywood, and finally London. In an age starved for illusions, none surpassed Alexander Korda's "best show": his life.

※

IN THE CORRIDORS of the Institute for Advanced Study in the 1950s—which he shared with its director, J. Robert Oppenheimer, and with Albert Einstein, until Einstein's death in April 1955—John von Neumann was called "The Great Man." High tea at the institute, held in Fine Hall between three and four, with faculty wives in white gloves pouring tea from antique silver pots, had a special charge when von Neumann appeared. More accessible than the enigmatic Oppenheimer, von Neumann was the inspiration and role model for many of the next generation of mathematicians.

One of the most famous was John Nash, the eccentric future Nobel laureate who was celebrated in the film *A Beautiful Mind*, which won the Oscar for Best Picture in 2002, based on Sylvia Nasar's award-winning book of the same name. Like everyone else at Princeton, Nash observed von Neumann at the institute, and he dreamed of a career as ground-breaking and a life as glamorous as his. Nash idolized von Neumann, but their early relationship was marred by an unfortunate incident. In October of 1949, the brilliant young mathematician "cockily" demanded to see von Neumann to discuss a new theory he had. According to Nasar, von Neumann, seated behind an enormous desk, looked "more like a prosperous banker than an academic in his expensive three-piece suit, silk tie, and jaunty pocket handkerchief." Nash, who was on the verge of making historic contributions of his own to Game Theory, told von Neumann about a proof he felt he had discovered for equilibrium in games of more than two players. But von Neumann interrupted him, "jumped ahead to the yet unstated conclusion of Nash's argument, and said abruptly, 'That's trivial, you know. That's just a fixed point theorem.' "

Perhaps, as Nasar believes, the clash between these two geniuses was almost inevitable, given their vastly different backgrounds and styles: von

Neumann, "who had come of age in European café discussions" and was socially adept; Nash, already showing signs of his future insanity, seeing people "as out of touch with one another and acting on their own." Whatever the reasons, Nash never contacted von Neumann again, and began to pursue his own lines of investigation and theory. It was a shame, for science and for both men, that they did not work together; who knows what that intersection of wholly different kinds of genius might have produced? And how both fitting and ironic that the first mathematical prize ever awarded to John Nash, in 1978, was the John von Neumann Theory Prize, from the Operations Research Society. (Nash, then in the deepest throes of madness, could not accept the award himself; he was sitting in a corner of his Princeton office, according to an eye witness, "functioning at the sub-adolescent level.")

EVERYONE at the institute had a von Neumann story—usually about his astounding memory. The favorite ones had to do with von Neumann's beating computers in feats of calculation. To Johnny's old friends from Budapest, who recalled that at six he could divide two eight-digit numbers in his head, there was nothing astounding about Johnny beating a machine. The joke about von Neumann being an extraterrestrial imitation of a human was a favorite in the institute tearoom. "It all came so easily for him," Herman Goldstine mused, "and he was so far ahead of everyone else that he was like Mozart."

He was already the acknowledged midwife of the computer. For von Neumann, that was not enough. Elected to the General Advisory Committee of the Atomic Energy Commission in 1954, he joined the world's most influential policy-makers. He was a consultant to nearly two dozen government and industrial organizations. His devotion to reason, born in the optimism of his Budapest childhood, found its clearest expression in Game Theory. The notion that you could reduce human conduct to a rational scheme, mathematically predicting how adversaries would react across a poker table or on a battlefield, is pure von Neumann and would influence American military and strategic thinking for the next half-century and more, finally winning a Nobel Prize for one of von Neumann's descendants, Thomas C. Schelling, in 2005.

By the 1950s, Game Theory formed the basis for Washington's nuclear war planning. At the Air Force's Los Angeles think tank, the RAND Corporation, von Neumann shepherded the development of the nation's defense policies. The culmination of his Game Theory was the balance-of-terror strategy known as MAD—mutual assured destruction. In fact, the American military still relies on Game Theory for choosing targets for maximum destructiveness, while simultaneously deterring the enemy's capacity to respond. Game Theory reduces human behavior to mathematical formulae. Whether millions of people would actually behave according to von Neumann's theory, once irradiated by nuclear weapons, has fortunately never been tested. But Game Theory remains the intellectual underpinning of the United States' nuclear strike plan.

Von Neumann's fellow scientist, Norbert Wiener, the father of cybernetics, rejected the Hungarian's primary assumption of the player as a completely intelligent, completely ruthless person. No man, Wiener maintained, is either all fool or all knave.

"MY FIRST inkling that my father was ill," Marina von Neumann Whitman recalled, "was when he started sleeping seven to eight hours a night. It was shortly after a spontaneous shoulder fracture in the summer of 1955." Bone cancer was diagnosed in August. He was only fifty-three and full of plans. He and his co-author of *The Theory of Games and Economic Behavior*, economist Oskar Morgenstern, were planning to start a mathematics consulting firm. Von Neumann dreamed of moving to the West, whose wide-open spaces deeply appealed to him.

Some of his colleagues thought his cancer was occupational. He was always interested in lab work, and scientists liked to show him what they were working on, because he always understood. Great care was taken against radiation from explosions, but fewer precautions were taken in labs. Most people simply could not believe that this man, so much faster, brighter, deeper, and livelier than anyone else, was dying.

For a while he continued to lead his hyperactive life, telling almost no one about his condition. Stan Ulam first suspected something during a visit to Los Alamos in 1956. "There was a sadness in him," Ulam remembered. "He frequently seemed to look around, as if, it occurred to me later, he might have been thinking that this was perhaps his last visit and he wanted to remember the scenery, the mountains, the places he knew so well where he had so often had interesting and pleasant times. . . . Watching him through the window I definitely had the feeling that somber and melancholy thoughts were in his head."

Within months, he was walking with a cane. Then, wheelchair-bound, he continued to dominate meetings with his wit and brilliance. As he weakened, meetings were held in his Georgetown home, then at the Walter Reed Hospital, where he occupied the VIP wing reserved for high government officials. At one point during his hospitalization, President Eisenhower, a recent heart attack victim, occupied the suite opposite von Neumann. The Hungarian was almost as heavily guarded as the president. He stayed in the game until the very last. "The brass came to talk to him when he was still entirely lucid," his daughter recalled, "before the disease appeared to affect his mind. They came not out of sentiment but because they wanted to continue to get his input on technical and policy issues, as they had been doing for a long time prior to his illness."

In January 1956, in a wheelchair, von Neumann received the Medal of Freedom from President Eisenhower. "I wish I could be around long enough to deserve this honor," he told the president. Von Neumann did not accept the loss of his mental faculties without a terrible struggle. Teller recalled "visiting him when he was dying, and he would try to argue with me as he always had. But he couldn't anymore. His brain wasn't functioning. I think he suffered more from this loss than I've ever seen any other human being suffer."

"When he was trying to finish his final paper," his daughter remembered poignantly, "he would ask me to test him on simple math problems, such as 4 plus 7. Doing this with John von Neumann was more than I could handle emotionally. I fled the room in tears."

A lifelong agnostic, von Neumann now sought solace in religion. "Dad was not a self-analytical person until he was desperately ill," his daughter noted. "He summoned first a Benedictine monk, then a Jesuit priest." But nothing, not his astonishing legacy, not the presence in his hospital room of the powerful, nothing brought him peace. "He was terrified of dying," his daughter remembered, "and of losing that for which he was best known, his brain."

Lewis Strauss recalled a meeting at Walter Reed Hospital in April 1956. "Gathered around his bedside and attentive to his last words of advice and wisdom were the secretary of defense and his deputies, the secretaries of the army, navy and air force, and all the military chiefs of staff."

Outside his hospital room an Air Force colonel and orderlies with top secret clearance stood vigil. Security officials were concerned that in his hal-
lucinations he might reveal sensitive information, but they need not have
worried; von Neumann hallucinated in Hungarian.

On February 8, 1957, the trustees of the Institute for Advanced Study
received the following telegram: "With deep regret must tell you of the
death after cruel illness of John von Neumann, long Professor at the Institute." It was signed, "J. Robert Oppenheimer."

"He darted briefly into our domain," economist Paul Samuelson noted,
"and it has never been the same since."

✦

I N 1963, the quietest and most modest of the four Budapest scientists
won the Nobel Prize for physics. Eugene Wigner was cited "for systematically improving and extending the methods of quantum
mechanics and applying them widely." Typically, he protested.
"Einstein, Max Planck, Max von Laue," he wrote, "these were men who
had clearly earned the Nobel. . . . Nobel did not sponsor a mathematics
prize so I was not really surprised that von Neumann had never won. But
I felt that Teller and Oppenheimer should have won the Nobel before I
did."

Wigner hoped he had won for his science, not his contribution to the
political history of the previous quarter-century. Indeed, Wigner's role
in the drafting of the Einstein letter to President Roosevelt and in agitat-
ing for the Manhattan Project could not have escaped the attention of
the Nobel committee, but the prize was also belated recognition of
Wigner's leadership of theoretical studies at the Met Lab in Chicago, and
his contribution to creating a nuclear pile for the production of plutonium.

Wigner was never fully honored by the country of his birth in his lifetime. But in his Nobel acceptance speech he credited the city with ignit-
ing his love of science and learning, and spoke movingly of Johnny von
Neumann. Some years later, looking back with nostalgia on those faraway
days, he said, "After sixty years in the United States, I am still more Hungarian than American. . . . Simple Hungarian poems and songs that I

learned before 1910 still come to me unbidden. . . . I begin thinking in Hungarian and cannot find my English again." Wigner saw a blessing in old age and the failure of memory. "I am amazed," he wrote, "that sometimes even the name Adolf Hitler escapes me."

Eugene Wigner died as he had lived, quietly in Princeton on January 1, 1995, at ninety-three.

※

AFTER HIS trio of immortal films—*Casablanca, Yankee Doodle Dandy,* and *Mildred Pierce*—Michael Curtiz seemed at the top of his profession. But the business was changing around him. By the 1950s, Curtiz was no longer one of Hollywood's money directors. The combination of talent, luck, and determination that propelled him in prior decades was no longer enough. Curtiz was a creature of the studio system, which was beginning to wobble. Directors with more of a signature style were emerging in what was called *cinéma des auteurs.* And the excitement surrounded the new medium of television, which did not interest Curtiz.

In 1950, Curtiz turned Ernest Hemingway's novel *To Have and Have Not* into *The Breaking Point.* In many ways, it is Curtiz's most mature film. Stripped of his usual visual pyrotechnics, *The Breaking Point* captures both the pathos and the cynicism of Hemingway's story of a man alone, a gunrunner (John Garfield) who decides to get involved in a crime because he has nothing left to lose. The hero is a man in decline, who cannot find his place in the postwar world. "Ever since I took that uniform off," the Garfield character laments, "the world hasn't been so great."

For once, Curtiz's subject was not success in the land of opportunity, but failure. A man fights temptation but is defeated. As always, Curtiz powerfully evokes mood and atmosphere, in this case a squalid California fishing town. In the memorable closing scene, his camera reveals a small black child, whose father has been shot, left alone, as the crowd gradually thins.

The *New York Times* heaped praise on Curtiz for his film's "beautifully crisp, commanding style." Other reviews noted Curtiz's "pizzicato direction, which has color, violence, and suspense." But *The Breaking Point* was released without the usual Warner Brothers fanfare, and quickly vanished from theaters and memory. Six years earlier, Howard Hawks had directed the same Hemingway story as a star vehicle for Bogart and Lauren Bacall. By any measure, except its legendary stars, Hawks's *To Have and Have Not* is a much less distinguished film. But Warners was no longer interested in promoting Curtiz's work. Hollywood was turning to escapist fare. *The Breaking Point* was spare, socially tough, and heartbreaking. Film critic David Thomson has also noted that Warners probably did not wish to promote John Garfield, who was under investigation by the House Un-American Activities Committee.

Film historian Jeanine Basinger remembered seeing Curtiz's film in her native South Dakota as a young girl. "It ran in what we called 'dog time'—during the bitter cold, dead of winter when only the most zealous or desperate people went to the movies." But she never forgot *The Breaking Point*. "I said, 'Wow, this is different. This is great.'" Slowly, similar appreciation has spread among film people. "It was proof of Curtiz's remarkable range: from *Yankee Doodle Dandy* to *The Breaking Point*," Basinger noted.

Films were still Curtiz's life. If his energy flagged, no one knew it. He still skipped lunch on the set, popping aspirins instead. He still rose at dawn, rode horseback, and stayed in fighting trim, ready for the next project. But scripts didn't come along every week anymore. He made an unsuccessful effort to form his own unit inside Warners. The hero's final words in *The Breaking Point*, "A man alone ain't got no chance," reflect Curtiz's later years.

OLIVIA DE HAVILLAND remembered precisely when the phone rang: it was her birthday, July 11, 1957, and the day she moved into her Parisian town house. "I'm sitting here with a great admirer of yours," Samuel Goldwyn, Jr., told her, calling from Los Angeles. "I'll put him on." It was her old nemesis from the Errol Flynn swashbuckling days, Mike Curtiz. "We had not spoken in seventeen years and his tone was quite different. He was perfectly charming. He asked me to read a script called *The Proud Rebel*." After reading it, the co-star of *Captain Blood* and *The Charge of the Light Brigade* was sufficiently moved by this small Western fable to give Curtiz another chance.

The Proud Rebel is the story of a Confederate veteran (played by Alan

Ladd) in search of a cure for his son (Alan's son, David Ladd) struck by sudden dumbness at the shock of seeing Union troops kill his mother. "Mike was on the set in the morning when I arrived," de Havilland recalled, "just as he had been thirty-five years earlier. And he was still there at night when I left. His English hadn't improved much, but he still had a miraculous way of acting out what he wanted. Alan was very worried about how Mike would treat his son, but in fact he was gentle with the boy and got a great performance out of him."

De Havilland plays Linnett, an old maid feeling stirrings of love for the Confederate soldier. "Mike had not lost that strong visual sense of his. He acted out Linnett with an old straw hat, primping in front of a mirror. In another scene my character was reading by gaslight. I was told how to turn down the wick. But Mike said no, you must blow it out. Technically that was wrong, but visually of course he was absolutely right."

What neither Olivia de Havilland nor Alan Ladd knew was that Curtiz was living his own drama off the set. At the end of August 1957, two weeks before he began shooting *The Proud Rebel*, a sharp pain woke him in the middle of the night. Typically, Curtiz refused to be hospitalized until producer Sam Goldwyn assured him that production could be postponed. He was operated on that night for acute appendicitis, but doctors diagnosed something far more serious: cancer of the prostate, too advanced for surgery. Since nothing could be done, his doctor and his wife decided not to tell him. Though Curtiz had difficulty walking and was in great pain, he was on the set one week later.

For what would be one of his final films, Curtiz chose a light sex farce starring Sophia Loren and Maurice Chevalier. His reasons were purely sentimental. Filmed in Vienna, *A Breath of Scandal* was by the great Hungarian playwright Ferenc Molnar. It would bring the director close to his origins. But in the chilliest days of the Cold War, nearby Budapest was a world away. A reporter for a Hungarian paper was dispatched to interview him. "What's new at home?" Curtiz greeted the journalist. "Would you consider a visit?" reporter Gyorgy Sas asked Curtiz. "I'm often nostalgic for Hungary," the director admitted, "for my childhood, for my youth. But I have no one left there. Still, if I were to receive an invitation from the Ministry of Culture, I would accept."

He did not live long enough. In 1960, three years after he was first diagnosed, Curtiz wrote an old friend in Budapest:

"A few days ago I was walking in the streets of Hollywood, when all of a sudden it seemed as if the palm tree lined pavement slid from under my feet and I was walking around the deck of a huge ship gliding back toward Hungary. My nostalgia for Pest threw me back to the scene of my fondest memories . . . looking at the hour hand of the clock at the New York Café in dawn's foggy mist. I have been wondering for decades, could I be buried in Pest? I wonder why it is that after so many years in America I still long for my home? Is it hopeless for me to be buried there? I know that death is the same everywhere and that the grave is the destination of all philosophies. The only difference may be that while in Hollywood the palm trees watch over graves, in Budapest, a weeping willow would greet the new arrival. If I could leave the palm trees, alive or dead, I would choose the humble willow."

He died on April 11, 1962, age seventy-three. Cary Grant, Danny Thomas, Jack Warner, and Alan Ladd carried his coffin to a grave under the palm trees of Beverly Hills's Forest Lawn cemetery.

Why, given this body of work, is Michael Curtiz not on most lists of great twentieth-century directors? "He was impossible to pigeonhole," according to Jeanine Basinger, "because he could do it all. Maybe that is what has held him back: his range." Inside the profession, however, Curtiz is a legend. "He was one of the great ones," Hal Wallis asserted in 1974, "doing things twenty years ago that a lot of new directors think they invented. He was a master with the camera, way ahead of his time. He could do anything. . . . He was never happy unless he was working. On the last day of shooting a film, he'd ask when he could start the next one." When, in 1961, producer Sam Spiegel berated David Lean, the fabled director of *Lawrence of Arabia*, for working too slowly, Lean shot back, "I am not Mike Curtiz, who can take over a script Saturday and start shooting on Monday."

IF VON NEUMANN was the quintessential insider, Szilard remained the essential outsider. "Leo thought he could change the world," his nephew John Silard said. Having failed to stop Hiroshima, Szilard applied his fury and passion to stop the spread of nuclear weapons. No institution could ever contain Szilard. Since the day in Berlin when the young new arrival from Budapest accosted Albert Einstein, Szilard had rarely gone through channels. This man, whom General Groves had called "amoral," had, in the words of Edward R. Murrow, "a driving purpose, and that is to try to help dismantle the era of terror he helped to create."

From the lobby of Washington's Dupont Plaza Hotel, which he called his "office," he badgered policy-makers from Washington to Moscow, tossing out ideas like pebbles. As part of his new crusade, Szilard helped pioneer that peculiar Washington institution known as the "lobby." A 1946 *Life* magazine photo of Szilard shows him, wearing his favorite rumpled trench coat, with two colleagues as they created the Federation of Atomic Scientists, the first of many organizations Szilard founded to attempt to control the arms race. Its publication, *The Bulletin of Atomic Scientists*, with its famous clock on the cover showing the number of minutes left until a nuclear midnight, went on to become one of the most important journals in the field of science and politics.

After General Groves sidelined Szilard from nuclear physics, he attacked biology. Like physics in the early part of the century, in the late 1940s, biology lacked a theoretical framework. The challenge appealed to Szilard, who spent hours soaking in the bath, where he continued to do some of his best thinking. He was still homeless, preferring hotels and clubs like Chicago's Quadrangle Club, to an actual home. "Any thoughts?" was Szilard's typical morning greeting to colleagues. They knew better than ever to ask him the same question.

His eccentricities were the stuff of legend. At the University of Chicago, the wife of law professor Edward Levi* was accustomed to Szilard silently walking through her house, taking a chair from her kitchen, and setting it under a large tree in the Levis' garden. Szilard would then sit and think, sometimes for many hours. Eventually, having found the solution he sought, he brought the chair back to the kitchen and, with a mumbled thank-you to Mrs. Levi, returned to the university.

Following the first H-bomb explosion, Szilard raced between New York, Chicago, and Princeton, too agitated to settle anywhere for long, distraught by the nuclear world he helped create. In August 1953, when the

---

* Later President Gerald R. Ford's attorney general.

Soviet Union tested its first hydrogen bomb and the United States un-
veiled a policy of "massive retaliation," Szilard saw the doomsday scenario
that he had first read as a ten-year-old, *The Tragedy of Man*. He tried frantically to engage the country's brightest minds to focus on arms control.
But there was no chance that this brilliant outsider could ever control the
weapons he had helped to create.

He could, however, claim small victories. In 1955, he helped bring to
life the annual Pugwash Conference on Science and World Affairs, at
which, for the first time, American and Soviet scientists met face-to-face.
Forty years later, in 1995, Pugwash was awarded the Nobel Peace Prize.

Among his proudest achievements was the Council for a Livable
World, which he started and which still continues its work for Szilard's
goals: a rational approach to humanity's essentially irrational nature.
Szilard proposed the creation of a "Hot Line"—a direct telephone line—
between the Kremlin and the White House, to prevent a Dr. Strangelove–
type accidental nuclear war. After the 1962 Cuban Missile Crisis proved
the value—indeed, the necessity—of this idea, President Kennedy and
Soviet Premier Nikita Khrushchev set it up. To this day, the hotline, much
upgraded in quality, is used for vital direct communications between the
world's two largest nuclear powers.

Szilard attacked food the way he attacked ideas: voraciously. Friends
were used to Leo eating off their plates, as well as his own, all the while
telling them how to run their lives. Though Szilard and Teller could not
have been further apart politically, a joint television appearance on NBC
in the fall of 1960 revealed their affection and sense of humor. "We were
in agreement," Szilard told the audience, "that the danger of nuclear war
was great, but Teller meant this danger is great if the U.S. government
should listen to me, and I meant the danger was great if the U.S. government should listen to him."

To his first meeting with Soviet premier Khrushchev, Szilard took
an unusual gift: a Schick injector razor and some extra blades. "The
blade must be changed after one or two weeks," Szilard instructed Khrushchev. "If you like the razor, I will send you fresh blades from time to
time. But I can only do this," Szilard said with a smile, "as long as there is
no war."

Late in 1960, Szilard and his wife, Trude Weiss, en route home from

Moscow, stopped off in Vienna, tantalizingly close to Budapest. Like all of our Hungarians, once they got that close, their thoughts turned to their birthplace. Leo picked up the phone and dialed a childhood friend in his hometown, Joseph Litvan. Why not come for a visit, Litvan asked him. But Leo's memories of the thugs who had pushed him down the university stairs in 1919 were more powerful than the pull of nostalgia. Like Korda and Curtiz, he would never return to Budapest.

During the 1962 Cuban Missile Crisis, Jack Rosenthal, a young Oregon reporter who later became a senior editor at the *New York Times*, called Szilard to confirm a dinner date, only to learn from Szilard's housekeeper that the scientist had suddenly left the country. Expecting a nuclear holocaust, Szilard had moved to Geneva, Switzerland. Since 1933, he had kept two bags, his "Big Bomb Suitcases," containing family, academic, and patent records, always packed.

In 1964, Leo Szilard finally unpacked his suitcase. From his new home in La Jolla, California, he could see the Pacific, hear its waves crashing on the rocks below. He was offered lifetime residence and financial security at the Salk Institute for Biological Studies, which he had helped nurse into life. But even with new personal security, Szilard found reason to worry. "What if I should outlive the institute?" he asked friends only half in jest.

But he did not. Several months after settling into a place he said gave him "a foretaste of paradise," on May 30, 1964, Leo Szilard, age sixty-six, died of a massive heart attack. A front-page *New York Times* obituary the next morning called him "one of the great physicists of the century." Szilard would have preferred the London *Times* obituary, which noted, accurately, "He left his mark on history, as well as physics."

With the passage of years, Leo Szilard's subversive brilliance remained a favorite topic among his colleagues. In 1985, the Nobel laureate physicist Hans Bethe told Szilard's biographer, William Lanouette, that "Leo was one of the most intelligent people I have ever known. His mind worked quickly and profoundly, and he was able to come to ideas that most of us appreciated only after many hours of talk. This was his strength, and, of course, also his weakness. He was always ahead of his time."

A T DAWN on November 4, 1956, Soviet tanks rumbled over the beautiful bridges of Budapest. Within days, they had crushed the first armed revolution against the Soviet Union. Twenty thousand Hungarians were dead, 200,000 fled across the suddenly (but briefly) open Iron Curtain. In London, an enraged and helpless Arthur Koestler rushed to the Hungarian Legation and had to be restrained by friends when he threatened to hurl bricks.

Koestler had not been in Hungary since 1935. But, however painful his memories, he had never abandoned the dream of an eventual return. In 1964, while vacationing in the Austrian alpine village of Alpbach, he met a Hungarian cultural envoy. "What would happen," Koestler asked, "if I came back for a visit?" "We would welcome you with pride," the envoy assured him. Koestler soon presented himself to the Hungarian consulate in Vienna, to collect his visa. Before the consul stamped Koestler's passport, he mentioned a "small condition" to the visit. "You cannot speak or write about your trip." Koestler retrieved his passport and walked out.

From the day in July 1914 when he joined a Budapest march, until the end of his life, the ability to speak, to act, and to write gave meaning and purpose to Koestler, who described himself as a "typical . . . Central European member of the educated middle class," whose rites of passage had been "the rise of National Socialism and the rival lure of the Great Soviet Experiment . . . the mass migration of the Central European intelligentsia to western Europe and America, Palestine and Auschwitz, the surrender of Europe to the swastika and lastly the Second World War."

Koestler continued to write and speak out. For a while, he campaigned to ban the death penalty, a natural outgrowth of his months in a Spanish jail. Then, toward the end of his life, parapsychology became a new fascination.

He was an international celebrity, a Commander of the British Empire, a Companion of the Royal Society of Literature, a friend to luminaries such as Margaret Thatcher. But success could never fill his well of pessimism. "A dispassionate observer from a more advanced planet," he wrote, "who could take in human history from Cro-Magnon to Auschwitz . . . would come to the conclusion that our race is . . . a very sick biological product . . . there is the striking disparity between the growth curves of science and technology on the one hand, and of ethical conduct on the other. . . . Since the day when the first atomic bomb outshone the sun over Hiroshima," he concluded, "mankind as a whole has had to live with the prospect of its extinction as a *species*."

Koestler's pessimism was behind his decision not to father any children. When one of his many mistresses, Janine Graetz, disobeyed this stricture, Koestler refused ever to see his daughter, Christina.

IN 1977 Eva Striker's nephew, Sandor Striker, a young man in his twenties, was on a London visit from Budapest. When the Hungarian authorities in London seized Striker's passport, claiming it was invalid, Eva urged the penniless young man to call her old friend Arthur. "Eva told me Koestler did not like children," Striker recalled, "so I was a bit worried about calling. But he invited me for dinner that night." Arriving at Koestler's elegant Knightsbridge town house, Striker found the famous South African author Nadine Gordimer and Koestler's close Hungarian friend George Mikes. "After dinner, the ladies separated from the gentlemen," Striker recalled. "Until that moment Koestler seemed the perfect English gentleman. Very tweedy, dry sense of humor. But then the three of us switched to Hungarian. Mikes and Koestler began to reminisce about the Budapest of their youth: the cafés, and the intellectual life of the city. It seemed," Striker noted, "as if life had stopped for them, then and there. Koestler had such strong recollections. And no bad memories of the city."

Koestler never did return to Hungary. Nor did he live to see *Darkness at Noon*, translated into over thirty languages, published in Hungarian. That would only happen after the empire he helped unmask breathed its last in 1989. But he knew *Darkness at Noon* would outlive its critics. Even Harold Bloom, a leading contemporary critic who once predicted that *Darkness at Noon* was likely to last only three generations, later included it in a series containing the *Iliad* and *Great Expectations*.

Only old age and infirmity slowed him down. Suffering from Parkinson's and leukemia, Koestler felt his hard-won personal freedom slip away. An infirm body was simply one prison too many for the man who prized freedom above all else, and who had followed his inner voices wherever they led for sixty years. On March 4, 1983, the seventy-seven-year-old Koestler took a lethal dose of tranquilizers. His third wife, Cynthia, twenty years his junior and in perfect health, apparently helped him. Then, in an act that has never been fully explained or understood, she, too, took a fatal dose. Their deaths stunned the world but, at least for Koestler, it was a characteristic act—a final assertion of control over his own fate.

§

T HE SECURITY of a steady income and the institutional support of Condé Nast appealed to a man who had experienced as much instability as Andre Kertesz. So from 1945 until 1962 he accepted what amounted to a sanctuary, a well-paid staff job at *House & Garden*. But for Kertesz the artist, photographing the houses of the rich for a glossy American magazine was the equivalent of driving a taxi. "I felt," Kertesz said later, "like I was buried alive." Every moment he was aware that while he, the Old Master, was working for *House & Garden*, photographers he had groomed, among them Brassaï, Cartier-Bresson, and Capa, soared.

The convoluted subject of his Jewish roots had surfaced in 1946 when he learned the awful truth about the Hungarian Holocaust. After a long silence, his brother Imre wrote to him about the family's ordeal. In June 1944 the Nazis had forced the most dashing and elegant of the three Kertesz brothers, Imre, into the Budapest ghetto. There, with thousands of others, he and his wife, Greti, lived amid "filth, bugs, vermin." On October 15, following Horthy's overthrow by the fanatically fascist Arrow Cross, Imre and Greti barely escaped Eichmann's roundup. In January 1945 along with thousands of other survivors, they staggered from their cellar into daylight—to search for food. With picks and axes they hacked meat off the carcasses of frozen horses. Of the beautiful city of Andre Kertesz's memories and early photographs, very little had survived.

Even as he took competent, uninspired photographs of grand houses for *House & Garden*, Kertesz continued on his own photographic explorations of New York. He may not have liked America, but the Andre Kertesz of Budapest and Paris was becoming Kertesz of New York. His *Washington Square*, 1954, shows a sensibility different from that of the

Kertesz of Paris, but the master is still in command. From his twelfth-story Fifth Avenue apartment, Kertesz seized upon a lone figure in an urban landscape—a serene, human moment in Manhattan's bustle.

Late in May 1954, Kertesz heard that Robert Capa had been killed in Indochina. As he always did when he wanted to express deep emotions, Kertesz reached for his camera, and from his balcony he photographed the Manhattan skyline. It is twilight, darkness is dropping fast, like a curtain on a life. But beneath the skyline, the city lights flicker, life surges. Kertesz called it *Homage to Capa*.

BUT NEW YORK, and his *House & Garden* assignments, stifled him. When his former protégé and sometime rival, the poet of Parisian night, Brassaï, visited New York in 1956, Kertesz greeted him morbidly. "You are looking at a dead man."

But a dramatic revival of his muse was still to come. On January 13, 1962, for the first time in over thirty years, Andre heard the familiar voice of his beloved younger brother, Jeno, calling from Argentina. The brother who had believed in Andre from the beginning, who had spent hours leaping in the air or standing frozen against a shadowy wall for him, told him, "You are still Andre Kertesz. You can still be the world's greatest photographer." The brother's voice, tender, determined, yet still hopeful, triggered something powerful in the dejected man. Andre Kertesz, age sixty-eight, declared his independence.

"As I give up the slave work," Andre wrote his sister-in-law in Budapest, informing her that he had quit *House & Garden*, "I start again where I stopped before I stepped onto this sacred land. In the little time that I have left, I want to live according to my own taste, if possible. Or rather, to work according to my own style."

It takes a powerful will and great talent for a man to start over at the age of sixty-eight. But Kertesz, who could seem so gentle and poetic, was also propelled by his anger at America. From behind the camera, he could escape his burning resentment at having been shunted aside. I am back, he declared in 1962. Within months, his name began to reappear in articles and books and inside the tight international network of photography.

Ironically, his revival was spurred, in part, by the man he professed to despise, Brassaï. In "My Friend Andre Kertesz," the title of his April 1963 article in *Camera* magazine, Brassaï credited his career to Kertesz. "I was not yet a photographer and gave no thought at all to photography about which I knew nothing and even despised," he wrote, "when, about 1926, I met Andre Kertesz." Andre, he said, had "two qualities which were essential to a great photographer: an insatiable curiosity of the world of life and of people and a precise sense of form. . . . But rarely are the two qualities found in the same person."

In 1964, Kertesz returned to Paris, the scene of his greatest triumphs, with a one-man show at the Bibliothèque Nationale. It was immensely gratifying to be treated like a long-lost son. Here, no one seemed to mind his mangled French, here he was Andre, *"artiste extraordinaire."* For two months, he basked in a long-denied adulation. For the French, Kertesz's rejection by the vulgarians across the Atlantic was additional proof of his genius. Rejuvenated, he applied himself like a hungry youth. "Worked [in Montmartre] and after that like in a trance," he wrote in his journal. Then, miraculously, the negatives he had confined to a friend's care three decades earlier, and which he thought lost in the war, were rediscovered. Journalists and photographers recorded the dramatic moment when the master reclaimed his lost legacy, still buried, largely undamaged, underground.

Fusing his past with his present, Kertesz now reinterpreted his earlier work to reflect his evolving taste and personal history. In 1964, he cropped his famous 1933 portrait of himself and his wife, *Elizabeth and I,* so that only half of her face is left, and only his hand on her shoulder. Perhaps it was deliberate symbolism; Elizabeth now seemed only half his, as she devoted more and more time to her friend and partner in her cosmetics firm, Frank Tamas. For Andre, *vision* was his most singular attribute; her affection for a man who was legally blind must have been particularly hurtful. Elizabeth did not accompany Andre to his Paris opening. But she continued to give him the practical advice she had always provided. Reach out to the press, she urged him. "Go and see everyone . . . try to make a new career in Paris and then we will go over and live there. . . . I only see now how ugly it is [in New York] and how much I dislike it."

THE WORLD came calling. Prestigious museums—from New York's Museum of Modern Art to Stockholm's Moderna Museet—staged

Kertesz retrospectives in the 1960s and 1970s. In 1964, Cornell Capa, president of Magnum from 1956 until 1960, offered Kertesz a coveted place in the ranks of the agency and included him in a landmark international exhibit he organized, *The Concerned Photographer*, dedicated to the memory of Robert Capa and others who had died in the line of duty. Along with Capa and Kertesz, it included the work of Werner Bischof, Leonard Freed, David Seymour (Chim), and Dan Weiner. Traveling to Tokyo, Paris, London, and many other cities, the exhibit introduced Kertesz to a global public. Together, photography, "the most contemporary of art forms," and Andre Kertesz, were accorded a central role in the shaping of the twentieth century's sensibility.

John Szarkowski, the new curator of photography at MOMA, mounted a Kertesz retrospective in November 1964. "The photographic world," Szarkowski wrote, "has begun to realize again that in much of what it values it is the heir of Andre Kertesz. Fortunately, this rediscovery has come while Kertesz is still working, still seeking to express all that he sees and feels, and while his colleagues can not only be grateful for his past but look forward to his future." Kertesz, the curator of MOMA concluded, "possesses an intuitive understanding of the realism of the camera—of its ability to imprison the telling detail, the convincing texture, the climactic moment."

No artist could have hoped for greater affirmation from one of the high priests of world photography. He stayed in New York, the city he professed to despise. In the 1970s, Eva Besnyo asked him why he didn't return to Europe. "He said he needed the money," she told me shortly before she died in 2004. "He said he just didn't have the strength to start all over again."

THE ERUPTIONS of violence and anger that Kertesz's lens had always filtered out would explode in his conversation in the final decade of his life. "We would be walking through Washington Square," Hungarian-born photographer Sylvia Plachy, Kertesz's friend and protégée, recalled, "and Andre would suddenly mutter, 'God damned son of a bitch America.'" His venom was directed at those whom he blamed for his long delayed recognition: Ernie Prince of the Keystone Agency, which first brought him to New York; Beaumont Newhall, the MOMA curator who once asked him to airbrush pubic hair from his nudes; and Brassaï, whom he called a "low life" for stealing his technique and not crediting him sufficiently. He poured out his anger to Hungarian reporter Laszlo Lugosi Lugo in January 13, 1981. When Elizabeth died of emphysema in October 1977, he blamed America. Oddly, he never railed against the country of his birth for forcing him into exile or persecuting his family. It was as if he had chosen a safe target, America, to channel a lifetime of rage.

In 1978, a young photographer, Robert Gurbo, asked to meet his hero. Stepping into Kertesz's Fifth Avenue apartment, he recalled a quarter of a century later, "was like entering another world. It was flooded with this incredible light, which changed every five minutes. He had arranged beautiful objects and artifacts from his past very carefully, to catch the light." Gurbo was so nervous he almost lost his voice.

Gurbo was struck by the contrast between Kertesz's elegance and his occasional explosions of anger. "Until the very end of his life, when he had Parkinson's disease," Gurbo remembered, "he would always dress carefully for his visitors. He was very courteous and gentle." But when Gurbo told Kertesz he must feel very fulfilled by what he had achieved, the old man "snapped." Glaring at Gurbo, Kertesz spat out angrily, "You don't know my story." But Kertesz invited him back. Although both men were unaware of it at the time, Kertesz was grooming Gurbo for his eventual role as curator of his estate, the man who would perpetuate Kertesz's legacy to the next generation after he was gone.

To Gurbo, Kertesz's photographs only partly mirrored his soul. The rest he held in tight control. "He never talked about being Jewish—or about the Holocaust. When we spoke of God he would say, 'Your God.' He considered himself an atheist." The century that had spared him had left him without religious faith. Once, Gurbo walked in on a heated conversation between Kertesz and "a religious Jew. With a Bible in hand, he was arguing with Kertesz about not identifying himself as a Jew."

If you want to understand me, Kertesz urged Gurbo, "you must read the poetry of Ady." Endre Ady, the hero of Kertesz's Budapest generation, was the greatest of the twentieth-century Hungarian poets. Like Kertesz, Ady had spent time in Paris, but remained a passionate Hungarian. Ady died in 1919, the year Budapest's revolutionary spirit was snuffed out.

Sylvia Plachy was astonished to find that Kertesz, then in his eighties, was a fan of wrestling on television. "You should watch," Kertesz urged her, "you can learn about life, about winning and losing." To the end, she noted, Kertesz's artistic sensibility was undiminished. One night, he slipped and fell. When Sylvia found him lying on the floor in the morning, his first words were, "What amazing shapes you can see from this angle!"

Kertesz died in his Fifth Avenue apartment on September 28, 1985. He left behind 100,000 negatives. Andre Kertesz's black-and-white images of New York City—the city he loved to hate—have become among the world's most enduring. Succeeding generations continue to rediscover Budapest and Paris, too, through Kertesz's lens. It is astonishing that such an angry man produced these perfectly composed, harmonious images. They are the images of the world as Kertesz would have liked it to be—not as he found it.

N O O T H E R scientist had as much impact on Cold War America as Edward Teller. Pique at what he thought was his insufficient status at Los Alamos drove him to start a competing major weapons laboratory, at Livermore, California. "He was the driving force at Livermore," former Defense Secretary Harold Brown noted, "which was established because Edward was unhappy with Los Alamos. The Air Force, of course, had its own reasons for wanting another weapons lab. Teller was always pushing, looking for another big breakthrough like his success with the Super."

In the summer of 1955, Freeman Dyson rented a house in Berkeley, where Edward Teller was teaching. "One Sunday evening," Dyson recalled, "we went for a walk up the hill, leaving the house open as usual. When we came back through the trees to the house, we heard a strange sound coming through the open door. The children stopped their chatter and we all stood outside the door and listened. It was . . . Bach's Prelude No. 8 in E flat minor. Superbly played. . . . Whoever was playing it was putting into it his whole heart and soul. . . . We waited until the music came to an end and then walked in. There, sitting at the piano, was Edward Teller. We asked him to go on playing, but he excused himself. He said he had come to invite us to a party at his house and had happened to see that fine piano begging to be played."

In 1957, when the Soviets launched Sputnik, the world's first orbital satellite, *Time* magazine's story about the state of American science featured Edward Teller on its cover. But even as his influence over Cold War Washington grew, his internal exile continued. Brown remembered Teller's "black moods alternating with ebullience," and suspected that Teller was "probably bipolar, before people knew about such things."

Szilard, Wigner, and von Neumann may have disagreed with Edward, but, Hungarians to the end, they always defended him. "Great men . . . have passionate opponents," Wigner wrote, "and Edward Teller has been a great man. I suppose that men like Teller are fated to live their lives on an open stage . . . but after the war, when a few people began accusing Teller . . . the criticism pained me."

Edward Teller's astonishing final comeback started in 1967, when he met an actor turned politician. In Ronald Reagan, Teller found "the savior of the nation," Harold Brown recalled later—and his own savior as well. Two outsiders, two men shifting their interests from, respectively, acting and science, to politics, two men who felt that the "liberal establishment," with which they were personally familiar, was too weak to stand up to the Soviet threat. Teller would supply the theory; Reagan would articulate it and sell it to the nation. They ultimately called it the Strategic Defense Initiative (SDI), today Missile Defense: its critics mocked it as Star Wars.

It is telling what most struck the Hungarian about Ronald Reagan. "I was most impressed," Teller wrote of their first meeting, "by Reagan's relaxed manner. The only thing that he obviously worried about was being late for his wife." As to how the former movie star regarded the Father of the Hydrogen Bomb, "Reagan," Harold Brown observed, "saw Edward as a character in a movie: a benign Dr. Strangelove." Teller's vision of an America secure from incoming nuclear missiles captivated Reagan, who, like Teller, rejected the concept of mutual assured destruction as inadequate against a surprise first strike by the Soviets.

The 1967 encounter began a string of meetings that culminated in President Reagan's March 20, 1983, address to the nation announcing the Strategic Defense Initiative, a speech that reflected Teller's messianic vision of America shielded by satellites able to destroy missile warheads as they came up out of the atmosphere. "What if free people," President Reagan asked, "could live secure in the knowledge ... that we could intercept and destroy ballistic missiles before they reached our own soil or that of our allies?"

"By force of Teller's personality and dedication," Brown noted, "he persuaded Ronald Reagan that a missile defense shield could work."

Two decades and more than $100 billion later, the dream is still only that. "Edward had a tendency," Harold Brown noted, "to describe things with a view to getting people to reach the 'right' conclusions. That is a particular sin for a scientist." Fantasy or not, weapons in space are now enshrined in the Pentagon's budget, a testament to the determination of the man who discovered security in the consistency of numbers, many years earlier. But today, with America's main threats coming not from outer space but from suicide bombers and hijackers, even in military circles there is some concern that continuing to pour so much money into unproven (and so far unsuccessful) space technologies is dangerous and wasteful.

For Henry Kissinger, Teller was a man "impossible not to like. He was so passionate, so vulnerable and so human, I found him to be a much warmer personality than Oppenheimer. Teller was brilliant," the former secretary of state recalled in 2005, "but he could not control his emotions." Still, Kissinger recalled Teller's generosity: patiently attempting to explain to the then little known Harvard academic the concept of the relativity of time, "how if you travel to Venus you age less than if you stay on Earth. I never really understood it, but he kept trying to explain it to me."

Others regard Teller's legacy in a harsher light. "Together," Priscilla McMillan wrote, "Livermore and Los Alamos created the vast arsenal of superfluous nuclear weaponry that curses us today."

"In the 1990s," Harold Brown recalled, "I saw him walking with a long cloak and a staff, and asked, 'Edward, where are the tablets?' He was not amused." At age ninety-five Teller may not have developed a sense of humor about himself but, having outlived his childhood friends from Budapest, most of his enemies, as well as the Soviet Union itself, he felt vindicated. What is more, the country that once shunned him now gave him a heroic fade-out.

Hungarian science historian Gabor Pallo recalled a moment during one of Teller's trips to Budapest late in his life. "I said to him, in Hungarian," Pallo recalled, "that nothing is less certain than the past—a typical Budapest quip. But hearing it, Teller threw back his head and roared with laughter. He had a look on his face which said, 'I'm home at last.' "

"I am very much satisfied," Teller said during his final visit, "because in Hungary it is recognized that I contributed to the Russians no longer being here. And that's enough for me. Whatever will be said about me after I'm dead," he said, recognizing that his name would always ignite debate, "is not important, as compared to the point that the Hungarian government and Hungarians appreciate what I have done."

On July 23, 2003, President George W. Bush presented Teller with his adopted country's highest civilian award, the Medal of Freedom. Teller died six weeks later. His bitter, and certainly brief, wish in the immediate aftermath of the Oppenheimer affair not to be remembered would be unfulfilled. Like him or hate him—and he had plenty of influential people in both camps—he would stand, with Szilard and von Neumann and Wigner, as one of the giants of the century just ended.

It was a long way from Budapest at the dawn of the twentieth century to the White House in the twenty-first, and Teller had outlasted all the others. At his passing, none was left to link our world to the distant sounds and rhythms of the Café New York and the intense intellectual ferment, the political turmoil, and terrible drama that had created a generation of Hungarians who, finding their native land suddenly hostile and dangerous, had left to make their mark in the larger world. Their astonishing successes, against all odds—their photographs and movies, their books and their science—would live on, enduring legacies that had helped shape our modern world, tribute to the excitement that gripped the city on the Danube for a brief, golden moment.

EPILOGUE

With Edward Teller's death in 2003, the long journey of Budapest's exiled giants drew to a close. But the lure of the West, and the danger of living in Budapest under Nazi or Soviet occupation, would create yet another generation of remarkable Hungarians who would achieve greatness only by escaping their homeland. Their historic benchmarks would be Eichmann's ruthless roundup of Jews in the terrible last year of World War II, and the heroic but failed Hungarian uprising against Soviet rule in October 1956. Several hundred thousand Hungarians would escape; while countless others would die in death camps and brutal fighting (in 1945 and 1956) or in the gulag.

Among those who reached the West and prospered were artists, writers, designers, scientists, economists, and a legendary philanthropist-financier. Their childhoods in Budapest would leave them with vastly differing memories, but for all of them, the story would begin in the city that would always define them.

For Imre Kertesz (no relation to Andre Kertesz), the first Hungarian winner of the Nobel Prize for Literature (in 2002), Budapest would always be the place that turned its back on its own dark history, the subject of much of Kertesz's work. "Hungarians have not learned from their past," he told me as we sat in a Berlin café. Kertesz is a warm, easygoing man who likes to laugh and enjoys small pleasures: strong espresso, champagne, smoking, and stroking his wife, Magda's, hand. But he is unable to forget or forgive. In his seventies, he has chosen to live in Berlin, where his work was first recognized, rather than in Budapest. In 1997 he returned to his gymnasium, the Madach, with a German television crew filming his life story. "The Germans were embarrassed," Kertesz recalled, "at how coldly the people there treated me. Hungarians find my preoccupation with the Holocaust obsessive. They want me to write about other, more 'positive' subjects. But I cannot."

Born in Budapest in 1929, Kertesz was deported to Auschwitz when he was fifteen. "When our transport reached the [German] border," he recalled, "the Hungarian gendarmes asked all of us Jews for any remaining valuables. 'Be Magyar patriots,' they urged us, 'don't let the Germans have it.' " Kertesz has mined such memories in works like *Fateless* (the subject of a recent film), singled out by the Nobel committee. "I have seen the true face of the dreadful century," he said in his Nobel acceptance speech. "I knew I would never be able to free myself from the sight; I knew this visage would always hold me captive."

In Berlin, where he is a much honored and recognized figure, Kertesz found the peace of mind that eluded him in Budapest. We parted just as the lights were coming on in the Kurfürstendamm. Tipping his fedora at passersby who recognized him, the elderly gentleman in a trench coat turned back and looked at me with a slightly ironic smile that said, Who would have believed this scenario? The scars of the Holocaust have not healed, and yet I have chosen to live in the capital of the country that invented Auschwitz.

. . .

ANDY GROVE, the legendary co-founder of Intel, was born Andras
Grof in Budapest in 1936. He spent his youth in the shadow of the New
York Café. His memoir, revealingly entitled *Swimming Across*, contains
anecdotes that explain why he has steadfastly refused to return to Budapest, why he fixed his eyes so determinedly on the future, and why he
rarely speaks Hungarian. (His wife and friends were amazed when he and
I conversed at length in our native tongue at several dinners.)

Grove listed his primary childhood experiences as "War, persecution,
hiding with false identity, revolution." He learned to act decisively in critical situations at a very young age in the crucible of wartime Budapest.
At age seven he realized that in the eyes of many of his countrymen, he
was born "guilty." "One day a little girl was playing [in the playground],"
he recalled in his memoirs. "We had never seen each other before but I
had sand toys and she had a doll, so we started to play together. We were
busily building sand castles and putting the doll next to them, when she
suddenly turned to me and said, very seriously, 'Jesus Christ was killed by
the Jews, and because of that, all the Jews will be thrown into the Danube.'
My mother was sitting on a bench nearby. I jumped up and ran to her,
bawling my head off. I told her what the little girl had just said. My mother
put her arm around me and said it was time for us to go home. . . . That
was the last time I played in this park."

At age eight, his parents changed his name and identity from Andras
Grof to the Slavic Andras Malesevic, to elude the Nazi manhunt. It was
1944, the worst time of all; Adolf Eichmann had arrived in Budapest to
carry out his orders to exterminate all the Jews of Hungary. Grove survived, as did his parents, who slipped him out of Budapest to hide in the
countryside. "My mother warned me," he recalled, "never, absolutely
never to pee in front of anybody or to wash myself in front of anybody. I
had been circumcised, as Jewish boys in Hungary typically were, but
Christian Hungarian boys were not. If anybody saw my penis, it would
have given me away instantly. I took this to heart and became extremely
private."

Then, a decade after Hungary exchanged a German occupation for a
Soviet one, the twenty-year-old Grove was forced to leave his parents and
his country, all that was familiar, for the unknown, following the failed

1956 revolution. Like 200,000 others—including my own family some-what later—he crossed the Austria-Hungary border during the brief weeks when the Iron Curtain was temporarily breached by the Freedom Fight-ers. He arrived in New York alone and speaking only a smattering of English, but soon earned a degree in chemical engineering, followed by a Ph.D. from the University of California at Berkeley. A decade later he helped found Intel, the high-tech pioneer whose memory chips are at the heart of the global communications revolution. By the century's end Intel was making 90 percent of the planet's personal computer micro-processors. Perhaps as much as any other person, Grove, scientist and business titan, shaped the digital age.

Grove admitted his fearless innovations, his ability to see around cor-ners in the rapidly changing high-tech world, were an outgrowth of the refugee's fear of failure. When *Time* magazine picked Andy Grove as its 1997 "Man of the Year" it noted that few CEOs in the world had Grove's early survival training as a Jew in Nazi-controlled Budapest. "His charac-ter traits," *Time* reported, "are emblematic of this amazing century: a para-noia bred from his having been a refugee from the Nazis."

Grove has often said that he has no interest in ever returning to Hun-gary. "My life started over in the United States," he said. "Whatever roots I had in Hungary were cut off when I left and have since withered and died."

Yet his published memoirs suggest a more complex tale. "Roots," as he defines them, may have died, but those memories that he recounts so vividly are roots, too, and more than a half century later he can recall them with the precision of yesterday's events; they have neither withered nor died. "In addition to the German soldiers on the street," Grove wrote in *Swimming Across*, "we saw members of the Arrow Cross Party. . . . They wore armbands with their emblem, two crossed arrows, one vertical, one horizontal, with points on both ends. I had seen Arrow Cross members on the street before, but I never had anything to do with them. Now I didn't want to look at them; they frightened me." And one can hear distant, but distinct, echoes of that fear in the famous title of Grove's best-known book, *Only the Paranoid Survive*.

GEORGE SOROS is far more open than Grove, and less depressed than Kertesz, about his Hungarian youth; unlike either of them, he returns to

Budapest regularly. "World War II shaped me," he told me in one of our many conversations. He was only fourteen when he faced the threat of extermination in 1944. Forced to hide behind a false identity as a Christian, young George grew up fast. Watching Jews who obeyed orders only to disappear, he learned not to trust, nor to play by the rules. He learned to calculate risk and to rely on his instincts in order to survive. "Nineteen forty-four was my formative year, as well as the most exciting time of my life."

By the end of the war, the seventeen-year-old Soros had a sense of near-immortality. After outsmarting Europe's most efficient killers, modest goals would not suffice. He abandoned his family, his country, and culture and set off for London in 1947, just as the Soviet Union was consolidating its power in Hungary. In 1956 he moved to New York and began to accumulate the fabulous wealth that would enable him to reinvent himself yet again, this time as the world's greatest philanthropist.

The qualities that he had mastered on the terror-filled streets of Budapest turned out to be useful in the world of finance. Coolness under pressure, deft risk calculation, a willingness to lay everything on the line and ignore conventional wisdom and behavior—these traits, which had once saved his life, defined Soros's style in the high-risk world of hedge funds, where he became a legend. Soros had even higher ambitions.

By 1979, Soros had begun his philanthropic activities, which ultimately led to his presence in over fifty countries. His primary foundation, the Open Society Institute, has supported civil society and social, legal, and economic reform on five continents, training and inspiring an entire generation of democrats, many of whom, like Georgia's thirty-seven-year-old president, Michael Saakashvili, are virtually personal protégés. "My goal," Soros admits openly, with a hint of irony, "is to be the conscience of the world." With an iron will and a net worth now estimated at over $11 billion, Soros is better positioned than most to fulfill his grandiose dreams. "Many people have messianic visions," he says. "The difference is, I've actually lived out my visions."

Soros attributed his relentless drive to "a feeling that I need to constantly prove myself, that you are only as good as your achievements." And yet—in contrast to Andy Grove—this hard-nosed realist who prides himself on an unsentimental approach to life keeps going back to Budapest. "It's the damned language," Soros gruffly explained. But of course it is much more than the pleasure of speaking his mother tongue. In the 1980s he chose Hungary as the first place to plant his Open Society; and he built his Central European University, now a respected institution of higher learning, in Budapest. (Full disclosure: I am a member of CEU's Advisory Board.)

IN *The Third Man*, Korda's stand-in, Harry Lime (Orson Welles), proclaimed, "In Italy for thirty years under the Borgias they had warfare, terror, murder, bloodshed. They produced Michelangelo, Leonardo, and the Renaissance. In Switzerland, they had brotherly love, five hundred years of democracy, and they produced the cuckoo clock." Soros and Grove echoed Lime's words. They credited their reaction to the "warfare, terror, murder, and bloodshed" of fascist and communist Hungary for their extraordinary achievements. Their outsider's drive, not only as Jews in anti-Semitic Hungary, but, later, as refugees, spurred their creativity, their hunger to make a mark. The complacent and the self-satisfied are not the ones who ask the hard questions or push for change. "This drive," George Soros explained with remarkable candor, "is a form of low self-esteem. It is the opposite of being self-satisfied. I'm still trying to prove myself at seventy-five."

Another remarkable survivor of Budapest's black days deserves a special mention—Tom Lantos, who as a teenager was given refuge by Raoul Wallenberg, survived Eichmann, and found his way to the United States in 1947. Today, as the only Holocaust survivor ever to serve in Congress, Lantos is the ranking Democrat on the House International Relations Committee. His district is in San Francisco, but when he speaks, the accent is one more familiar to me than it is to most of his Bay Area constituents. Lantos is unembarrassed to invoke the drama of his native land as he addresses current issues.

THE New York Café still looms like a cathedral over the Ring Road. "Coming soon!" promised the sign in its window in early 2006. Overhead, the clock that Curtiz recalled in his Hollywood exile tells time again. Beneath it, the gold letters, *Anno 1887*, are a reminder of the time when the New York first opened its doors, during another era brimming with promise. Inside its massive revolving doors, craftsmen labor to restore the luster that had disappeared during the dreary years of communism and decay. The gilded cherubs on the richly carved and frescoed ceiling of the old café are coming back to life. The New York's new owners, an Italian hotel chain, intend to restore the café to its mythic place in Budapest's life.

Down the Ring Road from the New York, the Hotel Royal, where Alexander Korda first lived beyond his means, also gleams with fresh gilt and marble. Korda would not approve of the inelegant crowd now milling in the Royal's lobby. In blue jeans and T-shirts that blur national distinctions, they lined up for a "Hong Kong Business Investors' Seminar" held in one of the Baroque chambers where Korda once schemed.

Can the restoration of the New York and the Royal, as well as other monuments from the city's glory days, revive the excitement of the past? Will a new generation of von Neumanns, Szilards, and Capas fill the grand chambers and cafés with big ideas, audacity, and impatience? Of course, a tolerant and creative city cannot be re-created simply with new plaster. There is no fixed formula for the magical blending of opportunity and adversity that made Budapest a furnace of creativity almost a century ago. Achievement—"innovate or die" in the words of the 1971 Hungarian Nobel laureate in physics, Dennis Gabor—substituted for personal security. The urgency to succeed as if life itself depended on it—because it sometimes did—vanished with the brutalities of the last century.

Budapest has more than bricks, mortar, and foreign investors pulling it toward the future. For the first time in its tumultuous history, Hungary is a "normal" place, a European country more or less like the others. As a member of the European Union and NATO, it no longer fears its powerful neighbors to the east and west. It is a democracy, forever out of the orbits of the Austro-Hungarian Empire, fascism, Moscow, and communism. It is, at long last, an integral part of the very "West" that had beckoned and lured so many of Hungary's brightest and best to leave in decades past. Will this new freedom mean that creative or ambitious Hungarians will stay home to achieve their dreams—or will the easy mobility of the new Europe result in another, if more benign, brain drain of Hungarian talent, drawn by opportunities to play on a larger stage in Berlin, Paris, London, or New York? Will Hungary, now a "normal" country, still produce visionaries able to imagine a nuclear chain reaction in the laboratory of their brain?

Despite its troubled history, I love my native city. I dream of the day when its cafés will be as animated and creative as they were eighty years ago, when Capa and Szilard, Koestler and Teller, Curtiz and von Neu-mann—and my own family—saw a hopeful new century stretching out before them, before Horthy and Hitler and Eichmann, before Stalin and Khrushchev and Kadar. It is possible, I think as I walk the streets of a now free Budapest, remembering my earliest childhood memories of Soviet tanks rumbling across the Chain Bridge to crush the 1956 Free-dom Fighters.

But if Budapest aspires to become an incubator of talent without once again driving its most promising abroad, it must make a fuller ac-knowledgment of its past. Its ambivalence toward those native sons who achieved greatness outside Hungary is not a good sign. Blocks from the newly refurbished Hotel Royal and the New York is the Madach Gymna-sium on Barcsay Street. Four alumni are still missing from the wall of "Our Famous Graduates" in the school's lobby: Alexander Korda, Robert Capa, Nobel laureate Imre Kertesz, and Andy Grove. When will they take their rightful place (next to lesser figures, one might note) in the school where they first dreamed, not yet realizing that to fulfill those dreams they would have to flee for their lives, taking with them only the magic of the city as it was before darkness closed in?

NOTES

MAGIC IN THEIR POCKETS

To document the story of the Hungarians' trip to Einstein's summer retreat in Long Island, the author used the following sources: William Lanouette with Bela Szilard, *Genius in the Shadows: A Biography of Leo Szilard, The Man Behind the Bomb*; George Marx, *The Voice of the Martians: Hungarian Scientists Who Shaped the 20th Century in the West*; Richard Rhodes, *The Making of the Atomic Bomb*; Sir Georg Solti, *Memoirs*; Leo Szilard, *Leo Szilard: His Version of the Facts: Selected Recollections and Correspondence*, Spencer R. Weart and Gertrud Weiss Szilard, eds.; Tekla Szilard's unpublished journal; interviews with Tibor Frank, Hungarian science historian; William Lanouette, Leo Szilard's biographer; Gabor Pallo, Hungarian science historian; Richard Rhodes; and John Silard, Leo Szilard's nephew.

PAGE

1 *On a muggy day in July*: Leo Szilard, *Leo Szilard: His Version of the Facts*, Spencer R. Weart and Gertrud Weiss Szilard, eds. (Boston: MIT Press, 1978), 81–114.

2 *"We did not know"*: Ibid., 84.

2 *"I believe"*: William Lanouette with Bela Szilard, *Genius in the Shadows: A Biography of Leo Szilard, the Man Behind the Bomb* (New York: Scribner, 1992), 205.

7 *"Since that time"*: Sir Georg Solti, *Memoirs* (New York: Alfred A. Knopf, 1997) 8–9.

11 *"Hungarians"*: George Marx, *The Voice of the Martians: Hungarian Scientists Who Shaped the 20th Century in the West* (Budapest: Akademiai Kiado, 1994), 319.

11 *"The city was growing"*: Unpublished journal of Tekla Szilard, courtesy of John Silard.

1. PLENTY

For background and documentation, the author found useful material in: Gordon W. Allport, *The Nature of Prejudice*; Silvano Arieti, *Creativity: The Magic of Synthesis*; Thomas Bender and Carl E. Schorske, eds., *Budapest and New York: Studies in Metropolitan Transformation, 1870–1930*; Marta Bolcsics and Lajos Csordas, *Budapesti Krudy-Kalauz*; Endre Czeizel, *Tudosok, Genek, Dilemmak: A Magyar Szarmazasu Nobel Dijasok Csaladfaelemzese*; Szentes Eva, *Irodalmi Kavehazak Pesten es Budan*; Tibor Frank, *Ethnicity, Propaganda, Myth-Making*; Judit Frigyesi, *Bela Bartok and Turn-of-the-Century Budapest*; Peter Hanak, *The Garden and the Workshop: Essays on the Cultural History of Vienna and Budapest*; Paul Ignotus, *Hungary*; Oscar Jaszi, *The Dissolution of the Hapsburg Monarchy*; Michael Korda, *Charmed Lives: A Family Romance*; Lencso Laszlo, Kalcsu Eva, and Kegli Balazs, *Budapestimozik*; John Lukacs, *Budapest 1900: A Historical Portrait of a City and Its Culture*; William O. McCagg, Jr., *Jewish Nobles and Geniuses in Modern Hungary*; Miklos Molnar, *A Concise History of Hungary*; Istvan Nemeskurty, *Word and Image: History of the Hungarian Cinema*; Gabor Pallo, *Zsenialitas es Korszellem*; Ignac Romsics, *Hungary in the Twentieth Century*; Carl E. Schorske, *Fin-de-Siècle Vienna: Politics and Culture*; Peter

Singer, *Pushing Time Away: My Grandfather and the Tragedy of Jewish Vienna*; Paul Tabori, *Alexander Korda*; and Stefan Zweig, *The World of Yesterday*.

In this section, the author drew on interviews with Gyongyi Balogh; Professor L. Braham; Henri Cartier-Bresson; Professor Istvan Deak; Miguel Fidalgo, Curtiz scholar; Tibor Frank; Robert Gurbo, curator of the estate of Andre Kertesz; Gabor Gyapai, the Lutheran Gymnasium, Budapest; Vera Gyuri; Istvan Hargittai; Imre Kertesz; Karoly Kincses; David Korda; Michael Korda; William Lanouette, Leo Szilard's biographer; Stefan Lorant; Endre Marton; Gabor Pallo; Atilla Pok; Noemi Saly, Hungarian café historian; Michael Scammell, Arthur Koestler's biographer; John Silard, Leo Szilard's nephew; Andras Torok; Erzsebet Vezer; Marina von Neumann Whitman; Nicholas von Neumann; Eva Striker Zeisel; and Vilmos Zsigmond.

PAGE

15 *It was in a place like Rick's*: Andre de Toth, *Fragments: Portraits from the Inside* (London: Faber & Faber, 1994), 1–44.

15 *"I am sometimes overcome by a feeling"*: Letter from Michael Curtiz to friend, from the Michael Curtiz file of Hungarian-language reviews, letters, articles, and assorted clips, translated by the author and courtesy of the Hungarian Film Archives.

17 *"In the hierarchy of social prestige"*: Franz Alexander, *The Western Mind in Transition* (New York: Random House, 1960), 25.

18 *"Why should we?"*: Peter Hanak, *The Garden and the Workshop: Essays on the Cultural History of Vienna and Budapest* (Princeton: Princeton University Press, 1999), 53.

18 *A popular joke*: Thomas Bender and Carl E. Schorske, *Budapest and New York: Studies in Metropolitan Transformation, 1870–1930* (New York: Russell Sage Foundation, 1994), 232.

18 *"It was an era"*: Alexander, *The Western Mind in Transition*, 25.

20 *"They spoiled you there"*: de Toth, *Fragments*, 5.

20 *"The foundation of all"*: Ibid., 107.

20 *"Many times we are hungry"*: Letter from Curtiz to friend, Hungarian Film Archives.

21 *"I can see amazing things"*: Curtiz file, Hungarian Film Archives.

22 *"The intoxicating joy"*: Ibid.

23 *"It is sufficient"*: Ibid.

23 *"Sadly," he wrote*: Ibid.

24 *In the words of historian*: Author's interview with Istvan Deak, and see also "Survivor in a Sea of Barbarism," *The New York Review of Books*, April 8, 1999.

24 *"Budapest"*: Charles Drazin, *Korda: Britain's Only Movie Mogul* (London: Sigdwick & Jackson, 2002), 10.

25 *From the start*: Paul Tabori, *Alexander Korda* (New York: Living Books, 1966), 3–12.

26 *If Budapest made*: Karol Kulik, *Alexander Korda: The Man Who Could Work Miracles* (London: Virgin, 1990), 13–27; and Tabori, *Alexander Korda*, 39–61.

27 *"Always penniless, but always smoking a big cigar"*: Transcript of an interview with Josef Somlo, courtesy of the Hungarian Film Archives.

28 *"I'd like you to star in my war picture"*: Tabori, *Alexander Korda*, 40–41.

30 *"Film people"*: Michael Korda, *Charmed Lives: A Family Romance* (New York: HarperPerennial, 2002), 63.

31 *"I look for the poetic"*: Unpublished journal of Andre Kertesz, courtesy of the estate of Andre Kertesz.

33 *"The couple"*: Video interview with Kertesz, estate of Andre Kertesz.

33 *"The train left"*: Unpublished journal of Andre Kertesz, courtesy of the estate of Andre Kertesz.

34 *"The water of the pool"*: Ibid.

35 *"We called ourselves 'Magyars' "*: Eugene Wigner as told to Andrew Szanton, *The Recollections of Eugene P. Wigner* (New York: Basic, 1992), 36.

36 *"At school"*: Unpublished journal of Tekla Szilard, courtesy of John Silard.

36 *"Other members"*: Ibid.

37 *"My childhood world"*: Wigner as told to Szanton, *The Recollections of Eugene P. Wigner*, 11.

37 *"My parents did not discuss the absence"*: Wigner as told to Szanton, *The Recollections of Eugene P. Wigner*, 13.

37 *"Once he got home"*: Unpublished journal of Tekla Szilard.

38 *"In such places"*: Wigner as told to Szanton, *The Recollections of Eugene P. Wigner*, 17.

38 *"More and more troop trains"*: Leo Szilard, *Leo Szilard: His Version of the Facts*, Spencer R. Weart and Gertrud Weiss Szilard, eds. (Boston: MIT Press, 1978), 5.

38 *"The guns were silent"*: Unpublished journal of Tekla Szilard.

39 *"The thought that I might convert"*: Ibid.

40 *"They had a presence"*: Wigner as told to Szanton, *Recollections of Eugene P. Wigner*, 46.

41 *"When Ratz saw"*: Ibid., 51.

41 *"I never felt"*: Ibid., 57.

41 *Once, on the way home:* Ibid., 45–62.

41 *"depth of mathematical knowledge"*: Ibid., 57–58.

42 *"My own history"*: Eugene Wigner, Banquet Speech, Nobel Banquet, Stockholm, December 10, 1963.

42 *"Tell me how"*: Herman Goldstine, *The Computer: From Pascal to von Neumann* (Princeton: Princeton University Press, 1993), 167.

43 *On July 28, 1914*: Arthur Koestler, *Arrow in the Blue: An Autobiography* (New York: Macmillan, 1952), 60–72.

45 *"One day during the summer"*: Ibid., 50.

2. HARVEST AT TWILIGHT

Background for this chapter came from: Max Born, *The Born–Einstein Letters, 1916–1955: Friendship, Politics and Physics in Uncertain Times*; Brassaï, *Letters to My Parents*; Brassaï, *The Secret Paris of the 30's*; Piers Brendon, *The Dark Valley: A Panorama of the 1930s*; Evan William Cameron, ed., *Sound and Cinema: The Coming of Sound to American Film*; Lee Congdon, *Seeing Red: Hungarian Intellectuals in Exile and the Challenge of Communism*; Janet Flanner, *Paris Was Yesterday: 1925–1939*; Gisele Freund, *Photography and Society*; Neal Gabler, *An Empire of Their Own: How the Jews Invented Hollywood*; Peter Gay, *My German Question: Growing Up in Nazi Berlin*; Peter Gay, *Weimar Culture: The Outsider as Insider*; Sarah Greenough, Robert Gurbo, and Sarah Kennel, eds., *Andre Kertesz*; Ernest Hemingway, *A Moveable Feast*; Charles Higham and Joel Greenberg, *The Celluloid Muse: Hollywood Directors Speak*; Alex Kershaw, *Blood and Champagne: The Life and Times of Robert Capa*; Harry Kessler, *Berlin in Lights: The Diaries of Count Harry Kessler (1918–1937)*; Arthur Koestler, *Darkness at Noon*; Klaus Kreimeier, *The UFA Story: A History of Germany's Greatest Film Company*; Thomas Levenson, *Einstein in Berlin*; John Meredyth Lucas, *Eighty Odd Years in Hollywood: Memoir of a Career in Film and Television*; Pierre Mac-Orlan, *Paris Vu par Andre Kertesz*; William R. Meyer, *Warner Brothers Directors: The Hard-Boiled, the Comic, and the Weepers*; Caroline Moorehead, *Gellhorn: A Twentieth-Century Life*; Sylvia Nasar, *A Beautiful Mind: The Life of Mathematical Genius and Nobel Laureate John Nash*; William L. Shirer, *20th Century Journey:*

The Nightmare Years, 1930–1940; Fritz Stern, *Einstein's German World*; Edward Teller with Judith Shoolery, *Memoirs: A Twentieth-Century Journey in Science and Politics*; Richard Whelan, *Robert Capa: A Biography*; Richard Whelan, *Robert Capa: The Definitive Collection*; Hal Wallis with Charles Higham, *The Autobiography of Hal Wallis*; and Eva Striker Zeisel, *Memories of Arthur.*

The author interviewed the following people for their expertise or, in some cases, eyewitness experiences: Lauren Bacall; Professor Jeanine Basinger; Eva Besnyo; Hans Bethe; Peter Bihari; Yvette Biro; Inge Bondi; Harold Brown; Henri Cartier-Bresson; Olivia de Havilland; George Dyson; Miguel Fidalgo, Curtiz scholar; Leslie Gelb; Professor Edward Gerjuoy, physicist, University of Pittsburgh; Rachel Gray, director, the Institute for Advanced Study; Robert Gurbo; Linda Leroy Janklow; Karoly Kincses; Henry Kissinger; Michael Korda; David Korda; Ferenc Kosari; William Lanouette, Leo Szilard's biographer; Dr. Peter Lax; Stefan Lorant; Suzy Marquis, Robert Capa's niece; John Morris; Gabor Pallo; Sylvia Plachy; Richard Rhodes; Michael Scammell, Arthur Koestler's biographer; Professor Fritz Stern; Peter Stone; Edward Teller; Wolfgang Theis, Deutsch Film Archive; David Thomson; Marcia Tucker, librarian, the Institute for Advanced Study; Erzsebet Vezer; Dr. Annette Vogt, the Kaiser Wilhelm Institute, Dahlem; Laszlo Voros; Richard Whelan, Robert Capa's biographer; Marina von Neumann Whitman; and Eva Striker Zeisel.

PAGE

50 *"I took this picture"*: Video interview of Andre Kertesz, courtesy of the estate of Andre Kertesz.

50 *"My being Jewish"*: Unpublished journal of Andre Kertesz, courtesy of the estate of Andre Kertesz.

51 *"All that is treasured in my life"*: Andre Kertesz, *Andre Kertesz: The Early Years* (New York: W. W. Norton, 2005), 24.

51 *"On one of them"*: Edward Teller with Judith Shoolery, *Memoirs: A Twentieth-Century Journey in Science and Politics* (New York: Perseus, 2001), 13–14.

51 *"My father could no longer"*: Ibid., 13.

52 *"Finding the consistency"*: Ibid., 7.

52 *"He read Euler"*: Stanley A. Blumberg and Gwinn Owens, *Energy and Conflict: The Life and Times of Edward Teller* (New York: G. P. Putnam's Sons, 1976), 25.

52 *"During my last two years"*: Teller, *Memoirs*, 37.

52 *Teller was younger than his*: Ibid., 33.

52 *"So you are a genius"*: Blumberg and Owens, *Energy and Conflict*, 16.

52 *"I walked along the Danube"*: Teller, *Memoirs*, 38.

55 *"On the way to Vienna"*: Evan William Cameron, ed., *Sound and Cinema: The Coming of Sound to American Film* (Pleasantville: Redgrave, 1980), 108.

55 *"The sight before us"*: S. Z. Sakall, *The Story of Cuddles: My Life Under the Emperor Francis Joseph, Adolf Hitler, and the Warner Brothers* (London: Cassell, 1954), 16.

55 *"The director"*: Richard Berczeller, "Sodom and Gomorrah," *The New Yorker*, Oct. 14, 1974.

57 *"Get this man to Hollywood"*: Jack L. Warner with D. Jennings, *My First Hundred Years in Hollywood* (New York: Random House, 1964), 160–61.

57 *Korda arrived by first-class*: Michael Korda, *Charmed Lives: A Family Romance* (New York: HarperPerennial, 2002), 441–86; and Lee Congdon, *Exile and Social Thought: Hungarian Intellectuals in Germany and Austria* (Princeton: Princeton University Press, 1991), 43–136, 137–212.

58 *"Ball Game"*: Arthur Koestler, "Ball Game," *Hungarian Quarterly*, Summer 1989 (published posthumously).

58 *For Koestler*: Arthur Koestler, *Arrow in the Blue: An Autobiography* (New York: Macmillan, 1952), 85–134.

60 *On April 1, 1926*: Ibid., 137–246.

60 *"It was as though"*: Elizabeth Jane Howard, *Slipstream* (London: Macmillan, 2002), 261.

60 *Even while*: Koestler, *Arrow in the Blue*, 146–60.

61 *"To go to Berlin"*: Joseph Roth, *What I Saw: Reports from Berlin, 1920–33* (London: Granta, 2003), 12.

62 *"Only on Sundays"*: Ibid., 192.

62 *"What I remember about him"*: Michael Powell, *A Life in Movies: An Autobiography* (London: Faber & Faber, 2000), 113.

64 *"Engineering"*: Leo Szilard, *Leo Szilard: His Version of the Facts*, Spencer R. Weart and Gertrude Weiss Szilard, eds. (Boston: MIT Press, 1978), 8.

65 *"Szilard was a regular"*: Nicholas Kurti, "Some Szilard Reminiscences," Feb. 5, 1998, unpublished.

65 *"Speaking Hungarian freely"*: Wigner as told to Szanton, *The Recollections of Eugene P. Wigner*, 93.

65 *"Johnny von Neumann"*: Ibid., 58, 59.

65 *Szilard discussed*: Szilard, *Leo Szilard: His Version of the Facts*, 9–14; and William Lanouette with Bela Szilard, *Genius in the Shadows: A Biography of Leo Szilard, the Man Behind the Bomb* (New York: Scribner, 1992), 81–102.

65 *"I went to von Laue"*: Szilard, *Leo Szilard: His Version of the Facts*, 9–14.

66 *"Einstein's thoughts alone"*: Wigner as told to Szanton, *The Recollections of Eugene P. Wigner*, 94.

67 *"I went to him"*: Szilard, *Leo Szilard: His Version of the Facts*, 10–11.

67 *Both found the highest joy*: Steve J. Heims, *John von Neumann and Norbert Wiener: From Mathematics to the Technologies of Life and Death* (Cambridge: MIT Press, 1980), 116.

68 *"When I reach Hollywood"*: Pete Martin, "Hollywood's Champion Language Assassin," *The Saturday Evening Post*, Aug. 2, 1947.

68 *"ran some scenes"*: Ibid.

69 *Impressed by his drive*: John Meredyth Lucas, *Eighty Odd Years in Hollywood: Memoir of a Career in Film and Television* (Jefferson, N.C.: McFarland, 2004), 52, 74, 84–86.

70 *"I see scenes"*: Martin, "Hollywood's Champion Language Assassin."

70 *"Ladies and Gentlemen"*: Michael Curtiz File, Hungarian Film Archives.

71 *In the mid-1920s*: Norman Macrae, *John von Neumann* (New York: Pantheon, 1992), 129–44.

71 *Even among the geniuses*: Heims, *John von Neumann and Norbert Wiener*, 129.

72 *"It is just as foolish"*: S. M. Ulam, *Adventures of a Mathematician* (New York: Charles Scribner's Sons, 1976), 102.

72 *On July 14, 1928*: Teller, *Memoirs*, 48.

73 *By 1930, Szilard sensed*: Szilard, *Leo Szilard: His Version of the Facts*, 13, 14.

73 *Another astute observer*: Harry Kessler, *Berlin in Lights: The Diaries of Count Harry Kessler (1918–1937)*, edited and translated by Charles Kessler (New York: Grove, 1971), 420.

73 *For the first time*: Teller, *Memoirs*, 90, 91.

76 *The center of Kertesz's universe*: Sandra S. Phillips, "Andre Kertesz: The Years in Paris," in *Andre Kertesz of Paris and New York*, Sandra S. Phillips, David Travis, and Weston

J. Naef, eds. (Chicago: Art Institute of Chicago, 1985), 17–57; and Sarah Greenough, "To Become a Virgin Again," in *Andre Kertesz*, Sarah Greenough, Robert Gurbo, and Sarah Kennel, eds. (Washington, D.C.: National Gallery of Art, and Princeton: Princeton University Press, 2005), 59–141.

76 *"My photographs were passed"*: Greenough, "To Become a Virgin Again," 59–140.

77 *"Loneliness is not for you"*: Letter from Jeno Kertesz to Andre Kertesz, courtesy of the estate of Andre Kertesz.

78 *"When we parted"*: Ibid.

78 *Kertesz's commercial breakthrough*: Greenough, "To Become a Virgin Again," 69–70.

78 *"has an artist's instinct"*: Phillips, "Andre Kertesz: The Years in Paris," 35.

78 *"Can we help it"*: Weston J. Naef, "Andre Kertesz: The Making of an American Photographer," *Andre Kertesz of Paris and New York*, 106.

79 *"I was successful"*: Video interview with Kertesz, estate of Andre Kertesz.

79 *Increasingly, even his magazine work*: David Travis, "Kertesz and his Contemporaries in Germany and France," *Andre Kertesz of Paris and New York*, 61.

80 *"Not one of us here"*: Naef, "Andre Kertesz: The Making of an American Photographer," 99.

80 *"Each time"*: Noel Bourcier, *Andre Kertesz 55*, translated by Vincent Homolka (London: Phaidon, 2001), 15.

80 *"I was not yet a photographer"*: Brassaï, *Camera 42* magazine, April 1963, 32.

81 *"the inhabitants"*: Travis, "Kertesz and his Contemporaries in Germany and France," 80–81.

81 *"I have found my counterpart"*: Henry Miller, *Tropic of Cancer* (New York: Grove, 1961), 171.

82 *"Who does that guy"*: Korda, *Charmed Lives*, 81.

82 *"Since you left"*: Paul Tabori, *Alexander Korda* (New York: Living Books, 1966), 88.

82 *"Wednesday [payday] is lovely"*: Tabori, *Alexander Korda*, 96.

83 *"Please, my dear Lajos, tell me frankly"*: Ibid., 97.

83 *"He was a paper millionaire"*: Warner with Jennings, *My First Hundred Years in Hollywood*, 192–93.

83 *"What'dya think"*: Korda, *Charmed Lives*, 84–85.

84 *"I was the only one"*: Josef von Sternberg, *Fun in a Chinese Laundry: An Autobiography* (New York: Collier, 1973), 174.

84 *"Sandor Korda is"*: Brassaï, *Brassaï: Letters to My Parents*, translated by Peter Laki and Barna Kantor (Chicago: Chicago University Press, 1997), 201.

86 *Leon Trotsky was responsible*: Richard Whelan, *Robert Capa: A Biography* (New York: Alfred A. Knopf, 1985), 40–44.

86 *Budapest, in its own bubble*: Hungarian newspaper from the 1930s, courtesy of Attila Pok from his personal collection.

91 *"I invented Capa"*: John Hersey, "The Man Who Invented Himself," 47, September 1947; and Capa radio interview, WNBC, New York, October 20, 1940, courtesy of the estate of Robert Capa.

92 *"Promising as I might be"*: Wigner with Szanton, *The Recollections of Eugene P. Wigner*, 128–29.

92 *"Jancsi felt at home in"*: Ibid., 132–35.

92 *"No other people"*: Michael Blumenthal, *When History Enters the House: Essays from Central Europe* (Port Angeles, Wash.: Pleasure Boat Studio, 1998), 43.

93 *"the town had no coffeehouses"*: Wigner with Szanton, *Recollections of Eugene P. Wigner*, 173.

93 *"Princeton's physics"*: Ibid., 166.

93 *"how little people"*: Robert Jungk, *Brighter Than a Thousand Suns: A Personal History of the Atomic Scientists* (New York: Harvest, 1986), 299.

93 *"But Johnny"*: Macrae, *John von Neumann*, 170.

93 *"various objects of silver, etc."*: John von Neumann file, courtesy of the Institute for Advanced Study.

93 *"ensconced in a large"*: Richard Rhodes, *The Making of the Atomic Bomb* (New York: Simon & Schuster, 1986), 196.

94 *"There is not much"*: John von Neumann file, Institute for Advanced Study.

94 *"It's naive"*: Miklos Redei, *"John von Neumann's Selected Letters,"* 2004, unpublished.

94 *"Johnny showed me Budapest"*: Ulam, *Adventures of a Mathematician*, 109.

95 *"Johnny used to say"*: Ibid., 111.

95 *Happy to be back in Europe*: Koestler, *Arrow in the Blue*, 208–15; and Michel Laval, *L'Homme Sans Concession* (Paris: Calmann-Levy, 2005), 61–89.

96 *In Berlin*: Koestler, *Arrow in the Blue*, 237–46.

96 *"My income was . . . not"*: Koestler, *Arrow in the Blue*, 239.

96 *"One day [journalism]"*: Ibid., 240.

96 *"I had sung"*: Ibid., 240–41.

96 *"We were Central Europeans"*: Ibid., 234.

97 *"Active resistance"*: Ibid., 258.

97 *"By the time"*: Ibid., 259.

97 *"I gave up my flat"*: Arthur Koestler, *The Invisible Writing* (New York: Macmillan, 1954), 21.

98 *"During that long"*: Ibid., 23.

98 *"At every station"*: Ibid., 51.

98 *"everything that shocked"*: Ibid., 53.

99 *"He had lost"*: Suzannah Lessard, *"The Present Moment,"* *The New Yorker*, April 13, 1987.

99 *"As I lay"*: Koestler, *The Invisible Writing*, 111.

99 *The famous African-American*: Langston Hughes, *I Wonder as I Wander: An Autobiographical Journey* (New York: Hill & Wang, 1964), 109–38.

99 *"By a strange hazard"*: Koestler, *The Invisible Writing*, 116.

99 *"The Judge and the public prosecutor"*: Ibid., 119.

100 *Time seemed to have come to a standstill*: Ibid.

100 *"It is a curious fact"*: Koestler, *The Invisible Writing*, 150.

100 *"They were all tired men"*: Ibid., 155.

101 *"What I noticed"*: Szilard, *Leo Szilard: His Version of the Facts*, 13–14.

101 *"Non-Aryans"*: Ibid., 14.

101 *"We were convinced"*: Lanouette with Szilard, *Genius in the Shadows*, 120.

102 *This activity suited Szilard's temperament*: Szilard, *Leo Szilard: His Version of the Facts*, 15.

102 *"The forecast of the writers"*: Leo Szilard file, courtesy of William Lanouette.

102 *Lord Ernest Rutherford*: Teller, *Memoirs*, 110.

102 *"I do not believe"*: John von Neumann file, Institute for Advanced Study.

103 *"We are scraping along"*: Letter from Andre Kertesz to Imre Kertesz, estate of Andre Kertesz.

105 *"It is difficult to live here"*: Ibid.

105 *In 1939, Life*: Naef, *"Andre Kertesz: The Making of an American Photographer,"* 103–4.

106 *Arthur Koestler arrived*: Koestler, *The Invisible Writing*, 163.

106 *"For us"*: Arthur Koestler, *Bricks to Babel: Selected Writings with Author's Comments* (London: Picador, 1982), 119.

106 *"The old waiters"*: Koestler, *The Invisible Writing*, 165.

107 *So Koestler returned to Budapest*: Ibid., 168–87.

107 *"After a year"*: Ibid., 174.

107 *"Hitler gave it a new"*: Ibid., 193.

108 *"The Falling Soldier"*: John Morris to author.

110 *On Sunday, July 25*: Alex Kershaw, *Blood and Champagne: The Life and Times of Robert Capa* (New York: Da Capo, 2004), 48–65.

112 *After a short-lived Republican victory*: Piers Brendon, *The Dark Valley: A Panorama of the 1960s* (New York: Alfred A. Knopf, 2000), 359–410.

112 *The fact that Britain's*: Karol Kulik, *Alexander Korda: The Man Who Could Work Miracles* (London: Virgin, 1990), 83.

113 *"Everyone wanted to know Korda"*: Powell, *A Life in the Movies*, 263.

113 *For three years*: Korda, *Charmed Lives*, 94–127; and Kulik, *Alexander Korda*, 69.

113 *"An enormous personality"*: Kevin Brownlow, *David Lean: A Biography* (New York: Wyatt/St. Martin's Press, 1996), 279.

113 *"I would go see Alex"*: Korda, *Charmed Lives*, 92.

114 *"Alex, you must be mad!"*: Powell, *A Life in the Movies*, 363.

114 *Korda [was] one of the most*: von Sternberg, *Fun in a Chinese Laundry*, 173.

115 *"Korda had been urging"*: Lucas, *Eighty Odd Years in Hollywood*, 148–49.

115 *"Largest gathering"*: *Variety*, Oct. 9, 1935.

115 *"The lucky Hungarian"*: Anne Edwards, *Vivien Leigh: A Biography* (New York: Simon & Schuster, 1977), 93; and Charles Drazin, *Korda: Britain's Only Movie Mogul* (London: Sidgwick & Jackson, 2002), 165.

116 *"The fact that we have lost"*: Memorandum called "Films" in Prudential Archives, Box 2353.

116 *"The films of the new company"*: Drazin, *Korda*, 201.

116 *Later that year*: *Chicago Herald-American*, Oct. 14, 1939.

116 *"Alexander Korda," Chaplin recalled*: Charlie Chaplin, *Charles Chaplin: My Autobiography* (London: The Bodley Head, 1964), 424–25.

117 *"Anyone who . . . lived through"*: Koestler, *The Invisible Writing*, 326.

117 *"I still had one last"*: Arthur Koestler, *Dialogue with Death* (New York: Macmillan, 1966), 45.

118 *"Let us hope"*: Ibid., 159.

118 *"I had actually"*: Ibid., 117.

119 *"We knew the truth"*: Koestler, *The Invisible Writing*, 387.

119 *"Closing time was approaching"*: Ibid., 375.

119 *"I saw my father"*: Ibid., 376.

119 *"No movement"*: Ibid., 388.

119 *"They walked past [me]"*: Ibid., 388.

119 *"I worked on my letter"*: Ibid., 389.

120 *"The Moscow trials"*: Ibid.

121 *Michael Curtiz escaped*: James C. Robertson, *The Casablanca Man: The Cinema of Michael Curtiz* (London: Routledge, 1993), 20–75.

122 *"I arrived"*: Rudy Behlmer, *Inside Warner Bros., 1935–1951* (New York: Fireside, 1987), 99.

122 *"When I see a lazy man or a don't care girl"*: Martin, "Hollywood's Champion Language Assassin."

122 *"Next time I send"*: Graham Lord, *Niv: The Authorized Biography of David Niven* (New York: Thomas Dunne/St. Martin's Press, 2004), 77.

122 *"High on the rostrum"*: David Niven, *Bring on the Empty Horses* (New York: G. P. Putnam's Sons, 1975), 119–20.

122 *"What the hell is this date"*: Lucas, *Eighty Odd Years in Hollywood*, 75.

123 *"I work because"*: Martin, "Hollywood's Champion Language Assassin"; and William R. Meyer, *Warner Brothers Directors: The Hard-Boiled, the Comic, and the Weepers* (New Rochelle, N.Y.: Arlington House, 1978), 75–107.

123 *"There is one thing"*: Hal Wallis memorandum, Dec. 3, 1937, Warner Brothers Archives.

123 *Paramount's Zukor*: Neal Gabler, *An Empire of Their Own: How the Jews Invented Hollywood* (New York: Doubleday, 1989), 46.

124 *Curtiz asked Jack Warner*: Warner with Jennings, *My First Hundred Years in Hollywood*, 275–76.

124 *"Nobody is going to hurt you"*: James Cagney, *Cagney by Cagney* (Garden City: Doubleday, 1976), 72–73.

125 *"I have seen hundreds of thousands"*: Robert Capa, *Death in the Making* (New York: Covici/Friede, 1938), unnumbered page proofs, courtesy of the estate of Robert Capa.

125 *"I know your modesty"*: Capa correspondence, estate of Robert Capa.

126 *"I was sure"*: Letter from Martha Gellhorn to Robert Capa, estate of Robert Capa.

3. DARKNESS

The author relied on the following publications to background this period: Stephen Ambrose, *D-Day: The Climactic Battle of World War II*; Rudy Behlmer, *Inside Warner Bros., 1935–1951*; Jennet Conant, *109 East Palace: Robert Oppenheimer and the Secret City of Los Alamos*; Charles Francisco, *You Must Remember This . . . The Filming of Casablanca*; Howard Koch, *Casablanca: The Complete Script and Legend Behind the film*; Richard Rhodes, *The Making of the Atomic Bomb*; Edward Shils, "Leo Szilard: A Memoir"; and Alice Kimball Smith, "The Elusive Dr. Szilard."

Essential background for this section came from interviews with: Professor Jeanine Basinger; Eva Besnyo; Inge Bondi; Benjamin Bradlee; Harold Brown; Cornell Capa; George Dyson; Freeman Dyson; Professor Edward Gerjuoy; Rachel Gray; Robert Gurbo; Henry Kissinger; Michael Korda; William Lanouette, Leo Szilard's biographer; Professor Ralph Lapp; Professor Peter Lax; Bernard-Henri Levy; John Morris; Gabor Pallo; Richard Rhodes; Jean Richards; Jack Rosenthal; Michael Scammell, Arthur Koestler's biographer; Arthur M. Schlesinger, Jr.; John Silard, nephew of Leo Szilard; Peter Stone; Sandor Striker; David Thomas; Richard Whelan; Marina von Neumann Whitman; and Eva Striker Zeisel.

PAGE

129 *"[We] knew well"*: Edward Teller with Judith Shoolery, *Memoirs: A Twentieth-Century Journey in Science and Politics* (Cambridge: Perseus, 2001), 143.

129 *"It seemed to us"*: Leo Szilard, *Leo Szilard: His Version of the Facts: Selected Recollections and Correspondence*, Spencer R. Weart and Gertrud Weiss Szilard, eds. (Boston: MIT Press, 1978), 53.

129 *"[Oppenheimer] brushed [us] off"*: Eugene P. Wigner as told to Andrew Szanton, *The Recollections of Eugene P. Wigner* (New York: Basic, 1992), 244.

130 *"I still had no position"*: Richard Rhodes, *The Making of the Atomic Bomb* (New York: Simon & Schuster, 1986), 301.

130 *"attempting . . . to make"*: Teller, *Memoirs*, 142.

131 *"The colonels kept"*: Wigner as told to Szanton, *The Recollections of Eugene P. Wigner*, 203.

131 *"After the meeting"*: Teller, *Memoirs*, 149.

131 *"Precious months passed"*: Wigner as told to Szanton, *The Recollections of Eugene P. Wigner*, 205.

131 *Szilard wrote with undisguised dismay*: Szilard, *Leo Szilard: His Version of the Facts*, 115.

132 *"I had assumed"*: Rhodes, *The Making of the Atomic Bomb*, 330.

132 *"I still think war"*: Gregg Herken, *The Brotherhood of the Bomb: The Tangled Lives and Loyalties of Robert Oppenheimer, Ernest Lawrence, and Edward Teller* (New York: Henry Holt, 2002), 24.

132 *"a terrible anxiety"*: S. M. Ulam, *Adventures of a Mathematician* (New York: Charles Scribner's Sons, 1976), 118.

132 *Now, a second alarm bell*: Kai Bird and Martin J. Sherwin, *American Prometheus: The Triumph and Tragedy of J. Robert Oppenheimer* (New York: Alfred A. Knopf, 2005), 180.

133 *"almost in tears"*: Rhodes, *The Making of the Atomic Bomb*, 381.

133 *"Compton," Wigner related*: Wigner as told to Szanton, *The Recollections of Eugene P. Wigner*, 209.

134 *Wigner lived in "constant fear"*: Wigner to Szanton, *The Recollections of Eugene P. Wigner*, 215.

134 *"I refused to give it to them"*: Ibid., 216.

134 *"His name is Wagner"*: Teller, *Memoirs*, 194.

135 *"I feel like"*: "Testing the President," *The New York Times*, December 10, 1998.

135 *"Once the opening scene"*: Arthur Koestler, *Bricks to Babel: Selected Writings with Author's Comments* (London: Picador, 1982), 181. Quotes from *Darkness at Noon* are from *Darkness at Noon* (New York: Bantam, 1968).

136 *As Europe edged toward war*: Arthur Koestler, *The Invisible Writing* (New York: Macmillan, 1954), 393–405; and *Bricks to Babel*, 180–202.

138 *"Yet a friendly voodoo seemed"*: Koestler, *The Invisible Writing*, 402.

139 *"Brilliant as this book is"*: Iain Hamilton, *Koestler: A Biography* (London: Macmillan, 1982), 69.

139 *"one of the few books"*: Ibid., 71.

139 *"the greatest foreign novelist"*: Harold Harris, ed., *Astride the Two Cultures: Arthur Koestler at 70* (London: Hutchinson, 1975), 93.

139 *Upon its American publication, in May 1941*: Ralph Thompson, "Books of the Times," *New York Times*, May 20, 1941.

139 *"[Koestler] is unfair to Russia"*: Malcolm Cowley, "Books in Review," *The New Republic*, June 2, 1941.

139 *In a later issue*: Malcolm Cowley, "Books in Review," *The New Republic*, July 20, 1942.

140 *"It is the only good one"*: Letter from Arthur Koestler to Eva Zeisel, courtesy of Eva Striker Zeisel.

140 *"I had been interested"*: Teller, *Memoirs*, 182–83.

140 *"We had all gathered"*: Michael Powell, *A Life in Movies* (London: Faber & Faber, 2000), 331–32.

141 *"Alex summoned a meeting"*: Ibid., 329.

141 *"Propaganda"*: Michael Korda, *Charmed Lives: A Family Romance* (New York: HarperPerennial, 2002), 150–54.

142 *"The Nelson film"*: Anne Edwards, *Vivien Leigh: A Biography* (New York: Simon & Schuster, 1977), 128–29.

142 *"The stature it has given"*: Charles Drazin, *Korda: Britain's Only Movie Mogul* (London: Sidgwick & Jackson, 2002), 243.

143 *"Over an excellent glass"*: Ibid., 268.

143 *"There was something grand"*: Graham Greene, *Loser Takes All* (London: Penguin, 1955), 15.

144 *"We were asked to dinner"*: Powell, *A Life in Movies*, 612.

144 *"I'd take my pajamas"*: Paul Tabori, *Alexander Korda* (New York: Living Books, 1966), 12.

145 *Curtiz was skeet-shooting*: John Meredyth Lucas, *Eighty Odd Years in Hollywood: Memoir of a Career in Film and Television* (Jefferson, N.C.: McFarland, 2004), 128.

145 *"I have discussed this"*: Rudy Behlmer, *Inside Warner Bros., 1935–1951* (New York: Fireside, 1987), 194–221.

145 *"Every day we were shooting"*: Ingrid Bergman with Alan Burgess, *My Story* (New York: Delacorte, 1980), 109–10.

146 *"Curtiz has an instinctual"*: Jack Edmund Nolan, "Michael Curtiz," *Films in Review*, undated, 525–35, Michael Curtiz File, Hungarian Film Archives.

146 *"These are turbulent days"*: Behlmer, *Inside Warner Bros.*, 209.

147 *The film was nominated for eight*: James C. Robertson, *The Casablanca Man: The Cinema of Michael Curtiz* (London: Routledge, 1993), 76–80.

148 *"I was so dog tired"*: James Cagney, *Cagney by Cagney* (Garden City: Doubleday, 1976), 106–7.

148 *Mildred Pierce*: Joan Crawford, *A Portrait of Joan: An Autobiography* (Garden City: Doubleday, 1962), 139.

148 *"This stinks!"*: Ibid., 139.

148 *"I didn't care what I wore"*: Ibid.

148 *"When I started the tests"*: Ibid., 140.

149 *One day in 1945*: A. E. Hotchner, *Doris Day: Her Own Story* (New York: Bantam, 1976), 99.

149 *Curtiz had his own bungalow*: Ibid., 100–102.

150 *"Some people," Curtiz told her*: Ibid., 107–8.

150 *"I have two hours"*: Ulam, *Adventures of a Mathematician*, 141.

150 *"Johnny loved looking out"*: Steve J. Heims, *John von Neumann and Norbert Wiener: From Mathematics to the Technologies of Life and Death* (Cambridge: MIT Press, 1980), 192.

151 *"At great expense"*: Laura Fermi, "That Was the Manhattan District," *The New Yorker*, July 31, 1954.

151 *"[Teller and von Neumann] were talking"*: Ulam, *Adventures of a Mathematician*, 146.

151 *Behind the barbed wire*: Kai Bird and Martin J. Sherwin, *American Prometheus: The Triumph and Tragedy of J. Robert Oppenheimer* (New York: Alfred A. Knopf, 2005), 179–94.

151 *"He had a completely sure"*: Herman Goldstine, *The Computer: From Pascal to von Neumann* (Princeton: Princeton University Press, 1993), 176.

151 *"When [Teller] could forget"*: Fermi, "That Was the Manhattan District."

152 *Hans Bethe sometimes wondered*: Steve J. Heims, *John von Neumann and Norbert Wiener* (Cambridge: MIT Press, 1980), 358.

152 *"I am thinking about"*: Freeman Dyson, *Disturbing the Universe* (New York: Basic, 1979), 194.

153 *"Von Neumann was the first"*: Goldstine, *The Computer*, 191–92.

154 *"the most important document"*: Rhodes, *The Making of the Atomic Bomb*, 250.

154 *"He was a good guy"*: General Gavin, letter to the editor, 47 *Magazine*, October 1947.

155 *"After the previous night's experience"*: Robert Capa, *Slightly Out of Focus: The Legendary Photojournalist's Illustrated Memoir of World War II* (New York: Modern Library, 2001), 44–47.

155 *"The first ride through"*: Alex Kershaw, *Blood and Champagne: The Life and Times of Robert Capa* (New York: Da Capo, 2004), 108.

155 *"Mr. Capa, by reason"*: Letter from General Matthew Ridgway to *Life*, estate of Robert Capa.

155 *"You are going great guns, Bob"*: Telegram from Wilson Hicks to Robert Capa, estate of Robert Capa.

156 *"When he was not"*: Irwin Shaw, "Robert Capa," *Vogue*, April 1982.

156 *"I decided," Capa recalled*: Capa, *Slightly Out of Focus*, 137.

157 *"The bullets tore holes"*: Ibid., 140–41.

157 *"Poor fellow"*: Charles Jarreau, interview transcript, Eisenhower Center, New Orleans.

157 *"I climbed aboard"*: Capa, *Slightly Out of Focus*, 148.

158 *"Are you a good Jew?"*: Capa, *Slightly Out of Focus*, 133.

158 *"The old arrogance"*: Letter from Robert Capa to his family, estate of Robert Capa.

159 *"The night of the 25th"*: Capa, *Slightly Out of Focus*, 179.

159 *"From the Rhine to the Oder"*: Capa, *Slightly Out of Focus*, 226.

159 *By the mid-1940s*: Koestler, *Bricks to Babel*, 215–22; and Hamilton, *Koestler*, 383.

160 *For Koestler, who described himself*: Koestler, *The Invisible Writing*, 423.

160 *"My mother and I"*: Andrew S. Grove, *Swimming Across: A Memoir* (New York: Warner, 2001), 32–49.

161 *"Six million," Koestler*: Arthur Koestler and Cynthia Koestler, *Stranger on the Square*, Harold Harris, ed. (London: Hutchinson, 1984), 35.

161 *"He died in 1940"*: Koestler, *The Invisible Writing*, 376.

161 *"Talk to those"*: Koestler and Koestler, *Stranger on the Square*, 36.

161 *He made a dangerous journey*: Ibid., 37.

162 *"While dead and dying Jews"*: Teller, *Memoirs*, 201.

162 *"We were all lying"*: Ibid., 211.

163 *Groves's deputy, General Thomas F. Farrell*: Robert Jungk, *Brighter Than a Thousand Suns: A Personal History of the Atomic Scientists* (New York: Harvest, 1986), 201.

163 *"I am become Death"*: Jungk, *Brighter Than a Thousand Suns*, 201; Ulam, *Adventures of a Mathematician*, 170; and Teller, *Memoirs*, 219.

163 *Observing Oppie's ambivalence*: Ulam, *Adventures of a Mathematician*, 170.

164 *"It was too cleverly written"*: William Lanouette with Bela Szilard, *Genius in the Shadows: A Biography of Leo Szilard, the Man Behind the Bomb* (New York: Scribner, 1992), 309, 313, 333.

164 *"The Subject is"*: Ibid., 250.

165 *"of a new explosive"*: Rhodes, *The Making of the Atomic Bomb*, 617.

165 *"[Szilard's] general demeanor"*: Ibid., 637.

165 *For his part, Szilard was shocked*: Szilard, *Leo Szilard: His Version of the Facts*, 184–85.

166 *"Scientists have no right"*: Lanouette with Szilard, *Genius in the Shadows*, 270.

166 *"The things we are working on"*: Herken, *The Brotherhood of the Bomb*, 135.

166 *"I don't want Kyoto bombed"*: Rhodes, *The Making of the Atomic Bomb*, 640, and Groves, *Now It Can Be Told*, 275.

166 *"He had a hidden admiration"*: Goldstine, *Adventures of a Mathematician*, 105; and Richard Rhodes, *Dark Sun: The Making of the Hydrogen Bomb* (New York: Simon & Schuster, 1995), 202.

167 *"The fires raging unopposed"*: Rhodes, *Dark Sun*, 355.

167 "always managed to learn": Fermi, "That Was the Manhattan District."

167 "Using atomic bombs against Japan": Lanouette with Szilard, Genius in the Shadows, 277.

167 "It is very difficult": Ibid.

170 "I left France": Koestler and Koestler, Stranger on the Square, 67.

170 As always, the black cloud: David Cesarini, Arthur Koestler: The Homeless Mind (New York: Free Press, 1998), 271.

4. FALSE DAWN

The author also relied on important documentation found in: Jeremy Bernstein, Oppenheimer: Portrait of an Enigma; Kai Bird and Martin J. Sherwin, American Prometheus: The Triumph and Tragedy of J. Robert Oppenheimer; Jacob Bronowski, The Ascent of Man; Flo Conway and Jim Siegelman, Dark Hero of the Information Age: In Search of Norbert Wiener, the Father of Cybernetics; Frances FitzGerald, Way Out There in the Blue: Reagan, Star Wars and the End of the Cold War; Peter Goodchild, Edward Teller: The Real Doctor Strangelove; Steve J. Heims, John von Neumann and Norbert Wiener: From Mathematics to the Technologies of Life and Death; Priscilla J. McMillan, The Ruin of J. Robert Oppenheimer and the Birth of the Modern Arms Race; George Mikes, Arthur Koestler: The Story of a Friendship; John Morris, Get the Picture: A Personal History of Photojournalism; Jack Rummel, Robert Oppenheimer: Dark Prince; Philip M. Stern, "Foreword," In the Matter of J. Robert Oppenheimer: Transcripts of Hearing Before Personnel Security Board and Texts of Principal Documents and Letters; and Herbert F. York, The Advisors: Oppenheimer, Teller, and the Superbomb.

The author conducted interviews with the following for this section: Professor Jeanine Basinger; Eva Besnyo; Inge Bondi; Benjamin Bradlee; Harold Brown; Cornell Capa; Freeman Dyson; George Dyson; Leslie Gelb; Professor Edward Gerjuoy; Rachel Gray, director, the Institute for Advanced Study; Robert Gurbo; Henry Kissinger; Michael Korda; Peter Lax; Suzy Marquis (Robert Capa's niece); John Morris; Gabor Pallo; Sylvia Plachy; Richard Rhodes; Jean Richards; Jack Rosenthal; Michael Scammell; Arthur M. Schlesinger, Jr.; John Silard, nephew of Leo Szilard; Sandor Striker; David Thomas; Richard Whelan; and Marina von Neumann Whitman.

PAGE

173 von Neumann, characteristically: John von Neumann file, courtesy of the Institute for Advanced Study.

173 "warmed both hands": Herman Goldstine, The Computer: From Pascal to von Neumann (Princeton: Princeton University Press, 1993), 177.

173 "expected to produce": Letter exchange between Freeman Dyson and Richard Kadison, May 16 and 18, 2002, courtesy of Freeman Dyson.

174 Many scientists were upset: von Neumann's video biography (1994), courtesy of the American Mathematical Association of America.

174 "I wanted him to be a mathematician": Ibid.

174 "He became more and more engaged": Bronowski, The Ascent of Man, 432–35.

174 "We will have to do things": Edward Teller with Judith Shoolery, Memoirs: A Twentieth-Century Journey in Science and Politics (Cambridge: Perseus, 2001), 163.

175 Always intense and obsessive: Ibid., 162–63, 193, 273–359; William J. Broad, Teller's War: The Top Secret Story Behind the Star Wars Deception (New York: Simon & Schuster, 1992), 23–64; and Stanley A. Blumberg and Gwinn Owens, Energy and Conflict: The Life and Times of Edward Teller (New York: G. P. Putnam's Sons, 1976), 76–78.

175 "I always felt uncomfortable": Teller as told to Szanton, Memoirs, 162–63.

176 *Into this indecisive mood:* Ingrid Bergman with Alan Burgess, *My Story* (New York: Delacorte, 1980), 141–48.

177 *He turned their chemistry:* Richard Whelan, "Introduction," Robert Capa, *Slightly Out of Focus: The Legendary Photojournalist's Memoir of World War II* (New York: Modern Library, 1999), xix; and David Thomas, "I Leica Danger," *The New Republic*, Aug. 18 and 25, 2003.

179 *"Only in the morning":* Letter to the editor, 47, *Magazine of the Year*, Oct. 1947.

179 *May 22, 1947:* Pierre Assouline, *Cartier-Bresson: L'Oeil du Siècle* (Paris: Gallimard, 1999), 242–47.

180 *"Capa never ran out":* Gisele Freund, *The World is My Camera*, translated by June Guicharnaud (New York: Dial, 1974), 205–10.

180 *Fourteen years after:* Robert Capa, "The Danube Is Red," *Illustrated Magazine*, March 26, 1949; and Alex Kershaw, *Blood and Champagne: The Life and Times of Robert Capa* (New York: Da Capo, 2004), 192–200.

180 *"Budapest," Capa observed:* Robert Capa, "The Danube Is Red," *Illustrated Magazine*, March 26, 1949.

180 *"As only one out of twenty":* Ibid.

181 *"Sad to say":* Eugene P. Wigner as told to Szanton, *The Recollections of Eugene P. Wigner* (New York: Basic, 1992), 259.

181 *"I think you will find":* Richard Rhodes, *Dark Sun: The Making of the Hydrogen Bomb* (New York: Simon & Schuster, 1995), 356.

181 *"I know. Never!":* David Halberstam, *The Fifties* (New York: Fawcett Columbine, 1994), 25.

182 *Shortly after hearing:* Blumberg and Owens, *Energy and Conflict*, 201.

182 *Knowing that the political winds:* Teller, *Memoirs*, 280–90; and Blumberg and Owens, *Energy and Conflict*, 213–31.

182 *"In this matter":* Halberstam, *The Fifties*, 91.

183 *"over my dead body":* Teller, *Memoirs*, 283.

183 *"With the Russians":* Clay Blair, "The Passing of a Great Mind," *Life*, Feb. 25, 1957.

183 *But for all his tenacity:* S. M. Ulam, *Adventures of a Mathematician* (New York: Charles Scribner's Sons, 1976), 209; and Richard Rhodes, *Dark Sun*, 461–63.

183 *"He hoped one way":* Ulam, *Adventures of a Mathematician*, 217.

184 *The Super was exploded:* Teller, *Memoirs*, 343–59; and Rhodes, *Dark Sun*, 482–512.

184 *"Now that you have":* Halberstam, *The Fifties*, 99.

184 *He did not much care about Oppenheimer:* McMillan, *The Ruin of J. Robert Oppenheimer and the Birth of the Modern Arms Race*, 13.

185 *"I think it would be":* Ibid., 351.

185 *While Oppenheimer would not:* Halberstam, *The Fifties*, 351.

186 *Shortly after the hearings:* Teller, *Memoirs*, 399.

186 *"Twice before":* Ibid., 397.

187 *In the 1950s:* Harold Harris, ed., *Astride the Two Cultures: Arthur Koestler at 70* (London: Hutchinson, 1975), 118.

176 *"Not one voice":* Arthur Koestler, *Bricks to Babel: Selected Writings with Author's Comments* (London: Picador, 1982), 201–2.

187 *"When I finished":* Ibid., 277–78.

188 *"What sort of table":* George Mikes, *Arthur Koestler: The Story of a Friendship* (London: Andre Deutsch, 1983), 12.

188 *"Listening to [von Neumann]":* Arthur Koestler and Cynthia Koestler, *Stranger on the Square*, Harold Harris, ed. (London: Hutchinson, 1984), 122.

188 *"Who would have thought":* Letter from Koestler to Eva Zeisel, courtesy of Eva Zeisel.

188 *"and New York makes me"*: Ibid., 156.

188 *"London was only a stone's throw"*: Ibid.

188 *"His regime"*: Elizabeth Jane Howard, *Slipstream: A Memoir* (London: Macmillan, 2002), 263.

189 *"The road was teeming"*: Arthur Koestler, *Promise and Fulfillment* (New York: Macmillan, 1949), 196.

89 *At the shabby*: Caroline Moorehead, *Gellhorn: A Twentieth-Century Life* (New York: Henry Holt, 2003), 276–78.

190 *"Here I am"*: Letter from Robert Capa to his mother, courtesy of the estate of Robert Capa.

191 *In 1953, the State Department*: Robert Capa's files, estate of Robert Capa.

193 *"This is going to be"*: "Forward Lies the Delta," *Time,* June 7, 1954; and Kershaw, *Blood and Champagne*, 246–51.

194 *"Korda over the dinner table"*: David Parkinson, ed., *The Graham Greene Film Reader: Reviews, Essays, Interviews and Film Stories* (New York: Applause, 1993), 429–32.

195 The Third Man *was produced*: Samuel Goldwyn Papers, Margaret Herrick Library, Academy of Motion Picture Arts and Sciences, Beverly Hills, California; and David Thomson, *Showman: The Life of David O. Selznick* (New York: Alfred A. Knopf, 1992), 532–39.

196 *"Alex was so lonely"*: Charles Drazin, *Korda: Britain's Only Movie Mogul* (London: Sidgwick & Jackson, 2002), 291.

196 *"We are in show business"*: London *Daily Express,* Jan. 24, 1956.

196 *"Don't you know how"*: Drazin, *Korda*, 355.

197 *"He managed the difficult"*: Ibid., 356–57.

197 *"With the death of Korda"*: Parkinson, *The Graham Greene Film Reader*, 439–40.

198 *In the corridors*: Directory for the Institute for 1956–57, the Institute for Advanced Study Archive, Princeton, New Jersey.

198 *One of the most famous*: Sylvia Nasar, *A Beautiful Mind: The Life of Mathematical Genius and Nobel Laureate John Nash* (New York: Touchstone, 2001), 93.

198 *Perhaps, as Nasar believes*: Ibid., 94–95.

199 *Nash, then in the deepest throes of madness*: Ibid., 339.

199 *"It all came so easily"*: Video biography of John von Neumann (1966), Mathematical Association of America.

200 *"There was a sadness"*: Ulam, *Adventures of a Mathematician*, 239.

201 *"I wish I could be around"*: Norman Macrae, *John von Neumann* (New York: Pantheon, 1992), 377.

201 *"visiting him when"*: Interview with Teller, video biography of John von Neumann (1966), Mathematical Association of America.

201 *"Gathered around"*: Steve J. Heims, *John von Neumann and Norbert Wiener: From Mathematics to the Technologies of Life and Death* (Cambridge: MIT Press, 1980), 371.

202 *"With deep regret"*: John von Neumann file, the Institute for Advanced Study.

202 *"He darted briefly into our domain"*: Norman Macrae, *John von Neumann* (New York: Pantheon Books), 1992.

202 *"Einstein, Max Planck"*: Wigner as told to Szanton, *The Recollections of Eugene P. Wigner*, 281.

202 *"After sixty years"*: Ibid., 313–15.

203 *"beautifully crisp"*: William R. Meyer, *Warner Brothers Directors: The Hard-Boiled, the Comic, and the Weepers* (New Rochelle, N.Y.: Arlington House, 1978), 99.

206 "A few days ago": Letter from Michael Curtiz to friend, Curtiz File, courtesy the Hungarian Film Archives, Budapest.

206 "I am not Mike Curtiz": Kevin Brownlow, David Lean: A Biography (New York: Wyatt/St. Martin's Press, 1996), 425.

207 After General Groves: William Lanouette with Bela Szilard, Genius in the Shadows: A Biography of Leo Szilard, the Man Behind the Bomb (New York: Scribner, 1992), 377–403; and Nova: "The Genius Behind the Bomb," WGBH-TV, Sept. 29, 1992.

208 "We were in agreement": Nova: "The Genius Behind the Bomb," Sept. 29, 1992.

208 "The blade must be changed": Lanouette, Genius in the Shadows, 421.

209 "What if I should": Lanouette, Genius in the Shadows: A Biography of Leo Szilard, the Man Behind the Bomb (New York: Scribner, 1992), 474.

209 Hans Bethe told Szilard's: Lanouette, "Szilardian Science and Politics: Evolution, Revolution, or Subversion," Nov. 10, 2005, World Science Forum, Budapest.

210 "typical . . . Central European member": Koestler, Bricks to Babel, 683.

210 "A dispassionate observer": Ibid., 508.

211 Only old age and infirmity: Mikes, Arthur Koestler, 72–80.

212 his brother Imre wrote to him: Letter from Imre Kertesz to Andre Kertesz, courtesy of the estate of Andre Kertesz.

213 "You are still": Unpublished diary of Andre Kertesz, estate of Andre Kertesz.

213 "As I give up the slave work": Letter from Andre Kertesz to Greti Kertesz, Nov. 6, 1962, estate of Andre Kertesz.

214 "Worked [in Montmartre]": unpublished journal of Andre Kertesz, courtesy of the estate of Andre Kertesz.

214 Fusing his past with his present: Andre Kertesz, Kertesz on Kertesz: A Self Portrait (New York: Abbeville, 1985).

214 "Go and see everyone": Letter from Elizabeth Kertesz to Andre Kertesz, estate of Andre Kertesz.

215 "The photographic world": John Szarkowski, The Photographer's Eye (New York: Museum of Modern Art, 1966), 8.

217 "One Sunday evening": Freeman Dyson, Disturbing the Universe (New York: Basic, 1979), 92–93.

218 "Great men . . . have passionate opponents": Wigner as told to Szanton, The Recollections of Eugene P. Wigner, 273, 317.

218 "I was most impressed": Teller, Memoirs, 509.

EPILOGUE

The author relied on the following works in the writing of the epilogue: Silvano Arieti, Creativity: The Magic of Synthesis; Andrew S. Grove, Swimming Across: A Memoir; Michael T. Kaufman, Soros: The Life and Times of a Messianic Billionaire; as well as interviews with the following: Andy Grove; Imre Kertesz; and George Soros.

SELECTED BIBLIOGRAPHY

Aizpurua, Juan P. Fisi, Richard Whelan, and Catherin Coleman. *Heart of Spain: Robert Capa's Photographs of the Spanish Civil War*. Bilbao: Museo Nacional Centro de Arte Reina Sofía, 1999.

Alexander, Franz. *The Western Mind in Transition*. New York: Random House, 1960.

Allport, Gordon W. *The Nature of Prejudice*. Reading, Penn.: Addison-Wesley, 1992.

Ambrose, Stephen. *D-Day: The Climactic Battle of World War II*. New York: Simon & Schuster, 1994.

Arieti, Silvano. *Creativity: The Magic of Synthesis*. New York: Basic, 1976.

Assouline, Pierre. *Cartier-Bresson: L'Oeil du Siècle*. Paris: Gallimard, 1999.

Bacall, Lauren. *By Myself*. New York: Alfred A. Knopf, 1979.

Baxter, John. *Hollywood in the Thirties*. London: A. Zwemmer, and New York: A. S. Barnes, 1968.

Beaumont-Maillet, Laure, ed. *Capa Connu et Inconnu*. Paris: Bibliotheque Nationale de France, 2004.

Behlmer, Rudy. *Behind the Scenes*. Hollywood: Samuel French, 1990.

———. *Inside Warner Bros., 1935–1951: The Battles, the Brainstorms, and the Bickering from the Files of Hollywood's Greatest Studio*. New York: Fireside, 1987.

Behrman, S. N. *The Suspended Drawing Room*. London: Hamish Hamilton, 1966.

Bender, Thomas, and Carl E. Schorske, eds. *Budapest and New York: Studies in Metropolitan Transformation, 1870–1930*. New York: Russell Sage Foundation, 1994.

Berczeller, Richard. "Sodom and Gomorrah." *The New Yorker*, Oct. 14, 1974.

Bergman, Ingrid, with Alan Burgess. *My Story*. New York: Delacorte, 1980.

Bernstein, Jeremy. *Oppenheimer: Portrait of an Enigma*. Chicago: Ivan R. Dee, 2004.

Bernstein, Peter L. *Against the Gods: The Remarkable Story of Risk*. New York: John Wiley & Sons, 1996.

Bird, Kai, and Martin J. Sherwin. *American Prometheus: The Triumph and Tragedy of J. Robert Oppenheimer*. New York: Alfred A. Knopf, 2005.

Blumberg, Stanley A., and Gwinn Owens. *Energy and Conflict: The Life and Times of Edward Teller*. New York: G. P. Putnam's Sons, 1976.

Blumenthal, Michael. *When History Enters the House: Essays from Central Europe*. Port Angeles, Wash.: Pleasure Boat Studio, 1998.

Bolcsics, Marta, and Lajos Csordas. *Budapesti Krudy-Kalauz*. Budapest: Helikon Kiado, 2002.

Bondi, Inge. *Chim: The Photographs of David Seymour*. Boston: Little, Brown, 1996.

Borhan, Pierre. *Andre Kertesz: His Life and Work*. Boston: Little, Brown, 2000.

Borhan, Pierre, ed. *Andre Kertesz: La Biographie d'une Oeuvre*. Paris: Seuil, 1995.

Born, Max. *The Born–Einstein Letters, 1916–1955: Friendship, Politics and Physics in Uncertain Times*. Translated by Irene Born. New York: Macmillan, 2005.

Bourcier, Noel. *Andre Kertesz 55*. Translated by Vincent Homolka. London: Phaidon, 2001.

Braham, Randolph L. *The Politics of Genocide: The Holocaust in Hungary.* Detroit: Wayne State University Press, 2000.

Brassaï. *Brassaï: Letters to My Parents.* Translated by Peter Laki and Barna Kantor. Chicago: University of Chicago Press, 1997.

———. *The Secret Paris of the 30's.* Translated by Richard Miller. New York: Thames & Hudson, 2001.

Brendon, Piers. *The Dark Valley: A Panorama of the 1930s.* New York: Alfred A. Knopf, 2000.

Broad, William J. *Teller's War: The Top-Secret Story Behind the Star Wars Deception.* New York: Simon & Schuster, 1992.

Bronowski, Jacob. *The Ascent of Man.* Boston: Little, Brown, 1973.

Brownlow, Kevin. *David Lean: A Biography.* New York: Wyatt/St. Martin's Press, 1996.

Cagney, James. *Cagney by Cagney.* Garden City: Doubleday, 1976.

Calder, Jenni. *Chronicle of Conscience: A Study of George Orwell and Arthur Koestler.* Pittsburgh: University of Pittsburgh Press, 1968.

Cameron, Evan William, ed. *Sound and Cinema: The Coming of Sound to American Film.* Pleasantville, N.Y.: Redgrave, 1980.

Cantham, Kingsley. *The Hollywood Professionals: Michael Curtiz, Raoul Walsh, Henry Hathaway.* London: Tantivy, and New York: A. S. Barnes, 1973.

Capa, Cornell, ed. *The Concerned Photographer.* New York: Grossman, 1968.

Capa, Robert. "The Danube Is Red." *Illustrated Magazine,* March 26, 1949.

———. *Death in the Making.* New York: Covici/Friede, 1938.

———. *Slightly Out of Focus: The Legendary Photojournalist's Illustrated Memoir of World War II.* New York: Modern Library, 2001.

Carter, Katy. *London and the Famous: An Historical Guide to Fifty Famous People and Their London Homes.* London: British Tourist Authority, 1982.

Cesarini, David. *Arthur Koestler: The Homeless Mind.* New York: Free Press, 1998.

Chalmers, Kenneth. *Bela Bartok.* London: Phaidon, 1995.

Clark, Ronald W. *Einstein: The Life and Times.* New York: World, 1971.

Cohen, Richard. *By the Sword: A History of Gladiators, Musketeers, Samurai, Swashbucklers, and Olympic Champions.* New York: Random House, 2002.

Conant, Jennet. *109 East Palace: Robert Oppenheimer and the Secret City of Los Alamos.* New York: Simon & Schuster, 2005.

Congdon, Lee. *Exile and Social Thought: Hungarian Intellectuals in Germany and Austria.* Princeton: Princeton University Press, 1991.

———. *Seeing Red: Hungarian Intellectuals in Exile and the Challenge of Communism.* DeKalb: Northern Illinois University Press, 2001.

Conway, Flo, and Jim Siegelman. *Dark Hero of the Information Age: In Search of Norbert Wiener, the Father of Cybernetics.* New York: Basic, 2005.

Conway, John, trans. *The Path to Dictatorship, 1918–1933: Ten Essays by German Scholars.* Garden City: Doubleday, 1966.

Corkin, Jane, ed. *Stranger to Paris.* Toronto: Jane Corkin Gallery, 1992.

Crawford, Joan, with Jane Kesner Ardmore. *A Portrait of Joan: The Autobiography of Joan Crawford.* Garden City: Doubleday, 1962.

Crossman, Richard, ed. *The God that Failed: Six Studies in Communism.* London: Hamish Hamilton, 1950.

Czeizel, Endre. *Tudosok, Genek, Dilemmak: A Magyar Szarmazasu Nobel Dijasok Csaladfaelemzese.* Budapest: Galenus Kiado, 2002.

Czettler, Antal. "Miklos Kallay's Attempts to Preserve Hungary's Independence." *Hungarian Quarterly,* Autumn 2000.

Czigany, Lorant, ed. *The Passionate Outsider: George F. Cushing, Studies on Hungarian Literature.* Budapest: Corvina, 2000.

Davis, Bette. *The Lonely Life: An Autobiography.* New York: G. P. Putnam's Sons, 1962.

Deak, Istvan. *Hungary from 1918 to 1945.* New York: Institute on East Central Europe, Columbia University, 1989.

Deak, Istvan, Jan T. Gross, and Tony Judt, eds. *The Politics of Retribution in Europe: World War II and Its Aftermath.* Princeton: Princeton University Press, 2000.

DeGroot, Gerard J. *The Bomb: A Life.* Cambridge: Harvard University Press, 2005.

de Hegedus, Adam. *Hungarian Background.* London: Hamish Hamilton, 1937.

de Toth, Andre. *Fragments: Portraits from the Inside.* Boston: Faber & Faber, 1994.

Diamonstein, Barbaralee, ed. *Visions and Images: American Photographers on Photography.* New York: Rizzoli, 1981.

Drazin, Charles. *Korda: Britain's Only Movie Mogul.* London: Sidgwick & Jackson, 2002.

Dreisziger, Nandor, ed. *Hungary in the Age of Total War, 1938–1948.* New York: Columbia University Press, 1998.

Ducrot, Nicolas, ed. *Andre Kertesz: Sixty Years of Photography.* Middlesex: Penguin, 1978.

Dyson, Freeman. *Disturbing the Universe.* New York: Basic, 1979.

Eby, Cecil D. *Hungary at War: Civilians and Soldiers in World War II.* University Park: Pennsylvania State University Press, 1998.

Edwards, Anne. *Vivien Leigh: A Biography.* New York: Simon & Schuster, 1977.

Elon, Amos. *Herzl.* New York: Schocken, 1986.

Eva, Szentes. *Irodalmi Kavehazak Pesten es Budan.* Budapest: Universitas Kiado, 1998.

Evans, Harold. *The American Century.* New York: Alfred A. Knopf, 1998.

Faludy, George. *My Happy Days in Hell.* Translated by Kathleen Szasz. Don Mills, Md.: Totem, 1985.

Fenyo, Mario D. *Hitler, Horthy and Hungary: German-Hungarian Relations.* New Haven: Yale University Press, 1972.

Fenyvesi, Charles. *When Angels Fooled the World: Rescuers of Jews in Wartime Hungary.* Madison: University of Wisconsin Press, 2003.

———. *When the World Was Whole: Three Centuries of Memories.* New York: Viking, 1990.

Fermi, Laura. *Atoms in the Family: My Life with Enrico Fermi.* Albuquerque: University of New Mexico Press, 1982.

———. *Illustrious Immigrants: The Intellectual Migration from Europe, 1930–41.* Chicago: University of Chicago Press, 1968.

———. "That Was the Manhattan District." *The New Yorker,* July 31, 1954.

Fermor, Patrick Leigh. *Between the Woods and the Water.* London: Penguin, 1986.

Fitzgerald, Frances. *Way Out There in the Blue: Reagan, Star Wars and the End of the Cold War.* New York: Simon & Schuster, 2000.

Flanner, Janet. *Paris Was Yesterday, 1925–1939.* Edited by Irving Drutman. New York: Popular Library, 1972.

Fleming, Donald, and Bernard Bailyn, eds. *The Intellectual Migration: Europe and America, 1930–1960.* Cambridge: Harvard University Press, 1969.

Ford, Colin, ed. *The Hungarian Connection: The Roots of Photojournalism.* London: National Gallery of Photography, Film and Television, 1987.

"Forward Lies the Delta." *Time,* June 7, 1954.

Fotográfica Pública: Photography in Print, 1919–1939. Bilbao: Museo Nacional Centro de Arte Reina Sofía, 2000.

Francisco, Charles. *You Must Remember This . . . : The Filming of Casablanca.* Englewood Cliffs, N.J.: Prentice Hall, 1980.

Frank, Tibor. *Ethnicity, Propaganda, Myth-Making.* Budapest: Akademiai Kiado, 1999.

Freund, Gisele. *Photography and Society*. Boston: David R. Godine, 1979.

———. *The World in My Camera*. Translated by June Guicharnaud. New York: Dial, 1974.

Friedrich, Otto. *City of Nets: A Portrait of Hollywood in the 1940's*. New York: Harper & Row, 1986.

Frigyesi, Judit. *Bela Bartok and Turn-of-the-Century Budapest*. Berkeley: University of California Press, 1998.

Frojimovics, Kinga, Geza Komoroczy, Viktoria Pusztai, and Andrea Strbik. *Jewish Budapest: Monuments, Rites, History*. Edited by Geza Komoroczy. Budapest: Central European University Press, 1999.

Furst, Alan. *Kingdom of Shadows*. New York: Random House, 2000.

Gabler, Neal. *An Empire of Their Own: How the Jews Invented Hollywood*. New York: Doubleday, 1989.

Gay, Peter. *My German Question: Growing Up in Nazi Berlin*. New Haven: Yale University Press, 1998.

———. *Weimar Culture: The Outsider as Insider*. New York: Harper & Row, 1970.

Gellhorn, Martha. *Two by Two*. New York: Simon & Schuster, 1958.

Gergely, Emro Joseph. *Hungarian Drama in New York: American Adaptations, 1908–1940*. Philadelphia: University of Pennsylvania Press, 1947.

Gilbert, Martin. *Jewish History Atlas: 121 Maps from Biblical Times to the Present*. New York: Macmillan, 1977.

Glimm, James, John Impagliazzo, and Isadore Singer, eds. *The Legacy of John von Neumann*. Providence: American Mathematical Society, 1990.

Goldstine, Herman H. *The Computer: From Pascal to von Neumann*. Princeton: Princeton University Press, 1993.

Goodchild, Peter. *Edward Teller: The Real Doctor Strangelove*. London: Weidenfeld & Nicolson, 2004.

Greene, Graham. *Loser Takes All*. London: Penguin, 1955.

Greenough, Sarah, Robert Gurbo, and Sarah Kennel, eds. *Andre Kertesz*. Washington, D.C.: National Gallery of Art, and Princeton: Princeton University Press, 2005.

Grove, Andrew S. *Swimming Across: A Memoir*. New York: Warner, 2001.

Groves, General Leslie M. *Now It Can Be Told: The Story of the Manhattan Project*. New York: Da Capo, 1962.

Gurbo, Robert. *Andre Kertesz: A New York State of Mind*. Chicago: Stephen Daiter Gallery, 2001.

Gyorgyey, Clara. *Ferenc Molnar*. Boston: Twayne, 1980.

Hajdu, Tibor, and Gyorgy Litvan. "Count Michael Karolyi in Wartime England." *Hungarian Quarterly*, Winter 2003.

Halberstam, David. *The Fifties*. New York: Fawcett Columbine, 1994.

Hamilton, Iain. *Koestler: A Biography*. New York: Macmillan, 1982.

Hanak, Peter. *The Garden and the Workshop: Essays on the Cultural History of Vienna and Budapest*. Princeton: Princeton University Press, 1999.

Handler, Andrew. *Dori: The Life and Times of Theodor Herzl in Budapest*. New York: Herzl Press, 1983.

Harmetz, Aljean. *Round Up the Usual Suspects: The Making of Casablanca*. New York: Hyperion, 1992.

Harris, Harold, ed. *Astride the Two Cultures: Arthur Koestler at 70*. London: Hutchinson, 1975.

Heims, Steve J. *John von Neumann and Norbert Wiener: From Mathematics to the Technologies of Life and Death*. Cambridge: MIT Press, 1980.

Hemingway, Ernest. *A Moveable Feast*. New York: Scribner, 1996.

———. *For Whom the Bell Tolls.* New York: Scribner, 1995.

Herken, Gregg. *The Brotherhood of the Bomb: The Tangled Lives and Loyalties of Robert Oppenheimer, Ernest Lawrence, and Edward Teller.* New York: Henry Holt, 2002.

Hersey, John. *Life Sketches.* New York: Alfred A. Knopf, 1989.

Higham, Charles, and Joel Greenberg. *The Celluloid Muse: Hollywood Directors Speak.* New York: Signet, 1972.

Hoffman, Eva. *Exit into History: A Journey Through the New Eastern Europe.* New York: Viking Penguin, 1993.

Hotchner, A. E. *Doris Day: Her Own Story.* New York: Bantam, 1976.

Howard, Elizabeth Jane. *Slipstream: A Memoir.* London: Macmillan, 2002.

Hughes, Langston. *I Wonder as I Wander: An Autobiographical Journey.* New York: Hill & Wang, 1964.

Huszar, Tibor. " 'The Cause Which Obliges Me to Live Here.' " *Hungarian Quarterly,* Winter 2002.

Ignotus, Paul. *Hungary.* London: Ernest Benn, 1972.

———. *Political Prisoner: A Personal Account.* New York: Collier, 1964.

Isaacson, Walter, and Evan Thomas. *The Wise Men: Six Friends and the World They Made.* New York: Simon & Schuster, 1986.

Jackman, Jarrell C., and Carla M. Borden, eds. *The Muses Flee Hitler: Cultural Transfer and Adaptation, 1930–1945.* Washington, D.C.: Smithsonian, 1983.

Janik, Allan, and Stephen Toulmin. *Wittgenstein's Vienna.* New York: Simon & Schuster, 1973.

Jaszi, Oscar. *The Dissolution of the Hapsburg Monarchy.* Chicago: University of Chicago Press, 1971.

Jungk, Robert. *Brighter Than a Thousand Suns: A Personal History of the Atomic Scientists.* New York: Harvest, 1986.

Kahn, Lothar. *Mirrors of the Jewish Mind.* New York: Thomas Yoseloff, 1968.

Karoly, Kincses. *Made in Hungary.* Edited by Frederico Motta. Budapest: Magyar Fotografiai Muzeum, 1998.

Kaufman, Michael T. *Soros: The Life and Times of a Messianic Billionaire.* New York: Vintage/Random House, 2003.

Keegan, Susanne. *The Bride of the Wind: The Life of Alma Mahler.* New York: Viking Penguin, 1992.

Kershaw, Alex. *Blood and Champagne: The Life and Times of Robert Capa.* New York: Da Capo, 2004.

Kertesz, Andre. *Andre Kertesz: The Early Years.* New York: W. W. Norton, 2005.

———. *Kertesz on Kertesz: A Self-Portrait.* New York: Abbeville, 1985.

———. *On Reading.* New York: Grossman, 1971.

Kessler, Harry. *Berlin in Lights: The Diaries of Count Harry Kessler (1918–1937).* Edited and translated by Charles Kessler. New York: Grove, 1999.

Klein, George. *The Atheist and the Holy City: Encounters and Reflections.* Cambridge: MIT Press, 1987.

Klemperer, Victor. *I Will Bear Witness, 1933–1941: A Diary of the Nazi Years.* Translated by Martin Chalmers. New York: Modern Library, 1999.

Koch, Howard. *Casablanca: The Complete Script and Legend Behind the Film.* Woodstock: Overlook, 1988.

Koestler, Arthur. *The Age of Longing.* New York: Macmillan, 1951.

———. *Arrival and Departure.* New York: Macmillan, 1943.

———. *Arrow in the Blue: An Autobiography.* New York: Macmillan, 1952.

———. "Ball Game." *Hungarian Quarterly,* Summer 1989.

_____. *Bricks to Babel: Selected Writings with Author's Comments*. London: Picador, 1982.

_____. *Darkness at Noon*. New York: Bantam, 1968.

_____. *Dialogue with Death*. New York: Macmillan, 1966.

_____. *The Invisible Writing*. New York: Macmillan, 1954.

_____. *Promise and Fulfillment*. New York: Macmillan, 1949.

_____. *The Yogi and the Commissar and Other Essays*. London: Hutchinson, 1983.

Koestler, Arthur, and Cynthia Koestler. *Stranger on the Square*. Harold Harris, ed. London: Hutchinson, 1984.

Korda, Michael. *Charmed Lives: A Family Romance*. New York: HarperPerennial, 2002.

Kosztolanyi, Dezso. *Anna Edes*. Translated by George Szirtes. New York: New Directions, 1991.

Kovacs, Laszlo. *Eugene P. Wigner and His Hungarian Teachers*. Szombathely: Berzsenyo College, 2002.

Kovacs, Maria M. *Liberal Professions and Illiberal Politics: Hungary from the Habsburgs to the Holocaust*. Washington, D.C.: Woodrow Wilson Center Press, and New York: Oxford University Press, 1994.

Kreimeier, Klaus. *The UFA Story: A History of Germany's Greatest Film Company, 1918–1945*. Translated by Robert and Rita Kimer. New York: Hill & Wang, 1996.

Kulik, Karol. *Alexander Korda: The Man Who Could Work Miracles*. London: Virgin, 1990.

Kurti, Nicholas. "Some Szilard Reminiscences." Feb. 5, 1998, unpublished.

Lacayo, Richard, and George Russell. *Eyewitness: 150 Years of Photojournalism*. New York: Oxmoor House, 1990.

Lanouette, William, with Bela Silard. *Genius in the Shadows: A Biography of Leo Szilard, the Man Behind the Bomb*. New York: Scribner, 1992.

Laszlo, Lencso, Kalcsu Eva, and Kegli Balazs. *Budapestimozik*. Budapest: Ernst Muzeum, 2000.

Laval, Michel. *L'Homme Sans Concessions*. Paris: Calmann-Levy, 2005.

Lazar, Istvan. *An Illustrated History of Hungary*. Translated by Albert Tezla. Budapest: Corvina, 1990.

Lee, Douglas. *Masterworks of 20th Century: The Modern Repertory of the Symphony Orchestra*. New York: Routledge, 2002.

"The Legend of John von Neumann." *American Mathematical Monthly*, Vol. 80 (1973).

Lendvai, Paul. *The Hungarians: 1000 Years of Victory in Defeat*. London: Hurst, 2003.

Lessard, Suzannah. "The Present Moment." *The New Yorker*, April 13, 1987.

Levenson, Thomas. *Einstein in Berlin*. New York: Bantam, 2004.

Levine, Allan. *Scattered Among the People: The Jewish Diaspora in Twelve Portraits*. Woodstock: Overlook, and New York: Peter Mayer, 2002.

Lorant, Steven. *I Was Hitler's Prisoner: Leaves from a Prison Diary*. Translated by James Cleugh. London: Penguin, 1939.

Lord, Graham. *Niv: The Authorized Biography of David Niven*. New York: Thomas Dunne/St. Martin's Press, 2004.

Lucas, John Meredyth. *Eighty Odd Years in Hollywood: Memoir of a Career in Film and Television*. Jefferson, N.C.: McFarland, 2004.

Lukacs, John. *Budapest 1900: A Historical Portrait of a City and Its Culture*. New York: Weidenfeld & Nicolson, 1988.

_____. "The Tragedy of Two Hungarian Prime Ministers." *Hungarian Quarterly*, Autumn 2000.

Mac-Orlan, Pierre. *Paris Vu par Andre Kertesz*. Paris: Librairie Plon, 1934.

Macrae, Norman. *John von Neumann*. New York: Pantheon, 1992.

Madach, Imre. *The Tragedy of Man.* Translated by Iain MacLeod. Edinburgh: Canongate, 1993.

Magris, Claudio. *Danube: A Journey Through the Landscape, History, and Culture of Central Europe.* Translated by Patrick Creagh. New York: Farrar, Straus & Giroux, 1989.

Manchester, William, ed. *In Our Time: The World as Seen by Magnum Photographers.* New York: W. W. Norton, 1989.

Mandell, Richard. *The Nazi Olympics.* Urbana: University of Illinois Press, 1987.

Marai, Sandor. *Memoir of Hungary: 1944–1948.* Translated by Albert Tezla. Budapest: Corvina, 2000.

Martin, Pete. "Hollywood's Champion Language Assassin." *The Saturday Evening Post,* Aug. 2, 1947.

Marx, George. *The Voice of the Martians: Hungarian Scientists Who Shaped the 20th Century in the West.* Budapest: Akademiai Kiado, 1994.

McCagg, Jr., William O. *Jewish Nobles and Geniuses in Modern Hungary.* Boulder: Eastern European Quarterly, 1972.

McFarlane, Brian, ed. *The Encyclopedia of British Film.* London: Methuen, 2003.

McMillan, Priscilla J. *The Ruin of J. Robert Oppenheimer and the Birth of the Modern Arms Race.* New York: Viking, 2005.

Meth-Cohn, Delia. *Budapest Art and Art History.* Prague: Flow East, 1992.

Meyer, William R. *Warner Brothers Directors: The Hard-Boiled, the Comic, and the Weepers.* New Rochelle, N.Y.: Arlington House, 1978.

Mikes, George. *Arthur Koestler: The Story of a Friendship.* London: Andre Deutsch, 1983.

———. *How to Be Seventy: An Autobiography.* London: Andre Deutsch, 1982.

Miller, Henry. *Tropic of Cancer.* New York: Grove, 1961.

Millet, Lydia. *Oh Pure and Radiant Heart.* Brooklyn: Soft Skull Press, 2005.

Molnar, Ferenc. *All the Plays of Molnar.* Foreword by David Belasco; Introduction by Louis Rittenberg. Garden City: Garden City Company, 1937.

———. *Companion in Exile: Notes for an Autobiography.* Translated by Barrows Mussey. New York: Gaer Associates, 1950.

———. *Liliom.* Translated by Benjamin F. Glazer. Studio City, Calif.: Players Press, 1999.

Molnar, Miklos. *A Concise History of Hungary.* Cambridge: Cambridge University Press, 2001.

Moorehead, Caroline. *Gellhorn: A Twentieth-Century Life.* New York: Henry Holt, 2003.

Morris, Jan. *The World: Travels, 1950–2000.* New York: W. W. Norton, 2003.

Morris, John G. *Get the Picture: A Personal History of Photojournalism.* New York: Random House, 1998.

Morton, Frederic. *A Nervous Splendor: Vienna, 1888–1889.* New York: Penguin, 1979.

Nadas, Peter. *Book of Memories.* Translated by Ivan Sanders and Imre Goldstein. New York: Farrar, Straus & Giroux, 1997.

Naef, Weston, ed. *In Focus: Laszlo Moholy-Nagy.* Malibu: J. Paul Getty Museum, 1995.

Nasar, Sylvia. *A Beautiful Mind: The Life of Mathematical Genius and Nobel Laureate John Nash.* New York: Simon & Schuster, 1999.

Nemeskurty, Istvan. *Word and Image: History of the Hungarian Cinema.* Translated by Zsuzsanna Horn and Fred Macnicol. Hungary: Corvina, 1974.

Niven, David. *Bring on the Empty Horses.* New York: G. P. Putnam's Sons, 1975.

Nolan, Jack Edmund. "Michael Curtiz." *Films in Review,* undated.

Nowell-Smith, Geoffrey, ed. *The Oxford History of World Cinema.* Oxford: Oxford University Press, 1997.

Pallo, Gabor. *Zsenialitas es Korszellem.* Budapest: Aron Kiado, 2004.

Paloczi-Horvath, George. *The Undefeated*. London: Eland, 1993.

Parkinson, David, ed. *The Graham Greene Film Reader: Reviews, Essays, Interviews, and Film Stories*. New York: Applause, 1995.

Parsons, Nicholas T. *Hungary: A Cultural and Historical Guide*. Budapest: Novotrade Kiado, 1990.

Pawl, Ernst. *The Labyrinth of Exile: A Life of Theodor Herzl*. New York: Farrar, Straus & Giroux, 1989.

Perenyi, Eleanor. *More Was Lost*. New York: Helen Marx, 2001.

Petrie, Graham. *History Must Answer to Man: The Contemporary Hungarian Cinema*. Budapest: Corvina, 1981.

Philips, Arthur. *Prague: A Novel*. New York: Random House, 2002.

Phillips, Sandra S., David Travis, and Weston J. Naef, eds. *Andre Kertesz of Paris and New York*. Chicago: Art Institute of Chicago, 1985.

Pinter, Tamas K. *Budapest Architectura 1900*. Budapest: Alma Grafikai Studio es Kiado, 1998.

Powell, Michael. *A Life in Movies: An Autobiography*. London: Faber & Faber, 2000.

Preston, Diana. *Before the Fallout: From Marie Curie to Hiroshima*. New York: Walker, 2005.

Radai, Eszter. "Another Dimension: Andras Schiff in Conversation with Eszter Radai." *Hungarian Quarterly*, Winter 2003.

Ratz, Laszlo, and John von Neumann. *A Gifted Teacher and His Brilliant Pupil*. Winnipeg: University of Manitoba, 2003.

Redei, Miklos. "John von Neumann's Selected Letters." 2004, unpublished.

Rhodes, Richard. *Dark Sun: The Making of the Hydrogen Bomb*. New York: Simon & Schuster, 1995.

———. *The Making of the Atomic Bomb*. New York: Simon & Schuster, 1986.

Robertson, James C. *The Casablanca Man: The Cinema of Michael Curtiz*. London: Routledge, 1993.

Rockwell, Theodore. *Creating the New World: Stories and Images from the Dawn of the Atomic Age*. 1st Books Library (no date/publisher).

Rollyson, Carl. *Beautiful Exile: The Life of Martha Gellhorn*. London: Aurum, 2002.

Romsics, Ignac. *Hungary in the Twentieth Century*. Translated by Tom Wilkinson. Budapest: Corvina, 1999.

Rosenzweig, Sidney. *Casablanca and Other Major Films of Michael Curtiz*. Ann Arbor: UMI Research Press, 1982.

Roth, Joseph. *What I Saw: Reports from Berlin, 1920–1933*. London: Granta, 2003.

Rummel, Jack. *Robert Oppenheimer: Dark Prince*. New York: Facts on File, 1992.

Sakall, S. Z. *The Story of Cuddles: My Life Under the Emperor Francis Joseph, Adolf Hitler, and the Warner Brothers*. London: Cassell, 1954.

Sarkozi, Matyas. *Hungaro-Brits: The Hungarian Contribution to British Civilization*. Ministry of Cultural Heritage (no date/publisher).

Sarris, Andrew. *The American Cinema: Directors and Directions, 1929–1968*. New York: Da Capo, 1996.

Sayag, Alain, and Annick Lionel-Marie, eds. *Brassaï: The Monograph*. Boston: Little, Brown, 2000.

Schlesinger, Jr., Arthur M. *A Life in the 20th Century: Innocent Beginnings, 1917–1950*. Boston: Houghton Mifflin, 2000.

Schorske, Carl E. *Fin-de-Siècle Vienna: Politics and Culture*. New York: Alfred A. Knopf, 1980.

Shils, Edward. "Leo Szilard: A Memoir." *Encounter*, December 1964.

Shirer, William L. *Berlin Diary: The Journal of a Foreign Correspondent, 1934–1941.* New York: Alfred A. Knopf, 1941.

———. *20th Century Journey: The Nightmare Years, 1930–1940.* Boston: Little, Brown, 1984.

Shnayerson, Michael. *Irwin Shaw: A Biography.* New York: G. P. Putnam's Sons, 1989.

Singer, Peter. *Pushing Time Away: My Grandfather and the Tragedy of Jewish Vienna.* New York: HarperCollins, 2003.

Sklar, Robert. *Movie-Made America: A Cultural History of American Movies.* New York: Vintage/Random House, 1976.

Smith, Alice Kimball. "The Elusive Dr. Szilard." *Harper's Magazine,* July 1960.

Solti, Sir Georg, with Harvey Sachs. *Memoirs.* New York: Alfred A. Knopf, 1997.

Sontag, Susan. *Regarding the Pain of Others.* New York: Picador, 2003.

Soros, Tivadar. *Maskerado: Dancing Around Death in Nazi Hungary.* Translated by Humphrey Tonkin. Edinburgh: Canongate, 2000.

Sperber, A. M., and Eric Lax. *Bogart.* New York: William Morrow, 1997.

Spoto, Donald. *The Dark Side of Genius: The Life of Alfred Hitchcock.* New York: Da Capo, 1999.

Stern, Fritz. *Einstein's German World.* Princeton: Princeton University Press, 1999.

Suleiman, Susan Rubin, and Eva Forgacs, eds. *Contemporary Jewish Writing in Hungary: An Anthology.* Lincoln: University of Nebraska Press, 2003.

Szarka, Laszlo. "A Protecting Power Without Teeth." *Hungarian Quarterly,* Autumn 2000.

Szarkowski, John. *Looking at Photographs, 100 Pictures from the Collection of the Museum of Modern Art.* New York: Museum of Modern Art, 1980.

———. *The Photographer's Eye.* New York: Museum of Modern Art, 1966.

Szep, Erno. *The Smell of Humans: A Memoir of the Holocaust in Hungary.* Budapest: Corvina, 1984.

Szilard, Leo. *Leo Szilard: His Version of the Facts.* Edited by Spencer R. Weart and Gertrud Weiss Szilard. Boston: MIT Press, 1978.

———. *Voices of the Dolphins and Other Stories.* Stanford: Stanford University Press, 1961.

Tabori, Paul. *Alexander Korda.* New York: Living Books, 1966.

Taylor, John Russell. *Strangers in Paradise: The Hollywood Emigrés, 1933–1950.* New York: Holt, Rinehart & Winston, 1983.

Teller, Edward, with Allen Brown. *The Legacy of Hiroshima.* Garden City: Doubleday, 1962.

Teller, Edward, with Judith Shoolery. *Memoirs: A Twentieth-Century Journey in Science and Politics.* Cambridge: Perseus, 2001.

Thassy, Jeno. "The Bad War." *Hungarian Quarterly,* Autumn 2000.

Thomas, David. "I Leica Danger." *The New Republic,* Aug. 18 and 25, 2003.

Thomas, Hugh. *The Spanish Civil War.* New York: Harper Colophon, 1963.

Thomson, David. *The New Biographical Dictionary of Film.* New York: Alfred A. Knopf, 2002.

———. *Showman: The Life of David O. Selznick.* New York: Alfred A. Knopf, 1992.

———. *The Whole Equation: The History of Hollywood.* New York: Alfred A. Knopf, 2005.

Tuchman, Barbara W. *The Guns of August.* New York: Bantam, 1980.

Ulam, S. M. *Adventures of a Mathematician.* New York: Charles Scribner's Sons, 1976.

United States Atomic Energy Commission. *In the Matter of J. Robert Oppenheimer.* Cambridge: MIT Press, 1971.

Varkonyi, Istvan. *Ferenc Molnar and the Austro-Hungarian "Fin de Siècle."* New York: Peter Lang, 1992.

Volgyes, Ivan, ed. *Hungary in Revolution, 1918–19: Nine Essays.* Lincoln: University of Nebraska Press, 1971.

von Dewitz, Bodo, ed. *Kiosk, 1939–1973: A History of Photojournalism.* Köln: Stadt-Köln, 2001.

von Karman, Theodore, with Lee Edson. *The Wind and Beyond: Theodore von Karman, Pioneer in Aviation and Pathfinder in Space.* Boston: Little, Brown, 1967.

Vonneuman, Nicholas A. "John von Neumann as Seen by His Brother." Meadowbrook, Penn.: unpublished.

von Sternberg, Josef. *Fun in a Chinese Laundry: An Autobiography.* New York: Collier, 1973.

Wallis, Hal, with Charles Higham. *The Autobiography of Hal Wallis.* New York: Berkley Books, 1981.

Warner, Jack L., with D. Jennings. *My First Hundred Years in Hollywood.* New York: Random House, 1964.

Weber, Eugen. *The Hollow Years: France in the 1930s.* New York: W. W. Norton, 1994.

Whelan, Richard. *Robert Capa: A Biography.* New York: Alfred A. Knopf, 1985.

———. *Robert Capa: The Definitive Collection.* New York: Phaidon, 2004.

Wigner, Eugene P., as told to Andrew Szanton. *The Recollections of Eugene P. Wigner.* New York: Basic, 1992.

Wigner, Eugene P., Walter J. Moore, and Michael Scriven, eds. *Symmetries and Reflections: Scientific Essays of Eugene P. Wigner.* Westport, Conn.: Greenwood, 1978.

York, Herbert F. *The Advisors: Oppenheimer, Teller, and the Superbomb.* Stanford: Stanford University Press, 1976.

Yoshioka, Eijiro, curator. *Capa's Life: Robert Capa Retrospective Exhibition.* Tokyo: Tokyo Fuji Art Museum, 1999.

Young, Lucie. *Eva Zeisel.* Edited by Marisa Bartolucci and Raul Cabra. San Francisco: Chronicle, 2003.

Zeisel, Eva Striker. *Memories of Arthur.* Unpublished.

Zinsser, William, ed. *Extraordinary Lives: The Art and Craft of American Biography.* New York: American Heritage, 1986.

Zweig, Stefan. *The World of Yesterday.* Lincoln: University of Nebraska Press, 1964.

ACKNOWLEDGMENTS

For the past four years, my husband, Richard Holbrooke, has lived with ten Hungarians: myself and the nine figures who make up this narrative. He has been an enthusiastic participant in my journey through these extraordinary lives, asking probing questions and helping me to put them in the context of their turbulent age. He was my first reader and most tireless spur in making the work stronger. No writer could ask for a more devoted partner. I cannot thank him enough.

My wonderful friend and indomitable editor, Alice Mayhew, loved this project from the first and cheered me across the finish line. It has been a privilege and a joy to work with such a great editor.

Also at Simon & Schuster thanks are due to Gypsy da Silva for her shepherding the manuscript, as well as Victoria Meyer and Serena Jones, as well as to Roger Labrie for his tireless work on behalf of this book. Fred Chase's careful copyediting improved the work. Brandon Proia did an outstanding job of finding photographs for this tome.

Amanda Urban, a friend and co-conspirator of two decades, was indispensable for this one, as she has been for the last four.

My researcher, Janna Slack, found no fact too obscure to trace, and her cool under pressure was inspiring.

I was fortunate to have a great many scholars and experts in the various fields this work embraces helping me along the way. Four deserve special thanks.

Robert Gurbo, the curator of the Andre and Elizabeth Kertesz Estate, spent hours bringing the great photographer and his life and work vividly alive for me. His passion for photography and for the master he knew intimately was contagious. This book owes a great deal to Gurbo's generosity and tireless grooming of the manuscript.

Richard Whelan, Robert Capa's biographer and executor of the Capa Legacy, made Capa's genius, both for photography and for life, very real for me. Whelan and Gurbo have also been generous in providing this book with the many photographs from the Kertesz and Capa trusts. I am enormously grateful to them both.

William Lanouette, Leo Szilard's biographer and himself a scientist and a scholar, gave unstintingly of his time and vast knowledge. He and Richard Rhodes, the award-winning author of *The Making of the Atomic Bomb*, helped me navigate the shoals of the birth of the nuclear age and the role played by four Hungarian scientists during its critical, earliest days.

Istvan Deak, the Columbia University scholar and professor of Hungarian history, engaged in a four-year-long conversation with me regarding our homeland's tragic destiny. He is a scholar in the old-fashioned sense, precise, careful, and generous with his knowledge. I could not have written this book without his guiding spirit.

Michael Scammell, though hard at work on his own biography of Arthur Koestler, took time for long conversations about his subject and read and improved my manuscript.

Eva Striker Zeisel, a key player in the Koestler saga and herself a historic figure, gave me several afternoons of priceless remembrances of her lifelong friend Arthur. Eva's daughter, Jean Richards, was a wonderful source on Leo Szilard, her childhood friend, and Koestler.

In Hungary, I was fortunate to have guidance and support from the following scholars, academics, and specialists: Vera Gyuri and Gyongyi Balogh were helpful at the Hungarian Film Archives, and Karoly Kincses and Andras Torok helped to unlock Hungary's rich contribution to the field of photography. Vajda Miklos was helpful in locating old issues of the *New Hungarian Quarterly*, of which he is the editor.

I am grateful to the following eminent Hungarian scholars and friends for sharing their insights into Hungarian culture, politics, and history: Ambassador Andre Simony; Professors Tibor Frank, Dr. Istvan Hargittai, Dr. Gabor Pallo, and Dr. Attila Polk; Zold Ferenc, George Litvan, Erzsebet Vezer, Laszlo and Judit Rajk, Ferenc Partos, Noemi Saly, Maria Schmidt, Peter Bihari, Istvan Teplan, Katalin Bogyai, Eva Besnyo, George Soros, Imre Kertesz, Andy Grove, Sandor Striker.

In Paris, Henri Cartier-Bresson honored me with one of his final interviews. Suzy Marquis and John Morris shared their memories of Robert Capa. I am also indebted to my friend Bernard-Henri Levy for his always provocative conversations, and to Christine Ockrent and Bernard Kouchner for their boundless hospitality during my research.

Other scientists and scholars who were of invaluable assistance in my research were Dr. Edward Gerjuoy, physicist at the University of Pittsburgh; Dr. Paul Hollander; Dr. Peter Lax, the great mathematician and protégé of John von Neumann, at New York University's famed Courant Institute; and Dr. Leonard Lerman.

A conversation with Martin Peretz regarding the remarkable Budapest talent explosion in the early part of the last century played a significant part in getting me started on this book. Early in my research, John Simon was informative and entertaining on the lost spirit of Budapest. David Trilling helped with Capa photo research, Yvette Biro with the history of Hungarian cinema.

Photographer Sylvia Plachy provided invaluable help in my research on the life and work of Andre Kertesz.

In Berlin, Dr. Gary Smith, the President of the American Academy, offered historic guidance and hospitality. Wolfgang Theis showed me around the Berlin Film Archives, and Dr. Annette Vogt guided me around the Kaiser Wilhelm Institute.

I am indebted to Marina von Neumann Whitman for her memories of her father, John von Neumann. The book benefited enormously from my interviews and conversations with Michael Korda. Frank Rich was typically creative and generous in my search for the perfect title.

Among those who made significant contributions to this book were David Thomson, Dr. Harold Brown, Henry Kissinger, Marie-Josée Kravis, Les Gelb, Luke Janklow, Morton and Linda Janklow, Strobe Talbott, Israel Singer, Nicholas von Neumann, Fritz Stern, John Silard, Mary Kaldor, Julia Marton-Lefèvre, Andrew Marton, Jeanine Basinger, Arthur Schlesinger, Jr., Norman Pearlstine, Professors Ralph Lapp, Paul Hollander, Freeman Dyson, and George Dyson. They were all generous with their time, their knowledge, and their wisdom. I thank each one of them. Philip Gourevich, Leon Wieseltier, Israel Singer, Lauren Bacall, Peter Stone, Alan J. Pakula, Elie Wiesel, Tom Lantos, Cornell Capa, Richard Perle, Richard Plepler, David Margolick, Ben Bradlee, Richard Bernstein, Roger Cohen, Stefan Lorant, George Stevens, Jr., Frances FitzGerald, Christopher Hitchens, Charles Glass, Frank Wisner, and Jon Meacham all contributed ideas and helped point the way forward.

Until the very last days of his life, my father talked to me about the Budapest of his childhood and youth, bringing the city and its Golden Age—as well as its torments—into the New York apartment he shared with me in his final year. It is impossible for me to imagine this book without those conversations.

Finally, I began to revisit the city of my birth over two decades ago with Peter Jennings, who encouraged this project. I deeply regret that he did not live to see the journey's end. This book is for our children, Elizabeth and Christopher Jennings, whose own history is contained in its pages.

INDEX

PHOTO CREDITS

Dallas and John Heaton © Free Agents Limited/CORBIS: 1. © Imagno/Hulton Archive/ Getty Images: 2, *13*. Courtesy of Estate of Andre Kertesz © 2006: *v*, *3*, *6*, *9*, *13*, *22*, *32*, *47*. © Hulton-Deutsch Collection/CORBIS: 4, 20, *221*. Courtesy of Michael Korda: 5, 21. Courtesy of Leo Szilard Papers, Mandeville Special Collections Library, University of California, San Diego: 7, *14*. Courtesy of Marina von Neumann Whitman: 8. Portrait by Gerda Taro, Spain, 1937, Capa Archives, International Center of Photography, NY: 10. Courtesy of Yale Collection of American Literature, Beinecke Rare Book and Manuscript Library, reprinted by permission of Harold Ober Associates Incorporated: 11. Courtesy of Yale Collection of American Literature, Beinecke Rare Book and Manuscript Library: 12. Courtesy of Lawrence Livermore National Laboratory: 15, *171* (upper left). Courtesy of Deutsche Kinemathek, Berlin: 16. Photograph by Fred Stein, courtesy of Cornell Capa: 17. Photographs by Robert Capa, copyright © by Cornell Capa/Magnum: 18, 19, 23, 25. Copyright © by Cornell Capa/Magnum: 24, *127*. Courtesy of Capa Archives, International Center of Photography, NY, photograph by Carl Goodwin, copyright © by Carl Goodwin: 26. © Bettmann/CORBIS: 27, 30. © Ralph Morse/Time & Life Pictures/Getty Images: 29. Courtesy AIP Emilio Segre Visual Archives, © Bulletin of the Atomic Scientists: 31. © Alan W. Richards/Bettmann/CORBIS: 28, *171* (lower left). © March of Time/Time & Life/ Getty Images: *171* (upper right). Courtesy of AIP Emilio Segre Visual Archives: *171* (bottom right).

ABOUT THE AUTHOR

Kati Marton, an award-winning former NPR and ABC News correspondent, is most recently the author of *Hidden Power*, a *New York Times* bestseller, as well as *Wallenberg*, *The Polk Conspiracy*, and *Death in Jerusalem*. She lives in New York City with her husband, Richard Holbrooke.